Out of the Whirlpool

Sue W. Martin

Out of the Whirlpool

a memoir of remorse
and reconciliation

Sue Wiygul Martin

WORKING WRITER
{Discovery<|>Group}

First Edition
1 2 3 4 5 6 7 8 9

ISBN EBook
978-1-940524-00-9

ISBN PDF
978-1-940524-01-6

ISBN Quality Trade Paperback
978-1-940524-02-3

Book & Cover Design by Myra Coffield
Illustrations Curated by Jane McGriff

www.outofthewhirlpool.com

To Jim

Contents

part one: REMORSE

01| the whirlpool	2
02| i choose life	12
03| intensive care	16
04| a changed world	19

part two: REHABILITATION

05| tabula rasa	24
06| a feel for braille	30
07| living again	33
08| with cane i'm able	40
09| daddy to the rescue	48
10| i did it	53
11| trying to keep up	60
12| it's a skill thing	63
13| the drop-off lesson	69
14| the right neighborhood	78
15| without attending class	83
16| so much potential	89
17| skinny dipping	95
18| a shining image	99
19| her name is sadie	103
20| not by half	108

21| a life together   114

22| on the rocks   120

23| beyond the call   125

24| maine things considered   131

25| a drive for perfection   138

part three: RECOVERY

26| two clients, one goal   148

27| at what price   155

28| bones of contention   161

29| her name is quoddy   169

30| you can't push a string   172

31| back in the saddle   178

32| a question of wheels   183

33| wheel life stories   187

34| with extended arms   194

35| if you can't beat 'em   200

36| winter on the coast   205

37| the competitive urge   210

38| paying the price   215

39| the trials   219

40| clear as a bell   223

41| log house, maine woods   230

42| ice and snow   236

43| the sacred and profane   243

44| the brattleboro retreat   248

45| a little humility 256

46| her name is beverly 261

47| the ice storm 268

48| when your heart breaks 272

part four: RESOLVE

49| home calls 280

50| you are going to change 285

51| where it all began 291

52| girls' night out 296

53| a new passion 301

54| her name is kismet 307

55| the 508 dream team 313

56| mama's decline 318

57| mama passes 326

58| whatever it takes 332

part five: RECONCILIATION

59| the company of friends 340

60| ecce quam bonum 344

acknowledgments 350

SALIX BABYLONICA

weeping willow

PART ONE

REMORSE

~~~~~

*It isn't for the moment you are stuck
that you need courage, but for the long
uphill climb back to sanity,
faith, and security.*

Anne Morrow Lindbergh

01 | the whirlpool

I WAS TWENTY SIX YEARS OLD AND LIVING IN ALABAMA when my story begins. My first marriage had failed after two years. I had made a complete mess of my first and second attempts at establishing a career. Having resigned from a disastrous stint in the insurance industry, I moved back in with my parents, into the home where I grew up. Everything I touched, thought, or did seemed to be ending badly.

Not surprisingly, my parents insisted that I see a psychiatrist. I tried, I really tried, but I just couldn't tell him the truth. After some fruitless sessions, he prescribed an antidepressant. The only effect this medication seemed to have was to turn getting out of the bed each morning into an ordeal. I'd wake up and just lie there staring up at the ceiling of my childhood bedroom. There was nothing I could think of that would make getting out of bed worthwhile.

I had been an exercise rider for a federal judge for the previous two years. He owned a steel gray thoroughbred named Knight Commander. My job was to keep the horse fit and in training for fox hunting. Knight Commander had developed the habit of setting his jaw against the bit and galloping, out of control, at any fence that the judge directed him to jump during a hunt. This was dangerous enough in itself but it was especially dangerous in a crowded hunt field. This behavior didn't manifest when I rode Knight Commander for exercise and the judge concluded that it must be the excitement of the hunt that was the problem. He invited me to hunt Knight Commander the second weekend in November to see if I could break the habit.

On the morning I was to drive to the judge's home I awakened to the familiar feeling of paralysis. *What was wrong with me?* I should want to do this. I should be excited. I should be leaping out of bed in anticipation of a thrilling challenge. But I was none of those things. I was a failure. I had failed at marriage. I had failed in my career attempts. Now, I was failing even to get out of bed.

With an enormous effort, I dragged myself to my feet. I crossed to the casement windows of my room. Drawing back the full-length draperies I looked out, through the branches of the silver maple, across the yard to Pump House Road. Our house was located in the suburb of Mountain Brook, just southeast of Birmingham. The sun was just beginning to top the tall trees across the street. I gazed out at the peaceful scene and then turned back to my room, the sun now glinting off of medals won in fencing meets and a trophy handed to me when I won my first kayak race. On the wall to the left was my diploma from the University of the South. How proud I had been when the vice chancellor intoned, "Lillian Sue Wiygul, cum laude"—the culmination of four glorious years. I remembered walking to the front of All Saints Chapel wearing the slightly tattered and faded academic gown which had been awarded to me at the start of my sophomore year.

On the other side of the bookcase was a photograph taken from the top of a mountain looking down on jewel blue lakes. While friends and family at home were celebrating our country's bicentennial I had been abroad, toasting the Queen at an opening convocation for a summer term at University College Oxford. I had taken the photograph on a weekend jaunt to the Lake District of northern England during that term.

None of it now meant very much. Surely these trophies and mementos belonged in someone else's life. They didn't seem to belong in mine.

I steeled myself for what I needed to do.

Right. I needed to get dressed. Pack my hunting gear. Get in the car, and drive the ninety miles from Birmingham to Montgomery, where the judge lived. It was like I was standing outside of myself just watching as I went through the motions. Somehow, I got myself together. I arrived at the judge's home Friday evening, and, early the next morning, I groomed Knight Commander. I then trailered him and stowed my tack in the car, and the judge drove us the sixty or so miles to the meet.

As the judge pulled into the frost-silvered field deep in the heart of Alabama's richest farmland, I saw the familiar sights of the hunt staff in their scarlet coats and the members of the hunt wearing black coats, some with the hunt colors on their collars. I got out of the car and sounds of greeting and laughter filled the chilly air. Horses snorted and whinnied. All of it familiar, yet all somehow alien. I didn't feel a part of it. I felt isolated. I felt alone.

After the judge backed Knight Commander out of the trailer he saddled him while I slipped the bit between his teeth and drew the bridle over his head. Positioning myself at Knight Commander's left shoulder I prepared to mount. He was a big horse, standing seventeen hands, one inch, but I had mounted him effortlessly many times. On that day though, getting myself into the saddle felt like climbing a mountain. I struggled, and slowly, oh so slowly, dragged myself into the saddle. I remember the judge placing a hand on my boot and looking carefully into my eyes. He said, "Are you going to be all right?" Without saying anything, I nodded, gathered Knight Commander's reins, and moved off to join the hunt.

The huntsman sent the pack into covert to draw for a fox. They shot off in ever widening circles. They soon picked up a scent, and, with the hounds in full cry, we were off.

We galloped across a bare winter field and approached the first fence.

I wasn't sure what I was going to do if Knight Commander got out of control but I trusted my instincts. One thing I needed though was space. Gently tightening my hands on the braided reins, I slowed Knight Commander down, the other horses—black, bay, chestnut, and white—flashed by. Then it was time. Leaning slightly forward, tightening my legs, I gave Knight Commander some rein. We gathered speed.

As we approached the fence Knight Commander pinned back his ears, threw his head in the air, and rushed the fence. I had no control at all. I stood in the stirrups. Leaning as far forward as I dared, I simply yanked down, hard, on the right rein. That got his attention. Back in the saddle, I gathered the reins and collected the horse by driving forward with my legs and seat and resisting slightly with my hands. Knight Commander gracefully vaulted the fence.

By now the hunt was ahead of me. Leaning forward, I gave Knight Commander his head. He could run; he could run fast. The trees flashed by, and I caught up with the rest of the field. That hunt was a long one. The fox outsmarted the hounds over and over again, and there were long periods of time when we had to stand still and wait for the hounds to pick up the scent. Then we'd be off again.

Over the course of the day, I followed the same routine of hanging back to give Knight Commander room for the next fence. But it wasn't necessary; he stayed calm and collected over every jump for the rest of the hunt.

As I approached the meet I unbuckled my helmet. Tucking it beneath my arm, I shook out my hair. "I did it," I said, as the judge approached and took Knight Commander's reins in his hands. Then I dismounted. My feet hit the ground with the finality of a gavel on its sound block. I felt diminished. I returned in the space of an instant to that small place my world had become.

What on earth was wrong with me? I should have been elated. I had lived up to the trust the judge had in me. I had ridden brilliantly. But all I felt now was hollow. There was no joy, no satisfaction.

Just hollowness.

I got back in my car to drive home. *What was I driving home to "do"? Aside from being able to cure a horse from rushing his fences, what strengths or talents did I possess?* I couldn't think of a single one. As I drove back into town the sun was setting. Honest to God, I felt it was setting on my life.

The week after the hunt saw little improvement in my mood or energy. My mood remained grim, and my energy nonexistent. I began to isolate myself from friends. Although I interacted and spoke with my parents and my brother, it was like I did it with only half of my attention. I didn't feel as though I could tell anyone the truth, least of all, any member of my family.

When I was growing up, we had all sorts of "no talk" subjects. One of the subjects that was off-limits was saying anything about anyone or anything that was negative. I think my parents (and, in particular, my mother) were trying to create a positive atmosphere. A laudable goal, perhaps, raising children with nothing but sweetness and light, but one that had a devastating effect on me. Whenever I spoke candidly, honestly about anything negative—someone with whom I was angry, for example, or perhaps a situation that I thought unfair—I was greeted with disapproval. Life should be wonderful and good and nothing bad should ever happen. If something bad did happen it couldn't be discussed or explored because that would make it real.

It was no wonder that I felt I couldn't tell my family the truth.

The following week, with the idea of trying to give some structure to my life, I signed up for a class in oil painting. I dragged myself to class two evenings a week and managed to produce a pretty good painting. Based on a photograph that I had taken in Scotland, it was of a lighthouse on a rocky promontory with a sea gull in flight. All of it was enveloped in an early morning mist which softened the rough edges and gave the entire composition an ethereal feel. Okay, I thought, this is good. This was something on which I could build.

I started my next painting with a glimmer of hope. It was a much smaller painting of two mushrooms joined at their caps. The stems and lower parts of the mushrooms were taupe in color. The tops of the caps were a deep, rich crimson. I was so proud, I framed it and gave it to my father.

Yes, the instructor praised me, my parents praised me, and my brother seemed quite surprised at my hidden talent. But there was something about the praise that grated on me. What I heard was an artificial note, as though they were all praising a child who had just produced something mediocre, a child who needed encouragement.

My third attempt at oil painting was terrible, a field of wildflowers. I knew it was awful. Add yet another failure to my ever growing list of things I had screwed up. I couldn't paint anymore. I just quit. One more activity was added to the pile of ashes my life had become.

I began to wonder what the point of living was. Nothing was interesting anymore. There was no one with whom I could share my ever lower spirits. When I sat around the dinner table with my family, I just listened. Gradually, even listening to other peoples' conversations took on that feeling of pointlessness. I just didn't care anymore.

A few nights after I gave up on painting, as I lay in bed, I found myself dwelling on something that had happened when I was five or six years old. My father was a surgeon. He was also the quintessential southern gentleman. My parents took my brother and me to a hospital picnic held on the grounds of Lloyd Noland hospital in Fairfield, just west of Birmingham. One after another his colleagues approached to greet him and ask to be introduced to his lovely children. "You must be so proud of them" I heard over and over again.

"Yes, they're wonderful children, and we are so proud of them," answered my mother or father over and over again. My father's colleagues, everyone, from fellow surgeons to hospital switchboard and elevator operators, showed him such respect. I was so proud of him, proud to be part of the family.

Where had my sense of pride gone? As a child, it came from simply being part of the family. But I was no longer a child. The reflected glory was over. Now, as an adult, it was up to me to be successful. *That's where pride came from, right?* It came from being successful. It came from being a successful wife or professional. It came from being successful economically. It came from being popular in the right social circles.

I was none of those things.

I had tried the route of a June marriage right after graduating from college. That was no good. It ended in divorce two years later.

I had tried the route of becoming a business professional. That was no good either. It ended disastrously, again, after two years.

Where could I go next? I couldn't think of anywhere. I felt that I had exhausted all of my options.

My mother had written a column for the *Birmingham News* and had been a DJ on a local radio station before marrying my father. For the next twenty something years, she had raised my brother, Jimmy, and me and had made a comfortable and peaceful home for us all. She had been president of the PTA.

She was on the board of the Children's Aid Society. The year before my father retired, she had become a representative for a luxury clothing manufacturer and rose to the rank of regional manager. She seemed to be able to succeed at just about anything . . . and I seemed to be able to fail at just about everything.

As I contemplated what I had made of my life to this point, it felt like what I imagined a whirlpool to be, lapping ever higher, sucking me down. Over and over again, I compared my life to my parent's lives. I kept thinking about that picnic. Were I to walk into such a situation as my twenty-six year old self I felt sure that people would not be coming up to me and asking to be introduced, either to me or to my nonexistent children. *Why would they?* I felt inadequate. I didn't measure up. I had failed.

I'm not sure of the exact point when I decided that life wasn't worth living any longer. I just fell into that train of thought. Going to sleep every night was the best thing that happened to me all day. Waking up the next morning was the worst thing that happened to me all day. I just wanted to go to sleep and stay there. It would be all right if I could just go to sleep and never wake up again. But how could I make that happen?

I began to obsess about the shotgun in my brother's closet. But I knew I couldn't use that gun in my father's house. I didn't care about myself but I couldn't bear the thought of putting my family through the ordeal of finding me. Every time I retreated from my suicidal thoughts for a period of time, they kept coming back. The struggle was becoming almost too hard to resist.

Then I remembered another gun.

This one was at the lake house of some family friends. I knew where the gun was and I knew where the key to the house was. Eventually, the plan came together. I had to have a reason to get out of the house for a while. I told my parents that I was going to take my lighthouse and seagull painting and get it framed. Then I got in my car and drove to the lake house. It was December and it was quiet at the lake. The key was still in the same place. And so was the gun.

The gun was a .22 caliber rifle. I took the rifle down from the shelf and put some bullets in my pocket. Then I walked down to the dock. I had a fleeting memory of all of the good times I had once had on that dock but the memories were not strong enough to pierce the misery that had become my reality. I loaded the rifle and shot, at nothing in particular, out across the lake. Then I went back up to the lake house.

I reclined on the sofa, facing out towards the lake. There was a beautiful weeping willow on a spit of land just across the lake. Salix Babylonica, I thought, remembering the Latin name of the tree. I gazed at its branches, sweeping gracefully down, for a long time. Although I had majored in English in college, I had taken forestry and botany classes as well. The joke on campus was that you could always differentiate the dendrology students from the systematic botany students. The former walked around looking up at trees while the latter walked around looking down at objects on the ground. How many times had I gazed up into the branches of a tree when my forestry professor would say, "Quiz that tree?" *How many times had I dropped to the ground while walking to class or Gaylor Hall for breakfast to investigate an unusual flower that caught my eye?* I had scoured books upon books in the library for the lore and culture of trees and flowers. I thrilled at learning the place and meaning they held in mythology and legend.

Still gazing at the tree, I suddenly remembered. The weeping willow is associated with death. There are other associations, but the death thing seemed the only one I could remember. How apt, I thought.

Pulling my thoughts back into the lake house, I looked

at the clock. It was 11:30 in the morning. Then I sank back down into the very tiny place that had become my reality. I positioned the gun and paused. If I did this, there was no turning back. This was going to be final. There was nothing, nothing else, nothing that was big enough to get me out of the whirlpool of depression. I both wanted to do this and not do it. I held my breath. I squeezed my eyes shut.

I clenched my teeth. I pulled the trigger.

02 | i choose life

I LAY, UNCONSCIOUS, ALONE AND BLEEDING FOR EIGHT HOURS. When I regained consciousness, I knew exactly where I was and what I had done. It was dark. Completely dark.

I sat up and tried to think of what I should do next. The first order of business was to figure out why it was so dark. Sitting up I felt my face. I was covered in blood, some of it dry and crusted and some still sticky. I widened my eyes. Nothing.

Thinking the blood had dried and was keeping my eyelids closed I placed two fingers, one on the upper and one on the lower lids of my right eye. I pried my eyelids opened. Still nothing.

I reached to follow the same procedure with my left eye but as soon as I touched it I drew my hand back. It was too painful.

Putting the question of the darkness aside for the moment, I pondered my situation. Deep inside me there was a spark of the survivor. *What did one do when one was injured?* I took the first step towards living again: I got to my feet and aimed for the kitchen. I knew that there was a phone just to the left of the refrigerator.

I found the phone and picked it up. I was going to have to dial the thing by touch because it was still dark, all dark. I tried to punch in my parent's phone number. I must have tried six or seven times but I just couldn't get it right. I had lost so much blood that I could barely stay on my feet. And I couldn't see the phone; I couldn't see it at all. I gave up. I put the phone back on the hook, turned, and with my back to the refrigerator tried to decide what to do next. The thought of finding the gun and finishing the whole sorry business was just forming in my head when the phone rang.

I picked it up and said, "Hello." It was Adam.

Adam, the family friend who owned the lake house. At that precise moment, at that precise and precious moment, I wanted to live. Here was my chance to start over again. To put the terrible sucking feeling of that whirlpool behind me and to live. The desire for life became a fierce burning flame in my being.

I told Adam what I had done and told him that I was a mess. He misunderstood me at first. He said, "You missed?" With a powerful longing, I wished that I could tell him that I had, in fact, missed. But I couldn't do it. I had to face reality. And the reality was that I had lost a lot of blood and it was still dark, completely dark. Adam took control. He spoke strongly and clearly. He told me to put down the phone, make sure the door was unlocked, and then to take the phone with me and lie down on the floor. After I had done these things he said he was going to hang up and call a man who lived across the street from the lake house and then he was going to call me back.

Then things started happening. Adam called me back. The neighbor came into the lake house. He took the phone from me. He told Adam that it didn't look good, not good at all. I told the man that I was cold. He took a blanket from the back of the sofa and laid it over me. The police came. An ambulance came. And then we were headed back to Birmingham. It was only later, much later, that I learned what had happened.

~~~

Adam and I went way back. His parents and mine had been fast friends for as long as I can remember. Our families had spent many happy days together at the lake house.

When I didn't come home that day, my parents became frantic. They contacted their friend who had been the mayor of our suburb for several years. A trained policeman, he might know how to find someone who was missing. He told them to call anyone and everyone with whom I was friends in an effort to locate me. They called Adam. In a twist of fate, Adam was home. He should have been at a concert but the concert had been cancelled. Adam shared the lake house with his brother. He called the lake house and got a busy signal. I was in the midst of my failed attempts to call my parents. Adam then called his brother and also got a busy signal. Surmising that his brother might be at the lake and be talking with his wife who was in town, he gave up. But then he told me, "A voice in my head spoke to me telling me not to give up." And so he kept trying until I answered the phone.

When the police and the ambulance arrived, things became frenetic. Eventually, I was loaded in the ambulance and we set out.

I faded in and out of consciousness for the next hour. The ambulance stopped once, and I heard people talking. Then the door was closed and the ambulance moved off again. I had this vague feeling that something was just odd. These people were moving around and doing things in the ambulance but how could they see what they were doing. It was still dark, all dark. I simply didn't have enough energy to try to figure it out so I quit trying. After some passage of time, I don't know how long, I began to grow agitated. I have no recollection of why that would be but I remember it clearly. The people in the ambulance with me seemed to think it was important though and the ambulance soon stopped. I found out later that the intention had been to take me to Lloyd Noland Hospital where my father had been a member of staff for forty years. However, we were approaching Birmingham from the east and, at some point, they had decided it was too risky to continue. They stopped at Baptist Montclair, the first major medical center they could get to. I have a vague memory of doctors beginning to examine me in the emergency room and that was all I can remember of that day and night.

I was in the intensive care unit for three days before I regained consciousness. As I gradually awakened I lay still. I tried to think of where in the world I was and what had happened to me. *I knew that something really important had happened, but what was it?* I must have moved because the next thing I knew, my mother was at my side.

"I'm right here, honey," said my mother.

I reached up and touched my face. The left side, including my left eye, was covered in bandages.

I opened my eyes. It was still dark. But that didn't make sense. My right eye wasn't bandaged but I still couldn't see.

My mother helped me sit up and asked if I was hungry. I said, "Sure," because that's what one says. They brought me some oatmeal. In typical hospital food fashion the oatmeal was terrible—lukewarm, no flavor, a gooey mess.

"Yuck," I said, "Is there anything else on the menu?"

My mother would tell me much later that that was the precise moment when she allowed herself to think that I might be all right.

03 | intensive care

MY MEMORIES OF THE DAYS IN ICU ARE HAZY. I had no way of knowing when it was day or night. There was no peace to be had because of the constant beeping of machines, voices of nurses and doctors, quiet conversations of those who kept vigil by my bedside. It seemed that someone was always there.

I was heavily sedated and that might have been the only thing that kept me from demanding to know why I couldn't see. I kept telling myself that I was, after all, in a hospital and hospitals are where they cure people. They were probably just letting me get a little stronger before they did some surgery or other that would restore my sight.

Then, on the fourth or fifth night in the ICU, the son of one of my parent's friends was visiting. He said that he thought he'd have no problem helping them sell my car. I sat bolt upright in bed and cried, "What? Why are you going to ...," and then I stopped. There could be only one reason they were going to sell my car. There was going to be no surgery to restore my sight. This was it. This was the nub around which everyone had been circling. Now I knew.

Slowly, I sat back in bed. I heard absolutely nothing else that was said in the room that night. This darkness, this total absence of light, had become my reality. And not just my reality until they could do some kind of surgery, oh no. This was it. This was going to be my life.

Could things get any worse? I was no less depressed than I had been when I put the gun to my head. And now I had blindness to deal with on top of everything else. In an attempt to end my mental and emotional anguish I had put myself in an infinitely more terrible situation. I was still grappling with these thoughts of my bleak future when a nurse came in with a shot. The narcotic took me gently back from the precipice of despair.

"Honey," began my father, "we're moving you to a private room this morning. This gentleman will take you in a wheelchair and then we'll go over to another part of the hospital. Oh, and here's John; he wanted to tell you goodbye and wish you well." John was one of the nurses. He had become my special friend. He was never in a hurry and always spent a little extra time with me, sometimes coming around for a chat when things were quiet on the unit.

"Thanks for everything, John," I said as he hugged me.

"I'm so glad I got to take care of you while you were here. Good luck; you'll be okay, I just know it."

As the orderly wheeled me through the hospital corridors, I kept trying to decide if I was catching a glimmer of light from time to time. I gazed up towards the ceiling, sure that there would be overhead fluorescents. We entered a spacious and blessedly quiet private room before I came to any conclusion about whether I could see lights or not. I had to let that hope go for the time being.

Once I was settled in the new room I asked my father to describe the layout of the room. He walked around the room tapping the door to the bathroom, the window sill, the door to the corridor. "Does that help?" he asked when he once again stood at my bedside.

"Yes, thanks, Daddy." I wasn't sure why the layout of the

room was so important to me but it was.

After a few days in the private room the ophthalmologist told us that he was ready to do surgery. But it was not to be a surgery to restore my vision. It would be a surgery to remove my left eye, which had been badly damaged by the bullet.

I think it was Christmas Eve when the judge came to see me. I was all alone in the room, my parents having taken their leave to attend the Christmas Eve church service, and I recognized his voice at once. I was filled with wonder and gratitude that this man, this man who had served as my unwitting mentor, had come to visit.

At first, following my childhood protocol of polite optimism, I tried to make light of my new circumstances, assuring him that I would be okay, even saying I was looking forward to learning braille and getting a guide dog.

Then, the judge knelt beside the bed so that we were on the same level. Taking my hands in his, he said, in a voice thick with emotion, "I am so, so sorry."

And that did it. For the first time, I let go of the emotions that had been building in me since I understood that I was going to be blind.

For the first time I broke through the walls I had built up around myself. As I held hands with the man who had taken me into his world of horses—as I witnessed the tears of the man who had so much confidence in my abilities with Knight Commander—I began to cry.

Finally, at long last, I wept.

I wept for the loss of my sight.

But we both knew, the judge and I, it was more than the loss of my sight for which we wept.

We wept for my lost way of life.

04 | a changed world

A WEEK AFTER THE SURGERY I CAME HOME AT LAST. To say that it felt strange to be home would be an understatement. I felt reasonably sure that nothing had changed. I felt equally sure that absolutely everything had changed. It was like starting all over again. There were no half-finished projects to which I could return. There was no half-finished book lying on my bedside table just waiting for me to pick it up again. I didn't even know if there were cookies in the tin on the counter waiting to be eaten. It was as though I was entering the house in which I had lived for twenty-something years for the first time. I had a history in this house but that history was now irrelevant.

That evening my brother, Jimmy, came over for dinner and I managed to eat in front of him without any major embarrassment. It was one thing to eat a meal sitting up in a hospital bed with no one around. It was quite another to be sitting at the table with my family. *How many evenings had we sat around the table discussing school, gardening, politics, and who knows what else?* We were all there together as a family, as we had been for many years. Yet, it was different. I tried to follow the conversation but found it took way too much energy to do that as well as trying to figure out whether my fork was aimed at the spinach or the potatoes.

It was a relief to climb into the protection of my bed that night.

My bedroom was on the front of the house, facing the street. Each morning I heard cars, most of them driving from right to left as they passed the house. People were going to work. It gave me an empty feeling to know that life was going on around me as though nothing had happened. I felt wistful as I listened to the cars rushing past. *Would I ever go to work again?*

I almost always awakened early before anyone else was stirring. I would lie there, wishing I could sink back into the oblivion of sleep. Eventually, I'd hear my parents moving around. Hating to leave the safe haven of my bed, I'd drag myself up and try to face the new day.

Each morning I struggled to figure out which shirt was which and which socks matched which. After dressing there was that long trip down the hallway to the kitchen. My parent's bedroom was at one end of the hallway and the kitchen at the other. I usually managed to walk to the kitchen without too many bangs on doorjambs, although I did sometimes brush against those little spring door stoppers. When I did this the spring would boing with its silly sound. I tried to laugh when things like this happened but it wasn't easy. When we were young my friends and I used to pull those springs back and turn them loose with great glee. But this wasn't fun. *If just walking down the hall was such an ordeal, what did that mean for the rest of my life? Were things that used to be fun but weren't any longer going to haunt me forever?*

I had a conformer in my left eye. It was just a blank piece of plastic that I needed to keep in the socket until all of the healing from the surgery was over. I could then be fitted with a prosthetic eye. At first, the eye was bandaged, but by the time I left the hospital they were able to take the bandages off and give me a patch. They told me not to get it wet. That meant that I couldn't take a shower but had to take a bath instead.

My mother offered to help me the first time I took a bath. I thought this a little ridiculous but didn't possess the fortitude to decline the offer. It was horrible. My mother knelt beside the bathtub and both helped and spoke to me as though I was a child. I was so humiliated. I was just hating this.

The next time bath time came around I summoned up some courage and independence from somewhere and just took a shower. I washed my hair and everything, getting my left eye quite wet during the process. My parents were alarmed, but it ended up causing me no harm whatsoever. From this experience I learned that rebellion is sometimes a good thing. Most importantly, I learned that there was absolutely nothing wrong with me intellectually or spiritually. By spiritually, I mean that my strong and independent spirit was still alive and well. It had been cowed, certainly, but it was still there.

I could nurture it.

I could build on this.

PRUNUS SEROTINA

black cherry

PART TWO

REHABILITATION

~~~~~

It is with the heart that one sees rightly;

what is essential is invisible to the eye.

Antoine de Saint-Exupéry

05 | tabula rasa

FRIENDS BEGAN TO VISIT. Some seemed completely unconcerned about the change in my life. Others seemed uncomfortable at first but became more relaxed as time passed. The one consistent change was that all of these visits were the sit down and talk kind of visits. No longer did friends call and ask me to go play tennis. There were no invitations to go out to dinner and then to a movie. Aside from medical appointments I rarely left the house.

Jane seemed the most matter of fact and relaxed of all of my friends. She began to come over a couple of nights a week and we would spend hours in the den while she read to me. My brother, Jimmy, spent time reading with me as well. In his case we listened to an audio recording of *The Confederacy of Dunces*.

Although I enjoyed visits from friends and the time I spent reading with Jimmy and Jane I always felt the burden of my future without sight. I awakened every morning and just lay there. I longed, desperately longed, that this time, when I opened my eyes, I would be able to see again. Once I did wake up, open my eyes and realize I was still blind, everything was a struggle. Always in the past, when I had some kind of physical injury, I knew the pain and forced inactivity was finite. But this was different. I struggled to find activities which would interest and engage me.

I also had the nagging worry of the rehabilitation teacher hanging over me. She had made an appointment to come and see me about two weeks after I returned from the hospital. What was she going to be like? What was she going to do with me?

My mother told me that my rehabilitation teacher's name was Vera. On the afternoon of her first visit I waited nervously in the living room. I was not at all looking forward to this. It smacked of taking me out of my comfort zone. Granted, my comfort zone was not all that comfortable and not very large but it was, at least familiar.

"Hello, Ms. McClain," I heard my mother say. "I'm Frances Wiygul and this is my husband, Harrison. Sue is in the living room. Here, let me show you the way."

"Please, call me Vera," I heard the newcomer say. "I'm very pleased to meet you both. You have a lovely home." Vera's voice was kind of husky but in a pleasing sort of way. It radiated confidence and energy. I stood as they entered the living room.

"Vera, this is our daughter, Sue."

I held out my hand to shake Vera's. Nothing happened. Uneasily, I said, "I'm sorry, I can't see to shake your hand."

Laughing, Vera said, "That's quite all right. I can't see either." I gaped. They had sent a blind woman to be my teacher? What were they thinking? Somehow our hands found each other and we shook. Mama stepped in and gracefully guided Vera to a chair. Slowly, I sat down.

My parents had evidently learned something about Vera before this visit.

"I understand that we have some friends in common," said my father.

He mentioned a name, and Vera said, "Yes, we had dinner together just last weekend." The three of them made conversation for several minutes. This was perfectly okay with me. I felt most comfortable being an observer these days. It meant that I could just listen without anything being expected of me. After discussing mutual friends the talk turned to other matters.

"I was about seventeen when I started losing my vision," said Vera. "It went pretty quickly, and I was totally blind by the time I entered college."

"Oh, where did you attend college?" asked my mother.

"I went to Montevallo," Vera answered.

"Oh, that's a marvelous school," my mother replied. "They have an excellent music program."

"Yes-s-s-s," replied Vera, drawing out the syllable. She had a way of drawing out her words when she answered a question. It was as if she were thinking as she answered. Vera went on to say, "I have several friends who were in the music program at Montevallo. I rather lost touch with them when I went to graduate school in New York City though."

Quite involuntarily, I cleared my throat.

"Yes, dear?" my mother asked.

"Oh," I said, "I was just surprised that you went to graduate school so, um, far away."

"I really enjoyed living in New York City. Transportation is so easy there with subways and buses going almost everywhere. The hustle and bustle is really quite exhilarating," Vera added.

A short silence followed this pronouncement. I think we were all astonished. I was astonished because I couldn't imagine that someone who was blind could be so independent. My parents had even more reason to be astonished. It was only later that I learned they had been told that I would probably need a personal attendant for as long as I lived. I can only assume that this pronouncement had been made before I regained consciousness and when there was still a fear of brain damage.

Taking up the slack in the conversation Vera said, "My

job is to teach you adapted methods of performing all of those tasks that you're having trouble with now. I can teach you the skills to do almost anything. Where would you like to start?"

"What do you mean," I replied.

"Well, what kinds of things do you want to learn to do?" I thought hard about this question. The truth was that I was having trouble doing almost everything but, "Everything," didn't seem a reasonable response to the question.

I settled on asking a question of my own. "Could you give me some examples?"

"Well," said Vera, "We can divide the skills I can teach you into several areas. Of course, there's always cooking but we can save that for later. What about clothing? You know, sorting your clothes for laundering and matching them once they're clean. Then there's the whole area of 'communications.' When you can't see, the trick is to store information in a format that will allow you to retrieve it later."

"How would I do that?" I asked incredulously.

"The tape recorder is an excellent means of information storage and retrieval for someone who can't see. You might also want to consider learning braille. Why don't you tell me a little bit about yourself and that might help us know where to start."

I hesitated for a moment and then said, "I love to read. I was an English major in college. I also did a lot of whitewater kayaking and mountain climbing. I like to go for long walks and I like to swim." I abruptly stopped speaking. Just thinking about those things gave me a feeling of despair. Surely all of those activities were impossible for me now.

"The recreational skills we can leave for later," said Vera. "I know it seems farfetched at this moment but, as time goes on, you'll be able to do all sorts of recreational activities.

"With your love of literature, why don't we start with reading and the broader area of communications? I've brought some braille instructional books with me and we can start now, if you like." This was more than I had bargained for, but gamely I agreed. I heard Vera rummaging in her bag. Then she handed me a braille book.

"Before we get into the book let me tell you how braille works. Each character is made up of a combination of six dots. These six dots comprise one braille cell. You can think of each letter of the alphabet being composed of one cell of dots. There are two columns and three rows. The dots are numbered, beginning with the top left dot. That is designated as dot 1. Dot 2 is below it, and dot 3 below that. Dot 4 is on the top right, with 5 below that, and 6 at the bottom on the right side. When we speak of the dots which compose each character, we can describe them by the numbers. So, for example, the letter A is composed of dot 1 only. B is composed of dots 1 and 2. Get the idea?"

"Yes, that makes perfect sense," I replied.

"Okay," Vera continued. "Now go ahead and open your book. Feel across the top of each page until you feel some raised letters. The first five letters we'll learn are A, B, C, D, and E. Can you find the page with these letters embossed across the top?"

"Well, no," I replied, puzzled. "I don't know what those letters look like in braille so I'm not sure what to look for."

Vera laughed. "No, the letters I'm wanting you to find are the regular letters, you know, not the braille ones."

I opened the book and began to feel across the top of the pages. Immediately I found what Vera described.

"Okay, got it."

"If you feel just below each embossed letter you'll find the braille representation for that letter."

I felt in the direction she had indicated.

"Okay, got it."

The lesson proceeded and at the end of over an hour I

was able to read words like "Cab," "Dad," and "Bad."

As Vera prepared to leave, she told me that the book was self-paced and that I could continue as far as I liked between now and her next visit. We set an appointment for the next week, and Vera left in a taxi.

It had taken enormous concentration just to get to the point where I could read simple three-letter words. While this feat gave me some small feeling of accomplishment, I couldn't help thinking that the whole thing was absurd. The part of me that flew over fences mounted on a huge thoroughbred, the part of me that kayaked the toughest whitewater rivers in the Southeast, the part of me who had zipped through college—that part of me was almost ashamed. I was almost ashamed that learning to do something so simple as reading a three-letter word in braille gave me satisfaction.

06 | a feel for braille

PUTTING ASIDE MY COMPLICATED EMOTIONS about learning to read three-letter words, Vera's visit was not what I had anticipated. She was charming and capable and, I had to admit, a little intimidating. The very thought of walking around New York City alone was beyond my comprehension. However intimidated I may have been—however absurd it seemed to be learning to read three-letter words at the age of twenty-six—Vera had managed to provide to me a direction for forward motion. *What choice did I have?* It was either sink back into that paralyzing depression or move ahead, however slowly.

I immersed myself in learning braille. I worked on it several hours a day and soon was able to read many more words. After I had learned about half the alphabet, the book presented some short sentences to read. I was so slow at this that I sometimes forgot the first part of the sentence by the time I got to the end. Vera assured me that the speed would come as long as I kept practicing.

A few days after Vera's first visit my mother was pulling some muffins out of the oven.

"You know what?" she asked, sounding startled. "What?" Daddy and I responded at the same time. "This muffin tin looks just like a big braille cell."

I pictured the muffin tin in my head. "You know, you're right," I exclaimed. I mulled over this interesting fact but didn't see its significance until Jane came over for our next book reading session. I showed Jane the muffin tin.

She thought for a minute and then said, "You know, I think we could use this to help you learn braille."

Puzzled, I said, "What do you mean?"

Jane asked if we had some tennis balls. Getting the idea, I dug up six tennis balls that were hiding in my abandoned sports bag. Jane took the muffin tin, the balls, and me back to my bedroom. We spread out on the floor.

Jane said, "Do you have the braille alphabet somewhere that I can look at?"

"Yes," I showed Jane the books that Vera had brought on her first visit. "It's in one of these books." After a few minutes she found it.

She said, "Okay, I'll place the balls in the muffin tin and you feel them and tell me what letter they represent."

And so we played a sort of braille flash card game. It worked great and it was fun. I progressed rapidly through the entire alphabet.

During Vera's third visit I had a surprise for her.

"Hi, it's good to see you," I said as she tapped her cane to her usual chair. "I've learned the whole alphabet!"

"Well, that's most impressive," she replied. She seemed delighted with my progress. "Now it's time to learn the numbers." Eagerly, I picked up my book asking if that was the next lesson.

"Yes, it's the next lesson. And after that you'll learn punctuation."

"And after that, I'll be done?" I asked. I had noticed how close to the end of the book I was getting and assumed I had almost finished learning the braille code.

Vera chuckled, "Oh, no, after that we move on to book two."

"Book two?" I deflated slightly.

"Yes, you see, braille has over two hundred contractions in addition to the alphabet, numbers, and punctuation."

"Okay," I said gamely, "Let's go." I wasn't at all distressed by the prospect of learning more braille. Learning braille had become a comfortable task. I looked forward to each day when I knew I would sit down with my braille book and spend several hours working through the new characters. Working on braille was an activity in which I found real purpose.

My days began to take on some structure, and I began to shed those feelings of hopelessness and pointlessness.

07 | living again

IT WAS DURING THIS SAME THIRD LESSON THAT I ASKED VERA about her cane and her use of the cane.

"My vocational rehab counselor told me that I'd need to have an orientation and mobility specialist to teach me how to use a cane," I began. "Is it hard to walk with a cane?"

"Oh, no," Vera replied, "I've been doing it for so long now, though, that it's kind of second nature."

"I feel like my VR counselor is copping out on me," I said. "He told me I'd need an O&M instructor but then he told me that I'd have to go to the School for the Blind in Talladega to get lessons. That seems kind of crazy. Surely there's someone here in Birmingham who could teach me to use a cane."

"Well, I do know a man who has just left his job with a private rehab agency to go to work at the Veterans Administration blind rehab center. Would you like for me to give you his phone number?"

"Yes, that would be great," I answered.

That's how I met Oscar. It was difficult to get in touch with Oscar. Vera gave me his phone number at the VA but the switchboard didn't seem to know he existed. Finally my father was able to ask enough questions to discover that the Southeastern Blind Rehab Center, SBRC, of the VA was just getting started. This being the case the main switchboard could be forgiven for their lack of information.

Finally, I managed to speak to Oscar on a cold January afternoon.

"Are you Oscar Thompson," I began.

"Yes, how can I help you?" he answered.

"My name is Sue Wiygul and I've been working with Vera McClain. She gave me your name."

"Oh, and how is Vera doing these days?"

She's fine and she's really helping me a lot. I'm calling because I need a mobility instructor. Vera said that you might be willing to work with me privately."

A long silence followed.

"Well, I'm just starting this new job and things are a little crazy just now. If you're working with Vera isn't the State rehab office going to assign an orientation and mobility instructor to work with you?"

"No," I replied. "They say I'll have to go to Talladega to get lessons and I'm not sure I can do that. I've only been blind for a few weeks and I just don't think I can handle that."

Another pause, and then, "Okay," Oscar said slowly, I'll see what I can do."

Relieved I said, "Great, what happens now?"

"I'd like to come and meet you and explain what orientation and mobility is and what I can teach you. Let's start there."

And so, we agreed to meet the following Tuesday afternoon. Once again, my mother, father, and I waited in the living room for another stranger to ring the bell.

"Hello, I'm Oscar."

"Nice to meet you, Oscar," said my father. "We really appreciate you coming to meet with us. Here, Sue and Frances are in the living room. Come on in."

Like Vera, Oscar radiated energy and confidence. *Was this some kind of job requirement for people involved in blind rehab?* I felt small and mousy compared to this energetic individual. I was still wearing a patch over my left eye and I hadn't come close to regaining the weight I had lost in the hospital.

"We really appreciate you agreeing to meet with us," began my mother. "I understand that you've just started a new job. Please, sit down and relax. Can I get you something to drink?"

"Yes, that would be great," Oscar replied. With a Coke in hand Oscar began to describe what he could teach me.

"Stated simply, orientation and mobility is a discipline which will allow you, as a blind person, to use cues from your environment to know where you are and how to get to where you want to be."

I felt that Oscar was not simply looking at me but looking into me somehow. His earnestness and belief in what he said was quite powerful.

Continuing, he said, "Then I can teach you a set of skills with a long cane which will enable you to move safely and independently through the world. You will learn to think very systematically. You'll find that this systematic way of thinking will serve you well in more areas than just traveling with your cane. In truth, you don't have the luxury of being anything other than systematic now that you are blind."

"What do you mean," I asked. Then, thinking I might have sounded rude, I added, "I mean, can you explain that a little more?"

"Of course." I heard a smile in Oscar's voice when he said this. "You've probably already discovered that you can't just leave things lying around like you used to."

"That's the truth," I almost groaned.

"You're probably finding that you need to have a place for everything and be very systematic about putting things in their place rather than just putting them down wherever. The same habits will serve you well when you travel with a cane.

For example, when you come to an intersection you need to run through a kind of checklist. Is your alignment correct? What is the traffic pattern? At which moment is it ideal to begin your street crossing?"

I suppose Oscar saw my "deer in the headlights" look because he continued quickly, "All of that will become second nature to you after a while. What's more, those skills are down the road a piece. There are many skills you'll need to learn before we start crossing streets."

"Could you explain that a little further," said my father.

"Sure," said Oscar. "The first set of skills, and probably the most immediately practical, are those involved in walking with a sighted guide."

"Yes," my father agreed, "We've been making it up as we go. Sue has had a number of medical appointments and, while we always manage to get there I'd be quite interested in discovering a way to do it more effectively and gracefully."

"We can do a little bit right now if you like," replied Oscar. In the silence that followed I felt quite sure that all eyes were upon me.

"Okay," I said a bit hesitantly, "let's give it a try."

Oscar stood and moved into the center of the living room. "Okay, Sue, stand up."

I stood and took a step towards Oscar.

"The first thing you need to learn is how to make contact," he said. "As your sighted guide it is my responsibility to make contact with you. This prevents you from groping around in space trying to locate me."

He stepped toward me and turned so that we were facing in the same direction.

"Now, I'll touch the back of your hand with the back of my hand," he continued. "I'm not going to grab your hand, just make a light contact. That's your clue to knowing where I am and knowing that I'm offering to let you take my arm. When I touch your hand you run your hand up my arm and then grip just above the elbow. Let's try it." I felt Oscar brush the back of my hand with his and I ran my hand up to just above his elbow. I gripped the inside of his arm.

"That's it," said Oscar. "Just one little correction. Hold my arm as though you are gripping a glass of water. Your thumb should be on the outside and your fingers on the inside."

Adjusting my grip I said, "Like this."

"Exactly. Now when I move forward let me get about a half step in front of you before you begin to move." He stepped forward and, after a second, I moved along with him.

"That's it," he said. "Now let's do a little walking together." We moved across the living room, into the dining room, out onto the porch, and then back into the living room.

"Okay, that's great," said Oscar. "How did that feel to you?"

"It feels fine," I said.

Addressing my mother and father he said, "This way you are just a little ahead of Sue and she knows that her path is clear as long as you are moving steadily forward. Want to give it a try?"

"Sure," said my father. He rose and we went through the same procedure. Then my mother gave it a whirl. When she made contact with the back of my hand she turned hers so that she grabbed my hand.

"Hang on," said Oscar. "That's the most common mistake I see. Just touch the back of Sue's hand with yours. Think of it as a kind of request. You're letting Sue know that you're there and offering to let her take your arm."

"Oh, sorry about that." I heard the smile in my mother's voice. Then she tried again.

"That's it," said Oscar. After we had all retraced the route that Oscar had taken with me earlier Oscar said, "Okay, that was great. Now we'll address passing through narrow places."

Oscar and I went through the routine of making contact again and then he led me out of the living room in the opposite direction to that we had taken earlier. "Now we're approaching this narrower passage in the entrance hall," he said. "I'm going to tuck my arm behind my back. That's your clue that we're entering a narrow passage. When you feel that you should straighten your arm and step directly behind me. Straightening your arm should place you far enough behind me so that you don't step on my heels."

We tried it. Then I tried it with both of my parents.

"Okay, that's great," said Oscar. "Now we'll take a look at passing through doorways together. Sue, when you pass through a doorway there are two things you need to know. First, is the door opening towards you or away from you. Then you need to know which side it's on."

With me holding Oscar's arm again, we approached the door into the kitchen. "This door opens away from you on the right," said Oscar. Your sighted guide should give you this information as you approach each doorway. What I want you to do as we walk through the door is take a little bit of control yourself. You're holding my right arm with your left. That leaves your right hand free to take control of the door as you approach it." We moved forward and, reaching out with my right hand I found the door and held it as we passed through.

"In a situation like this it's not that big of a deal, but you'll find this really helps a lot with doors that close automatically behind you."

Remembering more than one door that had hit my heels as I walked through it I said, "Oh, I get it. This will be much better."

After Oscar showed us how to handle doorways, we all put on sweaters and went outside where he demonstrated negotiating stairs.

Addressing my parents Oscar said, "A slight pause will

allow Sue to know that you're at the top or bottom of a flight of stairs. You might want to let her know whether the stairs are going up or down. Another slight pause when you've reached the end of the flight of stairs might be good at first but, Sue, eventually you'll be able to tell that you've reached the level ground again by the angle of your guide's elbow.

"Well, I think that's a good place to stop," said Oscar. I've already been here for two hours, and it's getting late."

Two hours? I couldn't believe it.

Over a light dinner we discussed the evening activities.

"He seems very knowledgeable," began my father.

"Yeah," I replied. "And I can't believe how much easier it is to walk with you using the things he showed us."

Later, alone with my thoughts, I looked forward. I looked forward to trying out the new sighted guide techniques. I looked forward to having a cane in my hand. The ability to simply look forward, let alone the act itself, had been a pretty scarce commodity recently. It felt good.

08 | with cane i'm able

THE FOLLOWING SATURDAY OSCAR CAME TO PICK ME UP at around 10:00. He had asked that I locate a place for us to work that day. He told me to find a place with long open hallways that wouldn't be very crowded on a Saturday morning.

We went to a church a little way from our house. "Okay," began Oscar. "Let's review the sighted guide techniques you learned last time." We walked up and down the hallways. I couldn't believe how fast Oscar moved and it was difficult, at first, to keep up with him.

"Yikes," I said. "You're flying. I haven't walked this fast in weeks."

"Yeah, I'm sure you haven't. But blindness is no reason to adopt a slower gait than usual."

Mulling over this announcement as we zipped down the halls, I wasn't so sure but I kept my silence.

Presently, though, Oscar said, "Now I'm going to walk a bit slower. We'll walk along the hallway together and I want you to listen carefully as we go. Tell me if you hear anything different as we go along."

"Hear anything, what do you mean," I asked.

"Just listen," replied Oscar. After a few minutes of walking in silence I began to notice something familiar. I had heard these changes when walking up and down the hall at home.

"Oh," I said, "We're walking past doorways and I can hear the difference when we pass one."

"That's it," said Oscar. "Keep listening."

"Whoa," I said after a few more minutes. "There's something on the left. Is it an intersecting hallway?"

"Exactly," said Oscar. "Now you're getting the idea."

"Now it's time for you to walk on your own a bit," he said.

"I don't know about that," I muttered.

"Trust me," he said. "Here's what you do. Reach out with your left hand until you feel the wall. That's it. Now, hold your right arm across the front of your body like this."

He positioned my right arm at an angle so that it was in front of my abdomen.

"This is called the lower hand and forearm protective technique," he said. "Now walk down the hall trailing your left hand lightly along the wall. Your right arm will contact anything blocking your way so you won't run into it."

I walked. As I passed by doors I'd lose contact with the wall for a couple of steps but it was always right there when I reached the other side of the doorway. Oscar showed me another position for my right arm, this time placing it so that it was in front of my chest and face.

Then it was time for lunch. My mother had packed us a picnic lunch and we found a room with table and chairs. Sitting down gratefully I asked, "What's next?"

"After lunch I'll cut your cane and then it'll be time for you to begin learning to use it," said Oscar.

"Cut it?" I asked.

"Yes, your cane needs to be the proper length for your height and your stride." It was pleasant, sitting there and munching our sandwiches together.

"Have you been doing this very long?" I asked.

"Yes, a few years," Oscar replied.

"Do you ever have people who have only been blind for a few weeks, like me?" I asked.

"Yes," and continuing he said, "But I seldom get people who seem so eager and willing to learn O&M like you are."

Startled, I asked, "But why wouldn't someone want to learn to walk independently?"

"Most of the time people who have been blind for such a short period of time aren't thrilled about learning cane travel."

"But why?" I asked. This didn't make sense to me. My reliance on others to move about had been driving me crazy.

"Blindness still has a pretty negative connotation in the world," said Oscar. "People seem to think it's something to be ashamed of."

"But why?" I asked again.

"Well, think about what you know about blindness and blind people," said Oscar. "The Bible is the worst. Blind people are depicted in the Bible as beggars. Or else they're only mentioned in connection with being cured of their blindness. If you think about it just the phrase, 'cured of blindness', makes it sound like blindness is some kind of sickness that everybody hopes they'll recover from."

This struck home. Into my mind rushed all of those early morning periods of wishful thinking before I opened my eyes. Finally, and very slowly, I said, "Yes, I see what you mean."

"The other thing," continued Oscar, "Is that most of the people I work with are losing their sight gradually. It's a lot more difficult to adjust to gradual sight loss than having it go all at once like you did."

"You're kidding!" I spluttered. "What do you mean?"

"When people lose their sight gradually they can pretend, up to a point, that they can still see. They don't necessarily have to learn to use a cane right away or make a great many other changes in their lives. We call it, 'passing'. You know, trying to pass as a sighted person."

"So, they fake it," I asked incredulously.

"Yep," said Oscar. "It can cause all kinds of problems too."

"I can't imagine," I said thoughtfully. "I wish I had had time to adjust gradually."

"Why?" asked Oscar. "You only have to go through the trauma of losing your sight once. You know that you, absolutely, have to learn braille and learn to use a cane. Believe me, you're further down the road to adjusting to or accepting your blindness than you know."

I hesitated for a minute and then blurted, "But this is so hard! Every morning when I wake up I think that maybe when I open my eyes again I'll be able to see." I rushed on, "Every time I go to do something I get drawn up short, forgetting that I don't know how to do whatever it is now that I can't see." And out rushed all of the worries and concerns about my future that I had been bottling up. There was something about Oscar that made me feel comfortable about pouring forth all of my doubts and fears.

Oscar listened calmly until I ran out of steam. "Well, that was quite a speech," he said when I finally fell silent. And suddenly I was laughing through my tears. Oscar laughed too. I don't know if it was the laughter or the tears but suddenly I felt a lot better.

"Time for dessert and then it's back to the grindstone," said Oscar with mock sternness. He handed me a cookie, took one himself and we ate them in silence. When we had finished our cookies, Oscar picked up a cane I hadn't realized he even had, and he said, "Let's go in that big room at the end of the hall."

Once there I asked to see my new cane. Handing it to me Oscar said, "It's way too long for you. Let me measure and then I'll cut it for you. Stand straight for a second."

Oscar placed the cane vertically in front of me and told me to hold still. I felt him touch my sternum and then he said, "Okay, forty eight inches should do it."

He cut the cane and then fitted a nylon tip on it.

"I'm using a marshmallow tip for you," he said. "It's larger than the old pencil type cane tips and it's not as likely to catch in cracks and stuff. Okay, here you go."

I took my cane feeling like Oscar was giving me the keys to some kingdom. I knew perfectly well that this cane would afford me independence once I learned to use it. I examined it carefully and then said, "The grip feels just like the grip on a golf club."

Laughing, Oscar replied, "That's because it is a grip from a golf club."

"Oh," I muttered. And then gripping the cane as though it really was a golf club I took a golfer's stance and pretended that I was going to take a swing at Oscar. "Watch out!" I said. "I used to swing a mean golf club."

"Okay, okay," he said. "I'm the boss here and there'll be none of that!"

"Right," I replied. "Is this better?" I stood with both feet together looking down at the floor pretending to be demure. "How's this?"

Putting on a voice like WC Fields, he said, ""That's better my little chickadee."

"Are you left or right handed?" Oscar asked.

"Right," I replied.

"Okay, here's how to hold your cane. You want the flat part of the grip to be on the right. Then you grasp it with your right hand. Extend your index finger straight down the cane. You can think of the cane as an extension of your index finger."

"Like this?" I asked, assuming the hand position that he

had described.

"Yes, exactly. Then you want to extend your right arm ahead and down at about a forty-five degree angle and try to hold your hand right at the center line of your body."

Adjusting the afore mentioned parts of my body I asked, "Like this? Hmm, feels kind of funny," I muttered.

"Don't worry, it will feel perfectly natural before long," Oscar said. "I want you to practice swinging the cane before you actually move. The movement of the cane should come from your wrist only. Your arm should remain relatively still and straight in the center of your body. You'll be tapping the cane from left to right as you walk. The distance you swing the cane should approximate the distance between your shoulders. Here, let me show you."

He stepped forward and, grasping my right hand, moved it from side to side showing me the correct distance to swing the cane on each side. Oscar had me tap the cane from side to side without moving until I got the feel of the correct arc. Then he showed me how to keep in step. With one hand on my shoulder and one on my right wrist he explained that I should tap the cane on the left side as I stepped forward with my right foot and vice versa.

I walked forward slowly thinking about keeping my hand centered, swinging the cane the correct distance from side to side, and keeping in step. It was difficult. Finally Oscar told me to go for it. It felt awkward. Oscar encouraged me to keep moving and pick up my pace. Eventually I hit a sort of rhythm. As I approached the end of the room Oscar told me to stop. Then he'd trot back to the other end and have me walk towards his voice. It was difficult to get started on each pass but got easier the more I did it.

"Okay," said Oscar, "How did that feel?"

"Um, okay, I guess." We stopped for a few minutes to review the various components of this cane travel deal.

And then we did some more walking. "Hang on," said Oscar. "You're not in step."

"Oh, sorry about that," I said, coming to a halt. "But what difference does being in step make? I mean, as long as I'm swinging wide enough to cover the width of my body, why do I have to be in step?"

"Because you're clearing the space where your next footfall will land," said Oscar. "Go ahead, take a step with your right foot and tap on your left side." I did as he instructed. "Now stop," Oscar said. "Think about where your next step will land. Your cane is touching right about where your left foot is going to be in a second. Because you've just touched there with your cane you know that space is clear of obstacles."

I had to think about this for a minute. Then finally, "Oh, I get it now."

"Hang on, I need to think for a second."

Once I had my mind wrapped around the concept I started walking again.

"Yes," said Oscar. "Now you've got it." I walked up and down the length of the room several times trying to get used to staying in step.

"Great," said Oscar. "Now let's go out in the hall here." Keeping my mind on staying in step, I followed the sound of Oscar's voice to the door.

"Okay, go for it," Oscar encouraged.

And, off, down the hallway I went. It felt great. I was walking by myself for the first time in weeks. Paying attention to nothing except keeping my hand centered and staying in step I was brought up short when my cane tip collided with the wall at the other end of the hall. "Hey," I called back to Oscar. "It works! It stopped me before I walked slap into this wall."

"Yes, great job," Oscar called back. "You're definitely getting the hang of it."

We spent the rest of the lesson with me walking up and

down the corridors. I loved the feeling that I was walking on my own. Finally, Oscar said that it was time to go. I opened the tactual watch that Vera had given me and felt the hands.

"Wow, how did it get to be so late?" I asked in astonishment.

"Time flies . . . " began Oscar.

"When you're having fun," I finished.

Laughing together, we left the church.

09 | daddy to the rescue

MY EDUCATION IN BRAILLE WITH VERA CONTINUED. She brought me another book which had braille on the right hand page and print on the left. Using this book I was able to work with my mother. She hadn't quite gotten the hang of the tennis ball and muffin tin trick but she did spend hours sitting on the couch with me as I worked through the two hundred and something braille contractions.

Vera moved on to tasks in other areas. Continuing in the realm of communications she brought me several hand writing guides. These were made of plastic and had strips cut out of them.

Handing me a clip board she said, "Here's a full-page writing guide. Take a look." The clipboard had several sheets of paper with a sheet of plastic clipped on top.

"You can see that there are long horizontal strips cut out of the plastic," she continued. "Here's a pen. Give it a try."

Taking the pen, I located the top strip, positioned the pen at the left end of it and began to write. It wasn't easy. When I lifted the pen at the end of one word I felt unsure about where to put it to start writing the next word.

"I feel kind of lost," I said.

"I know," said Vera. "It takes some practice. If you let the clipboard rest on your lap you can use your left index finger to follow the progress of the pen as you write. That will help you know how much space to leave between words and when to start a new line." I tried it. She was right but it felt awkward.

After a few minutes Vera handed me two other writing guides. One had cutouts strategically placed for addressing an envelope and the other was about the size of a credit card and had just one cutout. "The larger one is for envelopes and the smaller one is just a signature guide," Vera told me.

I tried each in turn. After a few minutes of serious concentration I burst out laughing. "You know what," I said in an astonished voice. "I'm staring down at this writing guide like I can actually see what I'm doing."

With a knowing laugh Vera said, "Yes, I still do the same thing. It's perfectly normal and you'll probably always do it."

Next came the typewriter. I had the typewriter I'd used in college and Vera told me to have it set up for her next visit. I knew I should be able to type without being able to see the keys. How many times had my high school typing teacher admonished me to not look at the keys?

"Okay," Vera began at our next lesson, "I know you learned to touch type a long time ago but let's just review the layout of the keyboard. Find the spacebar and then move up two rows from that. Feel along that third row up and you'll find two keys with little bumps you can feel."

It seemed to take about half an hour to accomplish this but I finally said, "Okay, got it. Hmm, I've never noticed these before. Have they always been here?"

"Yep, and what's more you'll probably find them on every typewriter you ever need to use. Now, settle your index fingers on the two keys with the bumps and the rest of your fingers should fall naturally on the home row keys."

Vera then spent quite a long time calling out keys for me to strike, all the time explaining and reacquainting me with the layout of the keyboard.

"This is just weird," I said after a while. "How do I know

if I'm hitting the right keys or not?"

"Well, let's see." She dictated a couple of sentences for me to type. It was slow going. When I finished Vera told me to take the page to my mother who was in the kitchen to see how I had done. To my amazement, I had only made a couple of mistakes.

"Now, typing is like braille in the sense that you can work on your own and at your own speed." Pulling an index card with braille on it out of her bag she said, "Here, this is the phone number for a free correspondence course in typing."

"But," I began.

Anticipating my concerns she added, "It's a school in Illinois that develops courses for people who are blind. The courses are tape recorded and you send in your lessons as you complete them. A teacher at the school will grade you and send your results back to you in a braille letter." I couldn't think of any other objections so I took the card.

"There are beginning, intermediate, and advanced courses. Even though you've had typing in your sighted life I'd suggest that you start with the beginner's course . . . just to brush up."

A week later, when my typing course on tape arrived, I was very glad that Vera had told me to start at the beginning. It was unexpectedly difficult. I set up the tape recorder next to the typewriter and began. I was supposed to be able to just start the tape playing and keep up with it. There were long pauses in which I was supposed to be able to type what the tape told me to type and then be ready when it began speaking again. At first I couldn't do it at all.

"Vera, this is impossible," I wailed at our next lesson. "I just can't do it."

"What you need to do, at first, is make liberal use of the pause key on the tape recorder," she soothed. "Here, let's give it a try."

Soon I got the hang of listening to a phrase, pausing the tape, and then typing the phrase. "But I feel like I'm cheating," I moaned.

"That's okay," Vera said. "Just do it this way until you get your accuracy and speed going again and then you'll be able to keep up."

As usual, Vera was right. Remembering something completely unrelated to typing I said, "Hey, I've been wondering. Is there a writing guide for writing checks?"

"Well, there are some check writing guides but they don't always fit every check." Digging into her bag, which always seemed to contain whatever was needed, Vera said, "Here's one. You'll have to get your father or mother to look at it and see if it fits your checks." It didn't.

"There's another way of custom making a writing guide for anything," Vera continued, completely unperturbed. "If you can get your hands on some clear plastic you can make your own guide. You lay the plastic over the check and then cut out the strips so they exactly match your checks."

This time it was my father who came to the rescue. I described the dilemma over dinner that night. After a few thoughtful minutes my father said, "I think I know just the thing." Although retired from his medical practice for a couple of years, my father still had plenty of colleagues and friends at the hospital. The next day he returned from an errand and came into the den where I was reading.

"I've got it," he said. "Let's go back to the bedroom. I have some exposed X-ray film. Here, I'll tack it over one of your checks on this cutting board."

He then took up a scalpel and carefully cut strips out of the film exactly over the places on the check where I would have to write in the date, amount, and so forth.

"Now, let's see," he continued. "I'll cut another piece of film for a backing." In his precise way he taped the two pieces of plastic together at the left edge. "Here you go," he said, handing me his finished product. "You can open the two pieces like a book and slip your check in between them. Then the cutouts will be perfectly aligned over the places where you need to write."

"Hey, this is great," I exclaimed." Pausing a moment I added, "And whose broken arm is pictured in my check writing guide?"

With a chuckle he said, "No one's. I had the X-ray technician just expose a blank sheet of film."

10 | i did it

A S MY LESSONS WITH VERA AND OSCAR PROCEEDED, life began to have a little bit of a rhythm. In no time at all I looked forward eagerly to each of my lessons. I liked the lessons with both of them but I think I liked the mobility lessons best. I loved the action and I loved that Oscar was teaching me why I did things in a certain way rather than just teaching me to do them.

Nonetheless I was still sleeping badly. In those hours when I lay awake my mind still wandered to everything I had lost and to the feelings of hopelessness that still plagued me. In late February my doctor suggested that I enroll in some classes at nearby Samford University. Although the suggestion seemed slightly ludicrous I agreed. Without a clear notion of why, I decided to enroll in a psychology class. Maybe I thought I would learn something that would help me understand myself better. Or maybe it was just that I thought a psychology class would contain fewer obstacles than an English or math class.

Whatever the reason, I found myself enrolled in a developmental psychology class that began in just three weeks' time.

Abandoning his systematic lesson plan in the face of this new endeavor, Oscar and I began to go to Samford University for the few remaining lessons before my class began.

The building in which my class was held was a five story building. On the first day Oscar and I scouted out the building. We walked, with Oscar as my sighted guide, all over the building. This was before the days of The Americans with Disabilities Act or any passing nod to universal access. There was simply no good way to get from the place where my mother or father would drop me off to the classroom.

"There could have been an easy route . . . b-u-t . . . n-o-o-o-. . . ," muttered Oscar, placing a big emphasis on the last two words. This was an expression I'd hear many times during our work together.

Deciding on a route at last, Oscar described it to me as we walked it together. I had to enter the building through the northeast door. Then I had to travel about thirty feet down a corridor while looking for the first door on the left. After locating this door, I had to pass through it into a stairwell. Up two flights of stairs and then back out into the hallway. Turning left I had to go to the end of that hallway, turn right and travel about half the length of it until I found an elevator on the right. Buttons in elevators weren't brailled in those days. I just had to memorize the layout of the buttons and press the one for the fifth floor. Once there I had to turn right, go to the end of the hall, take another right and walk all the way to the end of that hall and, so, into the class.

Upon hearing of this complicated route both of my parents suggested that they just walk to the classroom with me. To their credit, they backed down from this offer when Oscar and I both said that it was a challenge, the meeting of which would be a huge victory to me and my self-confidence.

And so we began. Over and over, Oscar and I worked the route to the classroom. The stairs were the most difficult for me. Locating the first step on the trip down the stairs was still a little frightening although I had done it many times. As I approached the top of the stairs I'd shorten my stride and slow my pace dramatically.

"Here," said Oscar, "I'll stand a couple of steps down to keep you from falling. Try to keep your head up. You won't see anything by tucking your chin and looking down and it's affecting your balance."

Although I had laughed when I looked down at the envelope I was addressing when Vera gave me the envelope guide, this was different. "I know I can't see anything but I just can't help trying," I said.

"Go back to the doorway into the stairwell," said Oscar. "Try walking forward with your normal stride. Most importantly, keep your head up and concentrate on what you can feel with your cane rather then what you can't see with your eyes."

Taking a deep breath I did as I was told. Although still frightening, my approach to stairs gradually became smoother and more confident. By now it was early March and the weather was becoming warmer. We were able to have our picnics outside and Oscar began to take advantage of the beautiful Samford campus. The University sits on a hillside with the buildings arranged in a semicircle around a huge sloping green lawn. Sidewalks described the semicircle with all kinds of intersecting walkways and entrances to the buildings. Oscar showed me how to stay on a curving sidewalk by "shorelining."

"It's called 'shorelining,' because orientation and mobility got its start as a profession during and immediately after World War II," Oscar explained. "A lot of veterans of that war returned with new blindness. The Veterans Administration was the birthplace of the profession of blind rehabilitation so you'll hear some military terms from time to time." In my case, 'shorelining' meant following along the edge of a sidewalk rather than walking down the middle. I could use this technique to follow a curving sidewalk or to locate an intersecting one.

Finally, the evening of the first class arrived. Oscar told me to call him when I returned from Samford to let him know how it went. My parents both came along for the ride and I cheerfully announced that I would see them in two hours when the class was over. Taking a deep breath I began the route.

With a huge sigh of relief and a warm feeling of accomplishment I entered the classroom at the end of the last hallway. The teacher, Dr. Kernan, met me at the door and assisted me in finding an empty chair. Everyone seemed relaxed as they chatted before the beginning of the class. Didn't they realize that I had just accomplished the impossible? Heart still pounding I removed my tape recorder from my bag and was ready when Dr. Kernan began.

"I did it!" I said triumphantly when Oscar answered the phone. I took him through the route describing each turn, how I had found the elevator, how I had found each of the first steps on my way down the two flights of stairs. I didn't mention the way my stomach squirmed as I approached each of these steps feeling that I'd rather keep that to myself.

"Okay, now it's time to get down to business again," Oscar said as he picked me up for our next Saturday lesson.

"Cool," I said. "What's next?"

"We're going to begin your training on the streets of Birmingham. Let's go."

As in the case of Vera and the matter of grade 2 braille, I was not disappointed to learn that I had much more to learn. We got in the car and Oscar drove to a quiet residential part of Birmingham. As we stood on the street corner wearing light sweaters, Oscar began describing the layout of streets and sidewalks. "Every block in this neighborhood is exactly square," he began. "There's a sidewalk running beside each street separated from the street by a grassy strip. I'm going to help you get lined up to begin with," he continued. "Then I want you to walk straight down this sidewalk until you get to the next intersection."

"How will I know I'm there?" I asked.

"There will be a down curb. You should be able to feel it with your cane. Now, get going."

Taking a deep breath and hesitating long enough to make sure all of my body parts were in the correct position I began. It seemed I had walked about a half a mile. Where was that darn down curb? I slowed my pace uncertainly.

Oscar, who seemed to have been expecting this called, "You're doing fine. Keep going."

Finally, I felt the tip of my cane touch nothing. I had arrived at the end of the block at last. So relieved I was to finally know where I was, I forgot to stop for a second or two. With toes dangling over the down curb, I teetered.

"Okay, great job," announced Oscar as he steadied me. "Step off of the curb and then turn 180 degrees. I want you to use this down curb to line-up and see if you can establish a line of direction to return to our starting point. Oh, and this time, when you feel your cane out there in mid-air, try to stop a little sooner than later."

Hearing the smile in Oscar's voice, I did as he directed. A couple of times, while walking back along the sidewalk, I felt my cane hit grass. Trying to correct the veer I had obviously made, I did a quick check to make sure that my hand was centered and that I was in step. This time I walked right off of the sidewalk into the street when I reached the end of the block. Gaining my balance I tried turning right around and stepping back up onto the sidewalk. The only problem was that the sidewalk wasn't there anymore. I stepped up onto grass instead. Knowing that Oscar had been right behind me during my walk down the sidewalk I called out, "Okay, I give up. What did I do wrong?"

Knowing a teachable moment when he saw one, Oscar

said, "Grab on. We'll go sit on this wall for a minute."

Taking Oscar's proffered arm I followed him over to a low stone wall. "'Kinesthetics,'" Oscar began, "refers to the ability to judge distances based on your speed of movement and the passage of time."

After our discussion of kinesthetics, Oscar showed me how to systematically search for the sidewalk if I veered during a crossing or if I did a one-eighty only to find that it was not there.

I was ready to try it again. Oscar had told me to tell him when I thought I was drawing close to the end of the block. He, in turn, said that he would tell me the same bit of information if I got within six feet of the down curb but had not said anything. I traveled the block a few more times and felt more comfortable approaching the down curb each time. On those occasions when I accidentally stepped out into the street, I learned to stay calm, turn around, and not panic if the sidewalk wasn't right in front of me. Using the systematic technique that Oscar showed me, I was able to relocate the sidewalk every time.

"Okay, good job," said Oscar as I found the end of the block and managed to stop before stepping off for the third time in a row. "Now we're going to begin crossing streets."

Oscar showed me how to bring my cane right up perpendicular to the curb and close to my body. "As you've probably noticed there's not much traffic on these streets so you can't really use the traffic to line up your crossing. Instead, find the drop off with your toes and try to move in a perpendicular direction from that of the curb."

Muttering something about hanging ten, I followed Oscar's instruction. With an affirmative nod to Oscar asking if I was ready, I set off across the street. Wham, my cane collided with the up curb on the other side and I screeched to a halt. "Great," called Oscar. "Now pop your cane up over the curb and see what you find."

"It feels like the sidewalk," I called back.

"Yes, exactly." Oscar replied, now right at my shoulder. "You found sidewalk at the end of your crossing meaning that you made a straight crossing and didn't veer. If you had veered, you would have found grass instead.

"Okay, cool," I replied. "Can I keep going?"

"Go for it," Oscar said. So, I went for it. We crossed street after street. Not every crossing I made was straight though. When I found grass instead of sidewalk I had to make myself stay calm. I was learning an important lesson. I was learning that I had a bit of the perfectionist in me. Okay, maybe I had a lot of the perfectionist in me. But life isn't perfect. And it's especially not perfect when you have to relearn how to do almost everything as an adult.

When I got home I carefully considered what I had learned that day. While I still preferred to feel the small victory of making a straight street crossing I had also learned that making a mistake was okay. Mistakes were going to happen. I just needed to accept that, learn what to do when it happened, and get on with it.

11 | trying to keep up

WITH ALL OF THE NEW SKILLS I WAS LEARNING and with my developmental psychology class my daily schedule was fuller than ever. The only problem was that it was spring. I loved the transition from the dormancy of winter to the vibrant lushness of spring in the south. I always scoured the yard and neighborhood for the first daffodils. I loved watching the march of spring colors across the hillsides. First came the distinctive dark red as the maples bloomed. Then the improbable fuchsia of the redbuds with the white of the flowering dogwood mixed in.

I'd never see any of that again.

I couldn't help feeling bereft when I dwelled on this new fact of my life. I'd never be identifying flowers, shrubs, or trees visually again. There would be no more swinging up onto my horse bareback to go tearing through the woods reveling in the rebirth of the natural world. I needed to talk about all of this with someone. It needed to be someone who knew about adjustment to blindness. I picked up the phone and called Oscar at the VA.

"I'm feeling kind of bummed out," I began. "I need to get out of the house. I need to talk about my feelings and fears."

"I understand," said Oscar promptly. "Hang on. I need to make a quick phone call and I'll call you back."

In just a few minutes he did so. "I'll pick you up at five o'clock this afternoon. Let's go out to dinner."

Later, seated at a table in a restaurant at the mall I tried to explain. "I don't know how to describe what's going on," I began. "I'm learning so many new things but it kind of feels like my brain and emotions aren't keeping up. This blindness thing is so hard. I don't know, I mean you work with blind people all the time. Is this normal? Will it get easier?"

After a long silence Oscar said, "Blindness might just be the most difficult disability to adjust to. Sight loss affects every area of your life. And, you're absolutely right, the emotional adjustment is sometimes the most difficult part."

I reached for my glass of wine and almost knocked it over.

"See what I mean," said Oscar, catching the glass before it tipped. "Keep your hand low and your fingers slightly bent. You have to learn a new way to do something as simple as picking up a wine glass. The skills that Vera and I are teaching you are only half the battle. Learning these skills will increase your competence and, at the same time, your self-confidence. This, unfortunately, is only half the battle."

It felt as though Oscar could read my mind. How many times had I had this exact train of thought? Oscar, however, seemed to be able to put it succinctly into words. Slowly, I said, "Tell me more."

"There's a book by a Catholic priest that I think you might be ready to read. It's called BLINDNESS, *What It Is, What It Does, and How to Live With It.*"

It was the second time I had been referred to this book. Into my mind flashed what Henry II had said about Thomas à Becket, "Who will rid me of this troublesome priest?" But I didn't want to be rid of him. I wanted to read what he had written.

"Vera mentioned that book too," I said. "She didn't seem to think that it was such a great idea to read it just yet."

"She may be right," said Oscar. "There is, however, one concept of Father Carroll's that I think you are ready for and might find helpful. He says that a person who becomes blind as an adult must let go of his sighted self in order to move forward and develop his life as a person who is blind."

We sat in silence while I thought about what Oscar had said. How could he be telling me to just forget about the twenty-six years I had lived? On the other hand, there were definitely parts of that twenty-six years I'd just as soon put behind me. I can't pretend that the idea of starting over didn't have some appeal. Feeling conflicted, I asked, "But how can I just pretend that my past life doesn't exist anymore?"

Oscar looked at me for a minute and then said, "That's the wonderful thing about Father Carroll's idea. You're still the same person once you've relinquished that old self. It's just that you're free to move forward with your life rather than dwelling with regret on the things you can't do or be anymore."

We finished our dessert and coffee in silence. Oscar had certainly given me something to think about. As I lay in bed that night I examined my feelings. I couldn't help compare Father Carroll's ideas to the death and rebirth of Jesus. But the man was, after all, a Catholic priest. I thought of all the other places where I had run across the death and rebirth concept. It was all over the place in various mythologies. I saw it every year in the turning of the seasons. Instinctively I knew that I could not really move forward with the hand I had been dealt without letting go of old notions, habits, and thought patterns. I had noticed, over and over again, that my most frustrating moments were those when I railed against the impossibility of doing things the way I used to do them, or when I was filled with resentment that I couldn't see the sunset or the huge cherry tree that was blooming in the front yard. There were to be many setbacks in the months and years ahead, but that was the beginning of my willingness to look forward instead of backwards.

12 | it's a skill thing

B Y THIS TIME I was several months into my rehabilitation program with Vera. She had shown me how to label my clothing with small braille tags which could be sewn onto the label of a garment. I even learned to thread a needle using either a wire needle threader or a dental floss threader. We had worked on some housecleaning tasks like vacuuming and cleaning a countertop in the kitchen. I learned to be very systematic when I cleaned something, using a pattern of horizontal and vertical swaths or ever widening concentric circles to make sure I covered the whole surface.

Finally, the cooking lessons began. "Bring volume two of your braille book into the kitchen," Vera instructed. "Do you remember that recipe for sugar cookies at the end of the book?"

"Of course I remember it," I said ruefully. "That was one of the most difficult parts of the whole book!"

Vera laughed, "I know. I hear that from all my students." Returning to the kitchen with the book, I opened it to the pages with the sugar cookie recipe.

"The first problem," Vera began, "Is to know what's what and what's where. Oh, you'll need your braille label maker too."

Fetching the labeler, I placed it on the chopping block in the middle of the kitchen.

"Where do you keep the flour and sugar," Vera began. Opening the drawer in which these items were kept I got out the two identical jars and placed them on the chopping block next to the braille labeler. Vera said, "Go ahead and make a label for sugar and one for flour." As I completed each label I handed it to Vera. She affixed each of them to the lid of the proper jar.

Next, Vera asked me to get out measuring cups and spoons. "Now, the measuring cups are graduated like this; the largest is one cup, the next is a half a cup, the next is a third, and the last is a quarter of a cup." She went on, "You'll always know which is which if they're all together, but they won't always be together. So, here's what we'll do."

She showed me a small file. "We'll leave the largest cup alone. Here, hand me the others." I heard her filing away for a few minutes and then she handed the cups back to me. "Feel along the right edge of each handle," she told me, "the half cup has two little notches, the third of a cup has three, and the fourth cup has four. Can you feel them?"

"Yes," I said in amazement. "How did you think of that?"

"Oh, it's just one of the tricks in my bag."

"Now, the next thing we need to do is mark the stove so that you can set it to the proper temperature. Yet again, Vera dug into her bag. This time she came out with some little bumps with adhesive backing.

"Mrs. Wiygul," Vera began. "Can you help us here?"

Mama was watching from a stool on the other side of the counter. "Yes, what do you want me to do?"

"If you can just stick this little bump on the pointer of the oven temperature knob . . . "

Taking the proffered bump, Mama walked over to the stove and affixed the bump to the knob.

"Next," continued Vera, "Here are three more bumps. Place them on the two-fifty, three- fifty, and four-fifty marks."

"Okay," said my mother, "I think I've gotten them all in the proper places."

"Sue, step up and tell me if you can feel them." I could and I said so.

"The only thing left now is to mark the 'bake' and 'broil' on the oven set knob." We proceeded as before, but this time Vera had me use the braille labeler to create two small pieces of Dymo tape. One had "Bk" and the other had "Br." Once these labels were in place, Vera had me set the oven to several different temperatures and asked my mother to confirm that I had done it properly.

"This is so ingenious," said my mother in amazement. "How do you think of all of these things?"

"Well, it helps that I live with blindness every day. You know, sometimes necessity is the mother of invention," replied Vera.

The preparation of the cookie dough proceeded. I found that I had to wash my hands constantly. They had to be clean each time I returned to the braille recipe so that I wouldn't soil the pages of the book. "How the heck am I supposed to measure a quarter teaspoon of vanilla?" I asked as I read the next line of the recipe.

"Do you have a very small wide mouthed jar?" Vera asked my mother.

After rummaging around for a minute, my mother asked, "Will this one do?"

Taking the jar, Vera said, "Oh, yes, this is perfect."

She poured the vanilla into the jar. Then, taking out another set of measuring spoons from her bag she said, "I'm going to bend the bowl of each spoon so that each one looks like a gravy ladle." When she was finished with this task she handed the spoons to me. "Now you can just dip the correct spoon into the jar and ladle out the proper amount of any liquid ingredient."

Amazed again at Vera's endless ingenuity, I measured the quarter teaspoon of vanilla and went on to the next ingredient.

When I had the cookie dough prepared I got out a cookie sheet. In the past I had always apportioned the dough using two teaspoons, one to scoop the dough and the other to remove any excess. I removed two teaspoons from the drawer and stopped.

"Vera." I said, "I don't think I can measure how much dough I'm placing on the cookie sheet using spoons like I used to. How should I do this?"

Well," Vera said, drawing out the syllable, as though she was thinking of what to say next. "God created hands before he created spoons, so just use your hands."

Startled, I said, "Is that okay?"

I could hear the knowing smile in her voice as Vera replied, "Oh, yes, you'll find that you will use your hands a lot more when you cook. Don't be afraid of it. Just dig in!"

The cookies were great. As Vera and I sat enjoying cookies and milk I asked, "You know the book you told me about, the one written by Father Carroll?"

"Yes," said Vera thoughtfully.

"Why does everyone say I shouldn't read it yet?" I questioned.

"Well, Father Carroll first goes into all of the things that you lose when you lose your sight and then goes into how these things are restored. The losses are first and I didn't think you or your parents needed to read about that so soon after your sight loss. There are twenty something of them and I thought that might not be the best place to start."

"Things like what?" I asked.

"Oh, things like the sense of the beautiful, the sense of

autonomy. You know, things like that."

Mulling this over I said, "But you don't seem like you've lost anything at all. I mean you've done all of those things like traveling, owning your own home, and having a job you're really good at."

"No, well, I don't feel any great sense of loss now, but I did when I was newly blind."

"How long did it take before you felt, well, normal I guess?"

"Oh, I don't know," said Vera. "Adjustment to blindness isn't something that just happens all at once. I mean I didn't wake up one day and say, 'poof', I'm adjusted. It's more of an ongoing process. Eventually the fact that you are blind will cease to feel like the most important thing about who you are."

"I don't know how that can be," I muttered. "I mean, my whole life has changed. It's kind of like I'm a new person."

"Yes, that's how many people describe their adjustment to blindness," said Vera. "In fact, that's Father Carroll's premise. You have to be willing to let go of your sighted life before you can embrace life again as a blind person."

"I don't think I've managed to do that," I said.

"No, you probably haven't. But I can see that process beginning in you."

"How?" I asked.

"I'll use an example," replied Vera. "When you want to look at something, do you consciously think of the fact that you can't see it with your eyes anymore?"

I had to think about this one for a minute. Finally I said, "No, not really. When I think of looking at something I think of looking at it with my hands."

"Exactly," interjected Vera. "Your means of interacting with the world around you have changed. It's becoming natural for you to think of interacting with your world in a different way than you used to. As time goes on you'll find that you become more and more comfortable with your blindness. It'll just become a part of who you are, but not the most important part."

I had to think about that one for more than a minute. Would blindness ever be that inconsequential to me?

At last Vera told me that our regular visits were coming to an end.

"I'll check in with you by phone and you can always call me if something comes up that you need help with," she said on a summer afternoon. "I've tried to teach you enough concepts for you to be able to figure out things as they come up. I know you'll be fine, but I'm always here if you need me," she concluded.

13 | the drop-off lesson

MY LESSONS WITH VERA ENDED long before my lessons with Oscar. I'm not entirely sure why this was the case. Perhaps it had something to do with the fact that Oscar was teaching a discipline in which I could get killed if I got it wrong. I rather think that it had at least a little bit to do with the fact that I loved the challenge and action of orientation and mobility training. I was really having a good time.

Whatever the reason my lessons with Oscar continued through the summer and on into the fall. Once I had the street crossing trick under my belt we moved into a busier residential setting. Here I learned to judge and respect traffic. I learned to use my parallel traffic surge as the cue to begin my street crossing. I learned that a light controlled intersection is a much safer proposition than an uncontrolled one. I became savvy to the right turn on red and the danger of an idling car that was just sitting still.

"Okay," began Oscar, as we moved on to training in a small business district. "This is going to be much more difficult and challenging. There's going to be a lot more traffic, more noise, and more complicated intersections."

We were standing at a relatively quiet street corner. I could hear the low rumble of traffic a block or two away. I remember the excitement of tackling something new. "I'm ready," I said, "What's the scoop?"

"At the end of this block we'll be moving into a business district. Instead of houses there will be stores and other businesses on both sides of the street. The first intersection is a simple light controlled one. I want you to cross it and continue straight to the next intersection. Wait for me when you get there and we'll talk about the traffic pattern."

So, off I went. The first street crossing was uneventful. I waited for my parallel traffic surge and made my crossing neatly. I was finding it easier to make a straight crossing when I had parallel traffic to help with my orientation. At the next intersection I waited as Oscar had requested.

"Let's step back a couple of steps and just listen for a minute," said Oscar, as he approached my right shoulder.

I stepped back and pulled my cane in so that it was vertical and out of the way of passing pedestrians. Then I listened. After two full cycles of traffic I ventured an observation. "Is there a left turn lane for the parallel traffic?"

"Exactly," Oscar confirmed. "What does that tell you about the timing of your crossing?"

"Well," I said, thinking through the process. "When I hear the parallel traffic begin to move I need to wait and see if it's the left turn cycle. Then I need to wait until I hear more of a surge and then I know it's okay to cross."

"You got it," said Oscar. "Now go cross that street."

So, I did. I crossed street after street with Oscar instructing and correcting as we went. At the end of one block Oscar approached me and said, "Do you know what you just did?"

"No," I replied, "why?"

Oscar laughed. "I wouldn't believe it if I hadn't just seen it with my own eyes. A store back there was having a sidewalk sale. There were racks of clothes all over the place on the sidewalk. You walked neatly between the racks without so much as stirring a sleeve."

Laughing, I said, "Well, heck, I knew you'd find out eventually. I've really been faking it all this time. I can see just fine." As the words left my mouth I realized that this was an extraordinary statement for me to make. A few short months ago the simple thought of being able to see again would have sent me into a complete decline because, of course, my blindness was permanent. When had I started to be able to laugh at my own blindness? I had no idea when it had happened. It felt good though.

At the end of the summer I finished my last class at Samford University. I transferred to the University of Alabama at Birmingham and signed up for three classes which began in September. Coincidental with this change Oscar suggested that I consider working as a volunteer at the blind rehab center at the VA medical center. The University is located adjacent to the medical center district of Birmingham so this combination afforded an opportunity for my training to progress to a complicated urban setting. Once Oscar helped me with an orientation to my classes he took me to the Southeastern Blind Rehab Center where he worked. He introduced me to Gina who helped me get signed up as a volunteer. My class schedule allowed me to attend my classes in the morning and walk over to the VA to do my volunteer work in the afternoon.

It never escaped my notice that my parents took what must have been, for them, a huge leap of faith every time they dropped me off at the University. Looking back I can appreciate the courage of my mother and father. I know that my safety was uppermost in their minds. I knew, too, that they wanted me to be able to develop the skills and attitudes that would lead to an independent life. I can remember my father telling me about one of his friends who had asked how I could possibly cross streets safely and navigate all around the medical district of Birmingham.

"Dr. Brown asked me, last night, how you can cross streets," my father began.

"What did you tell him?" I responded.

"Oh," said my father nonchalantly, "I just told him you cross with the light." I didn't have to be able to see the mischievous smile I knew my father would be wearing at the moment.

"And what did he say," I asked.

"Nothing at all for a full minute. But then I took pity on him and explained how you can read traffic and all of that business about crossing with the surge of traffic."

I knew that my father's nonchalant mention of my street crossing abilities reflected his pride in my accomplishments. Although I was happy to have such discussions relayed to me I knew that the truth was far more complicated. Many were the times that, as I began a street crossing, I felt a swooping sensation somewhere in the middle of my body. I still couldn't believe that I could do this thing and sometimes felt that I was crazy to try.

One afternoon, as I made my way from my last class to the VA, I was waiting to cross Eighteenth Street. A man beside me told me it was okay to make the crossing. So, I did. The trouble started half way across the street. I heard the cars on Eighteenth Street begin their movement. Frightened, I stepped up my pace. The cars were whizzing so close behind me that I was sure I was going to be flattened any moment. With a flood of relief I gained the sidewalk on the opposite side of the street.

"You're not going to believe what just happened," I began when I found Oscar in his office at the VA. I related the events of crossing Eighteenth Street. Seizing another teachable moment Oscar gave me a good talking to about taking the word of a stranger.

"It's your life and your safety that's at stake here," he began. "There's only one person who is going to be as cautious about your safety as you are. And that person is you. Doesn't matter if the Pope tells you it's okay to cross. You cross only when you know it's safe."

Chastened, I resolved to follow Oscar's instructions.

The day finally came for my "drop-off" lesson. Oscar had told me this was coming but I had never been entirely sure that he'd make me do it. It seemed crazier than anything we'd done yet. In a "drop-off" lesson, the instructor drops the student off at an unknown location and gives the student instructions about the destination only. There is no information relayed about the student's current location or any idea of exactly how to get to the destination.

Oscar picked me up on a Saturday morning and we set off in his car. We drove around for a much longer time than usual and I was completely confused by the time Oscar stopped and we got out of his car.

"Are you lost?" Oscar said.

"Well of course I'm lost. We could be in Georgia for all I know," I glared at him.

"Good," he said. I glared some more. Completely unmoved by my dirty looks he continued, "Your destination is that restaurant at Brookwood Mall. You know, the one where we had dinner together last spring. Bus Number 22 stops at the southwest corner of Twenty-second Street and Second Avenue North at 10:55. That's the bus you want. Got it?

I may have tried to look disgusted but both Oscar and I knew the truth. I had been looking forward to this lesson since Oscar told me about it two months earlier. "Okay, got it." And I turned away and started walking. When I reached the first intersection I stopped. "Okay," I said to myself, "You can do this." I took a deep breath. The first thing I had to figure out was the cardinal directions. I stood at the intersection and tried to decide where the sun was. I couldn't feel it at all. I crossed the street and stopped on the other side. And there it was, behind me and to the left. So, I was walking west on the south side of an avenue. I listened to the traffic carefully. My parallel street seemed to be one-way coming towards me. That meant it was moving east. For a minute I kind of panicked. What was I doing? What was the layout of the streets in Birmingham again? I couldn't seem to remember. Taking another deep breath, I had to stop doing that or I'd be hyperventilating next, I tried to summon the map of downtown Birmingham to mind. Not wanting to appear lost I decided to continue walking west while I evaluated the situation. Then I heard the train. I had listened to the trains all my life. Without knowing how I knew, I was positive that this train was a freight train moving through the industrial part of north Birmingham and it was to my right. By the time I reached the next intersection I had decided to hypothesize that I was on Third Avenue North. But where on Third Avenue North. Listening carefully I decided that there wasn't enough traffic for me to be in the middle of downtown which included Twenty-second Street, my destination. I couldn't be east of Twenty-second Street or I'd be slap in the middle of the post office. I had to be west. I turned right around making me, I was sure, look way more lost than I would have if I had just stood still. I didn't care though. I was on a roll. I had a mission.

I walked three blocks before I found anything to help me confirm or revise my hypothesis. As I made my fourth crossing I encountered an island half way across the street. Aha, I thought, Twentieth Street, Birmingham Green. Now, if the next street was one-way north I'd, at least, have one part of my location figured out. I proceeded. Yes, the next street had one-way traffic, and it was moving north. I went ahead and crossed Twenty-first and arrived at Twenty-second. If my hypothesis was correct I had to turn right and travel one block south, cross the street and that would be the bus stop. Arriving at, what I thought, was my destination I stopped. I looked at my watch. Thirty minutes to spare. I smiled. Then I started thinking. What if this was Fourth instead of Second? Running through what I had done so far and what I knew about the layout of the streets I suddenly realized that I could, in fact, actually be on either one of these streets. What to do? Picturing the street grid I realized that if I went one more block south that would tell me definitely where I was. If I was on Fourth, the next street south would be one-way west. If that street, instead, carried two way traffic it would be First Avenue.

The next street ended up being one-way west. Thankful that I had thought to double check myself I crossed Third and arrived, for sure, at the intersection of Twenty-second Street and Second Avenue North. I waited, thinking carefully about the mistake I had almost made. A car pulled up into the bus stop and a man emerged. I paid no attention until he spoke to me for the second time. "Are you waiting for a bus?" he asked.

"Yes, bus 22," I replied.

"That bus doesn't run on Saturday." He got in his car and left. *Oh, great, what to do now?* I thought. I stood there leaning on my cane and thinking vaguely of calling a cab. Then I heard a familiar voice in my ear.

"He didn't know what he was talking about," said Oscar. And then he vanished.

I continued to wait and the bus came. Hugely relieved I boarded and paid my fare. Then I confirmed that this was the bus to Brookwood Mall. Sitting down I sighed. Okay, one part done. I followed the movement of the bus carefully. We went to the top of the hill on Twenty-second, turned right on Highland and then left onto the Red Mountain Expressway. We then went straight through Homewood and took the looping exit onto Lakeshore. We turned onto Lakeshore heading east and then into Brookwood Mall. But which entrance? I questioned the driver before exiting the bus. After it pulled away I immediately realized that I hadn't understood his description. The traffic on Lakeshore was behind me. I had thought the driver told me I was in front of Rich's but this didn't jive with what I heard. Making another hypothesis I decided that I was on the long side of the mall instead of at the end, where the main entrance to Rich's was located. I gritted my teeth. I would have to cross this access street with no traffic control. I waited and waited. Finally I felt it was as good as I was going to get and crossed the street, almost running. Okay, now what? The only entrances to the mall on this side of the building led into parking decks. Pretending more bravery than I felt I walked ahead. I was walking up a ramp. That was the best I could have hoped for. There was only one deck that had a ramp up. With the end of this adventure in sight I hoofed it around the periphery of the deck, located the stairs and entered the mall right at the restaurant. I stood still for a moment.

"Super job!" said Oscar, at my right elbow. I hugged him and we both laughed joyfully. We entered the restaurant and had a celebratory lunch.

My formal rehabilitation training was drawing to an end. As Vera had done last June, Oscar assured me that he would always be available if something came up with which I needed his help. As the one year anniversary of my vision loss approached I reflected on the past year. I had gone from despair to triumph in just twelve months. I thought back to l and his concept of letting go of life as a sighted person in order to embrace it as a blind person. I never had gotten around to reading his book. Yet his concept of death and rebirth seemed to have carried me forward in a way that I could not have imagined. Oscar and Vera had taught me many skills. They had also done something for me which was quite intangible. It's hard to put my finger on exactly what this intangible thing was. It was attitude, certainly. But it was more than that. Perhaps I had been thinking of myself as a damaged version of my old self. Somewhere along the line that concept didn't fit anymore. I realized, quite clearly, that blindness had become, as Vera and Oscar had told me it would, just a part of who I was. It wasn't the most important part anymore. I had somehow become a whole and complete person who happened to be blind.

14 | the right neighborhood

I MUST GO BACK A FEW MONTHS TO CONTINUE MY STORY. In the fall, when Oscar took me to the VA to become a volunteer, an amazing process was set in motion. I remember Oscar telling me that his workplace might not be the best place to meet when I called him that time and asked to talk with him about my feelings and my adjustment to blindness. I envisioned a drab depressing place full of newly blind veterans all struggling with the same insecurities and fears that I, myself, was feeling. The truth couldn't have been more different.

I found the SBRC full of energetic professionals who were all working to teach their charges the skills needed to live with blindness. Even the veterans were an upbeat lot. There was banter and laughter. There was hard work and inner searching, yes, but there was also joy. There was camaraderie and even a little friendly competition. I heard one veteran ask another what he thought of that route up the hill on 21st Street. I heard another joshing with his friend about a cake that had evidently ended up on the sad side. It must have tasted good, though, as the chef was passing out pieces of the cake to all of his instructors.

Amazed at the positive atmosphere of the place, I entered into my volunteer work with enthusiasm. I had imagined myself interacting with the veterans, perhaps holding someone's hand while he talked of his losses. In truth, I did no work with the veterans. Gina introduced me to Steve, the head of the low vision department. Over the months, I had actually regained a little vision. Well, it might have been a stretch to call it "vision" at this point, but I could see and take direction from light. Steve showed me the closed circuit televisions (CCTVs), or "video magnifiers." These machines use a zoom camera lens to magnify and project on to a television screen whatever is placed beneath them. At first I thought I could do nothing with these CCTVs. However, with Steve's careful instruction I could soon see individual letters on the screen.

The annual convention of the American Association of Workers for the Blind was to be held in Birmingham that year. I was given the assignment of calling restaurants in the area and obtaining menus for transcription into braille. This could not have been a more perfect assignment. I had to engage all of the skills I had learned over the past year. First, I had to call the restaurants and get directions. Then, I had to take up my cane and walk to each restaurant. Upon my return, with menus in hand, I laboriously read each item on each menu using one of the CCTVs. I read each menu into a tape recorder. Then I took my tape into another room and brailled them into a machine called a VersaBraille. Once written into the VersaBraille, the menus could be sent to a braille embosser and printed out in braille. I was very slow with the CCTV but had a feeling of great accomplishment when I took the completed menus off of the braille embosser.

My interactions with the veterans who were in residence at the rehab center revolved primarily around recreational activities. They had square dances which were huge fun. Many of the veterans and volunteers did not know the steps to the dances very well and there were plenty of times that we completely missed each other when we were supposed to be doing a do-si-do or a "Swing your partner." It just didn't matter. Those with some vision helped the rest of us and the whole thing was lots of fun. Sometimes the recreational activity was simply a trip out to dinner at a local restaurant. There was lots of complaining about the hospital food so the trips out of the rehab center for meals were highly popular. We even took a trip to the local botanical gardens. I had been to the botanical gardens many times in my sighted life and could at least get someone in the right neighborhood to smell the roses.

The one consistency in the conversations I had with veterans concerned how much they were learning at the rehab center and how much their instructors were helping them. As these conversations mirrored my own feelings about what Oscar and Vera had done for me, I entered into them with the same gusto as the veterans. A couple of months after I began my volunteer work, Oscar tentatively suggested that I might want to consider a career in blind rehab. Although the idea had immense appeal, I hesitated. Selecting a new career seemed risky. I had only been blind for about a year at this point and still had occasional episodes of depression and fear about my future. The more I thought about it, though, and the more I was around the instructors at the blind center, the more appealing the idea became. After all, Oscar and Vera were having such a tremendous impact on my own life. What if I could do that for someone else?

I asked Oscar what it would take to enter the field of blind rehab. He told me about the master's program at Western Michigan University. It seemed that most of the instructors at the blind center had such a degree. "Okay," I finally said, "How would I go about getting into that program?"

"I'd suggest that you write a letter to Dr. Ponchillia," Oscar told me. "No, wait," he said, "he's blind, so maybe you'd better tape record your message and send it to him that way."

I mulled it over for a few days and then sat down in front of my tape recorder and began. I struggled over the message. It was hard to collect my thoughts and then say them into the tape recorder without inserting a lot of, "um's," and, "you know's." Finally I was satisfied with the recording and sent it off to Dr. Ponchillia. I was stunned when, two weeks later, the phone rang and it was Dr. Ponchillia, himself.

"I received your tape and just wanted to call you up and feel you out on this thing," he began.

I was immediately tongue tied and stammered out, "Oh, okay."

"Tell me a little bit about yourself," he began. "I understand that you've been working with Oscar Thompson." I knew this man lived in Michigan but I could have sworn he had a bit of a Southern drawl. "Oscar is one of our graduates," he continued. Well, about half the staff down there graduated from our program."

"Yes, that's what Oscar and Gina told me," I replied. We went on to discuss the other graduates of the Western Michigan program and then Dr. Ponchillia guided the conversation back to me and my motivation for entering the field. By the end of the conversation, I was ready to apply.

All of this took place in December. By February I was accepted into the class that began in late April. I think that Oscar and Dr. Ponchillia were the only people on earth who believed that I could do this. I think my parents had some hesitation but, to their credit, they wholeheartedly supported me. Most people, including my vocational rehab counselor, thought I had not been blind long enough to embark on a graduate level program of study. Nor did they think that I could possibly live on my own that far from home. I took a sort of perverse delight in their prophecies of doom and gloom. I just knew I could do it. What did they expect? Was I supposed to hang around for a few years getting used to being blind? I just didn't buy into that philosophy. So, in late April, my parents and I packed up the car and headed north.

15 | without attending class

Please, come in and sit down," said Dr. Ponchillia. My mother, father, and I entered his cramped office. Dr. Ponchillia dispatched a student to round up another chair. "How was your trip?" he asked.

"Oh, it was fine," said my father. We hooked up with some friends of friends last night and had a very enjoyable dinner."

After some small talk, Dr. Ponchillia addressed me. "I guess the first thing you'll need is an O&M instructor to help you get oriented to the campus and everything. Are you going to live in a dorm?"

"Yes," I replied. "I'll be in French Hall. We've already been by there and taken my things up to the room."

"Great," said Dr. Ponchillia. "I've assigned Dave as your O&M instructor. He'll help you learn the route from French over here and work with you on any other orientation or mobility needs you might have."

At that moment Dave, himself, stuck his head in the door. After introductions Dave agreed to begin right away. My parents had decided that they would take me back to the dorm before heading out but this changed their plans. Accepting Dr. Ponchillia's assurances that I would be just fine, they took their leave and headed back to Alabama.

"Please, just call me Paul," said Dr. Ponchillia after my parents had left. Then he asked me if I had ever heard of goalball.

"No," I replied, mystified, "What is it?"

Paul went on to tell me about the game. He seemed really enthusiastic as he related to me the concept of this team sport for blind athletes. "We're having a practice tonight," he concluded. "Why don't you come and see what you think?"

"Well," I began hesitantly, "I did used to enjoy competitive sports." At that moment Dave returned to begin my orientation. After working the route from French Hall to Sangren Hall, where all of my classes would be held, Dave took me by the dorm to grab some sweats and then dropped me off at the gym. I moved hesitantly into the cavernous gym, listening to the banter of the people within and wondering what the heck I was doing there. How could a bunch of blind people play a competitive game? I trailed around the wall of the gym with my cane and stopped when I was in what, I figured, was about the midpoint. At that moment I heard a woman's voice call my name.

"Hi, you must be Sue. Paul told me that you might be coming." She told me her name and I promptly forgot it. My attention was focused on the center part of the gym. I could hear a ball being rolled from side to side in front of me. The ball apparently had bells in it as I could hear them jingle each time the ball moved. It had become unnaturally quiet in the gym. I wondered about this until it dawned on me that, of course, it had to be quiet. How else could the players hear the movement of the ball. Observing the rule of silence I held my questions until the players took a break. The person who had introduced herself to me called to Paul who came over to the side of the gym.

"I'll take a pass on this next game and see if I can explain it to you," he said, sounding slightly winded. We withdrew from the immediate vicinity of the court and sat down. "Oh, wait a minute," Paul continued. "Dinah, hup!" he called out. Wondering what in the world he was talking about it immediately came clear when a dog ran up to him with much jingling of harness and leash. Paul had a guide dog. I hadn't even realized it when we were in his office. "Walk with me outside," he said, "I need to get Dinah out for a few minutes."

I took up my cane and followed him. It was easy to follow the clicking of Dinah's claws on the gym floor and the jingle of her harness. In about two seconds they were so far ahead of me that I almost had to run to catch up. "Do you always move that fast or does Dinah have to go really bad?" I asked, panting slightly.

"Nah," said Paul, "This is just our normal pace." Coming to a halt on a spot of grass, I heard Paul say to Dinah, "Okay, park time, Dinah dog." While Dinah circled around Paul, he asked, "Did you learn the route from French to Sangren?"

"Yes," I replied. "It's not too bad. Dave's a good teacher, too. Will he be able to help me with orientation to other places like stores and stuff?"

"Oh, yes. He's a second semester O&M student, and he'll be able to work with you as much as you like. Let's just sit down out here so we can talk without worrying about interrupting the next game."

Paul then described the game of goalball. "There are three players on each team," he began. "Everybody is blindfolded so that we're all on the same visual footing. The court is laid out on the floor using either ropes that are taped down or some other tactually discernible way. The court's about the size of a volleyball court. There's a box on either end, and players have to stay inside that box. The box is outlined by the ropes, and it has short orientation lines that run into the middle of the box so you can keep track of where you are."

As Paul paused for breath I asked, "How can you feel the ropes? I mean, can you feel them through your shoes and stuff?"

"Oh, yeah, you'll definitely be able to feel them through your shoes, although many players play on their knees and feel the ropes through their knee pads and with their hands."

"Knee pads," I began.

"Yep, most of us wear knee and elbow pads and most of the women wear hip pads as well," Paul continued, "It's a pretty rough game."

Startled, I said, "How is it rough? I mean, how do you play it?"

I heard the smile in Paul's voice as he continued, "Well, you heard the bells in the ball, right? The object of the game is to roll the ball down the court and get it past the opposing team and over the back line. If the ball's coming at you, you have to listen until you think you know where it is and then try to block it by throwing yourself across the floor into the path of the ball." Anticipating my next question, he said, "The center plays towards the front of the goal box and the two wings play back a little. That way we don't crash into each other when we're trying to block the ball."

"Oh," was all I could say.

Come on," Paul said, "Let's go watch a game." And off we went, back into the gym.

We reentered the gym. I could hear the sound of the ball being rolled back and forth between the two teams. Paul was right, the ball was moving very fast. I could also hear the sound of people crashing to the floor as they tried to block it. What I couldn't understand was that the players would occasionally call each other's name. Then I'd hear someone slap the floor followed by the sound of the ball being rolled a very short distance. "What's happening when they call each other's names?" I whispered to Paul.

"That's how the players pass the ball back and forth to each other," Paul replied. "Sometimes you're out of position when you catch the ball and it's quicker to pass it to a teammate rather than trying to get up and oriented so you can throw the ball yourself." I listened to the players interacting with one another and the sound of the ball as it zipped down the court. There also seemed to be a referee. He blew his whistle sometimes and I soon figured out that one blast of the whistle meant the ball had gone out of bounds and two quick blasts meant that someone had scored a goal.

"Okay," came Paul's voice next to me. You'll play in the next game. Go straight down the gym, along the wall that's to your right and you'll walk right into the women's locker room."

When I came back from changing into sweats, the current game was over. Paul helped me find knee, elbow, and hip pads. Then he showed me how to position my body when I tried to block the ball. "You'll want to have your head back with your arms held straight up and in front of your face. Go ahead, lie on your side and I'll show you."

Then I was on the court with Vicki and Kathy. I was playing right wing, Kathy was center, and Vicki was playing left wing. Knowing that I would be diving across the floor to block the ball I decided to play on my knees at first. I figured I wouldn't have as far to go to hit the floor. The referee called, "Ball in play," and we began. It took a lot of concentration. I had to keep track of my position on the court, the speed and direction of the ball, and the location of my teammates. It was wild and fast, but I was doing it. I was playing a competitive sport again.

I played in two games that evening. Then we all went out to dinner. It didn't matter that we were all hot and sweaty and more than a little disheveled. All that mattered was that I had found friends and a new sport that I could play. Without having attended a single class, I decided that I was going to love graduate school.

16 | so much potential

A FEW DAYS LATER CLASSES BEGAN. I'll never forget my first walk to class. It was raining and the wind was blowing a gale. Having no option, I bundled up, packed my tape recorder and extra tapes in a light backpack and set out.

Twenty minutes later, almost at my destination, a huge gust of wind almost knocked me off my feet. Arriving safely at Sangren Hall, I stood for a minute just inside the doors. I was drenched. My legs were so wet I might as well have climbed out of a swimming pool. I made my way up to the third floor and squelched down the hall to my first class. I didn't know it at the time, but my future husband, Jim, sat in the same classroom. His first glimpse of me was that of a disheveled, wet, and disgruntled student. Praying that my tape recorder was still in working order, I took it out and began my first class at graduate school.

Classes and homework became the framework of my days. Around that framework, my life seemed to come to life. I loved being on my own, able to plan my activities and quiet times as I fancied. The undergraduate classes I had taken in Birmingham equipped me with the skills and habits for academic success. I thrived on the challenge of both school and living on my own.

In one class, "The Dynamics of Blindness," we learned

about the social and emotional effects of blindness. One of our assignments was to participate in four recreational activities while wearing a blindfold. Paul, our instructor for this class, told me to choose four activities I hadn't done since I became blind. I'm not even sure what the other three activities were, but the one I do remember was tree identification. Having taken forestry and botany classes in college I was intrigued by the possibility of being able to identify the trees around me again. Paul had been a botanist before he became blind and had created a tree key on tape. The only problem I faced was that of finding someone with whom I could do this activity. It would have to be someone who knew the flora of southwestern Michigan so that my identifications could be confirmed or denied. I began asking around and was encouraged to introduce myself to Jim Martin and ask for his help. That's how Jim and I met.

Jim and I planned to go out in the woods on a Saturday afternoon. At noon on that day I was scheduled to take the English qualifying exam, a test that every graduate student had to pass in order to earn a graduate degree. On my way to the exam, I was walking along the sidewalk thinking about getting into the woods later. Suddenly, the bottom dropped out of my world. Someone had left the cover off of a manhole and I, walking along absent-mindedly and not swinging my cane widely enough to cover myself, stepped right into it. My cane flew out of my hand, and I somehow managed to catch myself with my elbows before falling in completely. I hung there, gasping for breath and trying to figure out what had happened. After a couple of minutes, I caught my breath and scrambled out onto the sidewalk. Where was my cane? I felt around and finally located it. There was absolutely no one around. No pedestrians came along to offer help and the person who had removed the manhole cover was nowhere to be seen. The only thing left to do was continue on my way.

Thinking vaguely that I wasn't in any shape to take an exam, I decided to go up to the blind rehab department instead. Dr. Kaarlela took one look at me and sent for a wheelchair. I was evidently white as a sheet and shaky on my feet. Instead of taking the English qualifying exam, I went to student health. After examining me, a doctor sent me back to my dorm with several ice packs and instructions to elevate my legs and keep ice on them.

That was the position in which I found myself when Jim called to see if I was ready to go out in the woods.

"Well, no, I don't think I can do it this afternoon." After explaining what had happened we both began to laugh uncontrollably. The whole thing seemed utterly hysterical to us.

"You know, if you didn't want to go out with me you could have just said so," quipped Jim. After a pause he continued, "There's a party at a friend's house tonight. Would you like to come?"

So, we went out that night and had a great time. We laughed and joked about my having fallen in a manhole. We talked about school and the reasons we had decided to go into blind rehab. We related to each other our hopes for our new careers. In short, we "hit it off."

We planned to go out in the woods the next day, and Jim dropped me off at my dorm. I thought about him that night and the next day until he came by to pick me up. Jim shared an old farmhouse with two or three others. The farmhouse was on forty acres and that's where we went for our tree identification expedition. As we walked out the door towards the hill up into the woods Jim said, "You know, your cane won't do much good on rough terrain. Want to just leave it here?" So, we walked, hand in hand, off into the woods.

At the top of the hill Jim stopped under a tree. "Okay, here's your first tree. Do you want to just give it a shot or do you want some help getting started?"

"Just show me to a branch and I'll see what I can do," I replied. Reaching up, Jim drew down a twig and placed it in my hand. The twig had opposite branching and the leaves felt a little papery to the touch. I could feel the serrated edges of the leaves. I thought back to my dendrology classes and tried to fit what I was feeling into some niche of my memory. Then something went, "clunk," in my head and I scratched the bark of the twig. I immediately smelled the aroma of almond. "It's a black cherry," I said confidently.

"Yeah, it is," replied Jim. I couldn't help but hear the astonishment in his voice. "Okay, let's keep going," he suggested. We looked at tree after tree. Some of them, I identified immediately and others baffled me. We walked deeper and deeper into the woods, stopping along the way to look at the trees.

Eventually, Jim started showing me some wildflowers. "This is a Mayapple," I said, laughing. "That one's too easy. Find some others." So, off we went with our attention directed downward instead of up towards the trees.

Soon, we sat on the ground beneath a huge oak to relax. It turns out that we were only six weeks apart in age. Jim grew up in Davison, a small town east of Flint, Michigan. He attended parochial school through eighth grade and then a public high school after that. His father worked as a millwright for Buick. With such different backgrounds we, each of us, found the other fascinating. We seemed to never run out of things to talk about.

Jim asked, "So, have you ever been in a serious relationship?"

Smiling, I replied, "Well, yes, I was married once."

A very long silence ensued, and Jim said simply, "Oh."

Feeling I had pulled his tail enough, I went on to describe my first marriage and how it had ended.

By this time, it was starting to get dark so we headed back to the house.

"There's a bar called the Hi-Lo just down the street," said Jim. "Would you like to grab a bite to eat before I take you back to French Hall?"

"Yes," I replied." Once we were settled at a table I found myself thinking that I had better tell Jim a bit more about myself. Specifically, I thought it best that he know about the cause of my blindness sooner rather than later. While blindness was becoming just part of who I was, I wasn't quite there with the suicide attempt. Taking a deep breath, I began. When I came to the end of my story I waited. Holding my breath, I waited for Jim's reaction.

"Oh," Jim said. Then he added, "Okay." And that was all he said.

"Is that all you can say?" I asked.

"Well, yes, what else should I say?"

"You're not horrified?" I said. And I thought, I might just fall in love with this guy. He knows what I considered, at the time, the most terrible thing about me and it was all okay.

While I was enormously attracted to Jim, I had conflicting feelings left right and center. I had already taken the very huge risk of enrolling in graduate school and moving about a zillion miles from everything which was familiar. There was no guarantee of success in this. It didn't come with a money back guarantee. There was the very real possibility that I would fail. Letting myself get involved with Jim, with anyone at this stage, seemed to expose me to another big chance for failure. And if we did get involved emotionally it was inevitable that physical involvement would follow.

And yet I felt so much potential with Jim. He encouraged me to explore my limits. He was gentle. He was accepting. I wanted to be with him. I wanted to explore what our lives together could become.

A few weeks later, at the end of the last class of the day, Jim said, "Want to grab a beer?"

"Sure," I said. "Where do you want to go?" We ended up at a pub near French Hall. There then ensued the most ridiculous conversation in which I have ever taken part. I tried to explain to Jim that I wasn't in any hurry to get into a relationship while, at the same time, I was hoping that a relationship between the two of us would develop. I further explained that I was particularly hesitant to get into any physical relationship.

An hour later, Jim waited in his car while I ran up to my dorm room to grab a change of clothes and a toothbrush. Then we went back to Jim's house for the night. So much for my protestations. But I never regretted that decision. Jim never betrayed me. He was patient and gentle. Growing together physically had the same sense of wonder and discovery that growing together emotionally had. I simply loved this gentle, quiet, fun loving man.

17 | skinny dipping

THE TERM I HAD STARTED AT WESTERN LASTED TWO
MONTHS. Then there was a week's break and another
two month term began at the end of June. I loved my
classes but hated life in the dorm. I felt like a grandmother.
With my focus on doing well academically, I found the constant
partying in the dorm distracting. I moved out of the dorm
after just one month. I spent the next month at the Lutheran
Student Center. Then, after the week long break, Jim and I
moved into a basement apartment in Kalamazoo.

Jim and I were getting along famously. We spent a
memorable day on the shore of Lake Michigan one Saturday in
June. Jim seemed to make no assumptions about what I could
and couldn't do and I loved him all the more for it. We drove to
South Haven where we had to scramble down a huge hill to get
to the beach. It was very steep and very rough. Jim went first
and I followed, using my long rigid cane more as a staff than a
tool of travel. But, when we got there, oh, what a glorious day
we had. The beach was completely deserted, so we just took
off our clothes and went skinny dipping. After swimming for
a while, Jim went up onto the beach.

"Join me," he said. "The beach is smooth, you can
maintain your orientation by listening to the water and we can
run together."

So, I joined him. "You go first and then I can follow you," I said.

He took off. I followed but had no chance of keeping up. Jim could run, fast. I dropped back and sat down in the sand. Realizing that I had stopped, Jim turned around. "What's the matter?" he called.

"I can't keep up with you," I replied.

So, he sprinted back in my direction. Simply listening to his feet as he zipped past me gave me a feeling of life and vitality. "Do it again," I yelled. And he sprinted back past me again.

Finally, we stretched out, naked, on a big towel. This was so, so far removed from anything I had ever done before, and I was loving it.

"Want to drive?" questioned Jim as we headed back to Kalamazoo.

"Yeah, right," I said, "Just move over and I'll drive us back," I said sarcastically.

"No, no, I'm serious," Jim said. "There's a wide straight road coming up on the left and there's almost never any traffic on it. You could do it, I'm sure."

I turned to him. "You're serious, aren't you?" I said.

"Yep, are you game?"

"I think you're nuts but, oh, what the heck, I'd like to give it a try."

A few minutes later, we pulled onto the deserted dirt road. Thinking this just about the craziest thing I had ever done, I got behind the wheel.

"Okay," Jim said, "Go ahead. I'll tell you if you need to steer left or right."

And so I drove. For the first time in eighteen months, I drove a car.

Later, when we were back in our apartment, Jim said, "You know those streets that you have to cross in order to get to campus?"

"What," I answered, "Stadium and West Michigan? Yes, what about them?"

"Well, you know that Dr. LeGrow said they were too dangerous, but I bet you could do it."

"Are you kidding?" I answered.

"No, not at all. Come on, if you can climb up and down that hill to the beach, if you can drive my car, you can do this."

"I don't know," I replied. "Let's go look at it again."

I grabbed my cane and we went to the intersection that our professor had judged too dangerous to cross. We stood at each corner and listened to the traffic through several cycles. Speaking at last, Jim said, "Okay, I think crossing Stadium is pretty straightforward. Then you can cross the railroad tracks and after about thirty feet, you'll come to the intersection of West Michigan. That's going to be the tough part."

There wasn't a lot of traffic on Lovell, which was my parallel street, so the time that Lovell had the green light was not very long. And West Michigan was a really wide street.

"West Michigan has a small island between the north and south bound lanes," began Jim. "If you had to, you could wait through a cycle there if you don't think you can make it all the way across in one cycle."

"I know," I replied, "But Dr. LeGrow thinks the island is too small for me to be really safe."

"Come on, let's go out there and wait through a traffic cycle together," Jim ventured. So, walking sighted guide, we went out to the island and waited through a couple of cycles of traffic.

"You know, I think it would be fine to wait here through one cycle if I had to," I said. "What do you think?"

"Let's take a shot at it," Jim said. We crossed and re-crossed West Michigan that day and by the time classes started up again on Monday, I was ready to do it for real. It all worked perfectly. There were a few times, when I was waiting through a traffic cycle on the island, that it felt a little scary. Those were the times when buses or trucks zipped by within a few feet. But I always made it across safely. Jim's belief in my abilities was exhilarating. And I loved him all the more for it.

18 | a shining image

WE ENTERED THE FALL SEMESTER. In one of our classes we studied the demographics of blindness. I listened, with growing horror, as the class progressed. From the discussion, I soon came to realize that the people with whom I would be working would be nothing like me at all. I had decided to become a rehab teacher thinking that I'd be working with people who were young, eager, and yearning to regain their independence. Or else people like the veterans who I had met at the blind center in Birmingham. But, no, that was evidently not to be. Most people in the U.S. who are legally blind are older folks or people who had additional disabilities.

When the class was over, I waited for Paul to get back to his office. Then I went in and closed the door. "This is not what I expected," I blurted through my tears. "I don't want to work with a bunch of old people. I don't want to work with people who have six other disabilities in addition to blindness. I thought I'd be working with people like me. People who are young and energetic. People who are thirsting to learn how to regain their independence."

"Are you done?" asked Paul mildly.

"Yes," I replied angrily.

"Then sit down and let's talk about this," he said.

I sat. He talked. I listened. I cannot honestly remember all that Paul said to me in the ensuing conversation. But somehow, he soothed me, assured me, and encouraged me to keep an open mind.

One of our classes that semester was Gerontology. It was an assignment for that class that found me reading "Heart Sounds." The book was about a man who was dying with congestive heart failure. It was written by his wife. She lucidly portrays the ever increasingly desperate attempts to save her husband's life. The end of the book, and the end of the man's life, take place in a hospital. The writer vividly describes the desperate attempts to save her husband's life. I read, with increasing horror, of the resuscitation attempts, the efforts to draw off the fluids in which the man was essentially drowning. And it was all for naught. The story had a profound effect on me. I came away from it with firmly fixed ideas about the end of life. It should be peaceful, not frantic. It should be dignified.

During this semester, the rehab teaching students took a field trip to Chicago. We visited the VA blind rehab center at Hines and the Illinois Visually Handicapped Institute, IVHI. The blind center at Hines mirrored the blind center in Birmingham where I had worked as a volunteer.

The highlight of the trip, for me at least, had nothing to do with Hines, IVHI, or anything related to the purpose of the trip. It took place in the hotel. Our class was staying in rooms that were all located adjacent to each other so we pretty much had an entire hallway to ourselves. We were hanging out in the hallway, just chatting and relaxing. Paul said, "Hey, Sue, want to take a spin with Dinah?"

"You serious?" I answered.

"Sure," said Paul. Come here." Paul showed me how to hold Dinah's leash and harness, described the verbal commands to use and demonstrated the hand signals. "Use a calm firm voice when you command her to move forward," he said.

Picking up Dinah's harness, I positioned the leash around my hand, stood to Dinah's right and said, "Dinah, forward," using the hand signal Paul had shown me. And Dinah moved out. She moved out fast. Wow, this was amazing. In no time flat, we were at the end of the hallway.

"Now, drop the harness, turn around, and come back down this way," called Paul. And we did. It was like flying.

I kept stammering my thanks to Paul when we reached the other end of the hallway. A good part of the rest of the evening, I peppered Paul with questions about guide dogs in general and about The Seeing Eye in particular.

Dinah was Paul's second dog. His first dog, Samantha, or Sam, was retired. Sam still lived with Paul and Sue, and Sue brought her to school with her every day. I had seen Sam take her leash in her mouth and go into the secretary's office when she needed to go out and Sue wasn't around. That was all very cool, but this? This was amazing. At that point, I decided that I wanted to go to The Seeing Eye to train with a dog. I wanted this freedom. I wanted to zip along with my own dog.

While the rehab teaching students were in Chicago, the orientation and mobility students were in New York and New Jersey. While I was falling in love with the idea of having a Seeing Eye dog, Jim was at the school itself. The Seeing Eye is in Morristown, New Jersey. It regularly hosts orientation and mobility students from the various graduate schools around the country. The students learn what is involved in training with a Seeing Eye dog and even get to walk with a dog. That was the beginning of what, to this point, has been a twenty seven year involvement with the school.

It was after that walk with Dinah that Jim and I spoke on the phone from our respective hotel rooms. I told him all about walking with Dinah and he told me all about walking with a Seeing Eye dog of his own. Then we started talking about our future. I had a shining image of our lives together.

Right along with that image was a dog wearing a harness. Without ever mentioning the word marriage, we eased into an understanding. We were going to be together for a long time to come.

On the drive back to Kalamazoo, I tentatively mentioned Jim's and my plans for the future. A fellow student, Sherry, pounced. When the van pulled up to the apartment that Jim and I shared, Sherry leapt from the van, dashed to the door of the apartment and yelled, "You're getting married!" Although I was slightly horrified, I had to laugh.

"Nice to keep these things private," I muttered to myself. After that, Jim and I, along with the rest of the class, fell into the same line of thought. We were, "an item." It was all good.

19 | her name is sadie

IN JANUARY OUR CLASS DISPERSED to all points of the compass to begin our internships. Jim went to the blind center at the Hines VA Medical Center in Chicago. I went to a private agency in northern Indiana. Jim lived in a grim dorm while I lived in a six-bedroom house all by myself. Almost every weekend, Jim either drove to Elkhart or, when there was a lot of snow, took a train.

Aside from beginning my real teaching, snow dominated my life that winter. Having grown up in the south, I had only experienced snow a few times. And even a little snow in Alabama usually brought everything to a screeching halt. Schools and businesses closed. People stayed home. Children made snowmen and hauled out sleds. It was all very exciting. But, in northern Indiana, snow was just what you had in the winter. I became used to ten and twelve foot snow banks. I learned that sometimes you just have to walk in the street because the sidewalks are buried beneath several feet of snow. I learned to cross country ski. I applied to The Seeing Eye for a dog.

As our internships drew to a close, Jim and I began our job hunt. A brand new blind rehab center was being established in Smyrna, Tennessee, and we both got jobs there. Jim began his job in mid-June just as I headed for The Seeing Eye and four weeks of training.

"Hello Ms. Wiygul, I'm Gary Matoon and I'll be your instructor," said the man as we shook hands. "Here, take my arm and I'll show you to your room. We're standing in the lobby right now and the student rooms are down this hallway to the right."

"Taking the proffered arm we zipped down the hallway, turned right, left, right again and went to the end of the hall.

"This is your room here, the last one on the right," said Gary, or Mr. Matoon as I was to call him.

At that time, students and instructors at The Seeing Eye addressed each other by surname. Men were required to change into slacks and a sports coat for lunch while women were required to change into nice slacks or a skirt. Why the formality?

The Seeing Eye was founded in 1929. At that time, individuals with blindness were thought only to be able to have menial and limited types of employment. They were often housed in institutions. Independence was just not a concept that applied to this population. When it opened its doors in 1929 The Seeing Eye began to change all of that. The school's tag line is "Independence with Dignity." These small things, being addressed by surname and being expected to dress nicely for lunch were small steps in that direction. But they had a profound effect on some students. For many, this was the first sign of respect ever shown them.

Why was the more formal dress required for lunch and not other meals? The Seeing Eye has many corporate donors. It was not unusual for a representative of these large donors to come to the school for a tour and to see how their donations were being used. These individuals often stayed for lunch with the students. The school recognized that its graduates, flush with new confidence and independence, might apply for jobs with companies that sent representatives to the school. The reasoning went something like this. If a company representative met a student at The Seeing Eye, dressed in ratty clothes, how would that effect the graduates possibilities of getting a job with the company?

After orienting me to my room, Gary said, "Okay, let's get started. The first thing we're going to do is a Juno walk."

"A what walk?" I asked.

"We use 'Juno' as a sort of generic name for a dog," said Gary. "I'm going to hold the harness body and walk in front of you. You're going to hold the harness handle as you will when there's a real dog in the harness. We'll do some walking together. This accomplishes several things. I'll be able to get an idea of your pace and how much pull you can take, I'll be orienting you to the building and grounds, and I'll be teaching you some basic commands. We always begin commands with the dog's name, so you'll be calling me 'Juno.'"

Gary placed the harness handle in my hand, positioned himself ahead of me and to my left, and said, "Now, use the command, 'Juno, forward.'"

"Juno, forward," I said. And I made a forward movement with my right hand.

"Whoa," said Gary, "How did you know that hand gesture?"

"Oh," I said, "Dr. Ponchillia showed me how to hold the harness and leash and explained all about hand gestures when I was in graduate school."

"Okay, cool," Gary said, "Now, let's get going."

And, get going, is exactly what we did. The pace of training at The Seeing Eye is, in a word, fast. After walking me all around the building, Gary took me outside to what he called the park, a large paved area where we would be taking our dogs at relief time.

"I'm going to really pick up the pace," said Gary. "I want to see what kind of pace you're comfortable with and how much pull you can take." We walked faster and faster. Gary started making, what felt like, swooping turns. It was very exciting. I couldn't wait until there was a dog in the harness.

When Gary brought me back to my room, I sat down on the bed for a minute before beginning to unpack my clothes. I remembered that shining image I had when Paul let me walk with Dinah. The image of Jim and me together with a dog in harness was about to become a reality.

As I placed the last item in the drawer, I heard chimes. Wondering what on earth they meant, it soon became apparent when folks who had trained at the school before began emerging from their rooms. "Time for dinner," I heard my next door neighbor say. So, I grabbed my cane and headed for the dining room.

There were three instructors in the class. Each instructor had six students. We sat at three long tables. It was the first time I got to meet the other five students in my class. Gary told us what the choices were for dinner.

"Hi," said a person at my elbow. "I'm Mary, what would you like for dinner."

When Mary put the plate down in front of me, she simply said, "There you are, is there anything else you would like?" It was fabulous. The staff at The Seeing Eye, all of the staff, seems to know exactly how much help or advice to offer. Students are provided with what seems like just the right amount of information. No molly coddling here. If you want or need more information than is offered, you simply have to ask for it.

The next morning, Sunday, we loaded into vans by class and went into Morristown. There, we did more Juno walks. When everyone got back to the school, the instructors went into a huddle. "They're deciding which person gets which dog," said my neighbor. She was training with her second dog and knew the ropes. Finally, the chimes sang out and we went to lunch, after which, we got the scoop on our dogs. My dog's name was Sadie. She was a two year old yellow Lab.

"Okay, Ms. Wiygul," called Gary. "Come down to the women's lounge and meet your dog." As I entered the room, Gary directed me to a chair and then brought Sadie to me. He placed a leash in my hand and said, "Here she is. She's a bundle of energy and I think the two of you will do very well together." I reached out to pat my new dog. Her ears were long and silky. She tentatively sniffed my hand and then moved closer to investigate this new person. It was real. I had my dog.

I will never forget my first walk with Sadie. On Monday morning, Gary drove us into town. He parked on a quiet street and took us, one by one, for our first walk. Standing to my right and slightly behind me, Gary insured that I correctly positioned the leash around my left wrist. Then he said, "Okay, pick up the harness and let's do it."

Picking up the harness handle, I said, "Sadie, forward," at the same time using the now familiar hand signal. We walked forward fifteen feet and stopped.

"We're at the intersection of Maple," Gary said at my right shoulder. "Command her forward." Sadie stepped off the curb, crossed the street, and paused at the up-curb. I commanded her forward again. "Now, tell her to turn right and then forward," said Gary.

And we flew. We flew down the sidewalk. I cannot express the wonder of it. This was as good as leaping a fence mounted on Knight Commander. No, it was better than that. That had been sport. This was life. Smiling, I walked into the future.

20 | not by half

THINK ABOUT ALL OF THE CHANGES your dogs have gone through," Gary began. "Four months ago, they came back into the kennel after a year and a half with their puppy raisers. They have to make the turnover of loyalty from their puppy raisers to their trainers. Then, after three months of training, they come to live in the house here. And suddenly there's this new person on the other end of the harness. About the time the dogs get used to things, you take them away from everything they've ever known and go to another completely new place. He paused and looked around at the class.

"Don't worry," he said, "Everything will work out but there are things you can do to make the transition easier. The one consistent thing in your dog's lives is work. When you get home, take your dog for a short walk. Make it an easy one. Set your dog up for success."

"Mr. Matoon," I began when the room had emptied. "I don't know how I missed this, but I didn't know about keeping things sort of quiet for the first two weeks home. I'm getting married two days after I get home."

"Oh," said Gary, and he paused. Recognizing that this was not something that I could change, he thought for a minute. "Okay, he said. "Okay, this changes things. But Sadie is a rock solid dog. Will you be getting married in a church," Gary began.

""No," I replied. "We're getting married at home.""

"Ah," Gary said, "Will the person who is marrying you be wearing vestments of any kind?"

"Yes, Grady is an Episcopal minister and he'll definitely be vested."

"In that case, will it be possible for Sadie to watch as he dons his vestments?" And continuing Gary added, "Dogs can be suspicious of people who are dressed differently, you know, like people who are wearing uniforms and things."

"Sure," I said, "That should be no problem at all." Gary made other suggestions to help Sadie make the transition and I felt much better by the end of the discussion.

"Good luck," said Gary as he shook my hand at the gate in the Newark airport. "You'll do great. I have complete confidence in both of you."

Shortly after that, I boarded the plane. When the plane landed I prepared to disembark. Gary had told me not to work Sadie off of the plane but to go sighted guide with a flight attendant. But that little imp, the one that sat on my shoulder and told me to take a shower when I wasn't supposed to all those months ago, said into my ear, "Go ahead and work her. It will be fine. And oh so much more impressive." So, I did. I was sitting near the front of the plane and I was the first person to come up the Jetway. My parents were there to meet me.

The emotions of our greetings all those years ago are still clear in my mind. If this wasn't a manifestation of all of the rebirth concepts that had helped me in those early days of blindness, nothing was. I walked back into my family as a new person. I walked back into life as a confident capable adult.

When we arrived home, I removed Sadie's harness, took her out to park, gave her some water and then, gratefully, sat down at the table for lunch. Afterwards, I realized how tired I was. Training with a Seeing Eye dog is exciting and exhilarating. But it's also exhausting. I must have been running on adrenalin much of the time.

Realizing that I was probably going to fall asleep if I didn't stay in a vertical position, I decided I'd better do the walk thing now. As I turned left onto Pump House Road at the end of our driveway, I thought this might be the first time a Seeing Eye team has ever been seen in this neighborhood.

I proceeded down Pump House Road to Abingdon Road and turned left. Abingdon is a dead end street so I walked the mile or so to the end of it and then returned home. I was now on the other side of the road from our house. Walking until I judged I was well past the house, I crossed the street and headed back in the other direction. When we got there, Sadie turned neatly into the driveway as though she had been doing it for years.

Jim arrived at about nine o'clock that night. He had to wait until the end of the workday at the Tennessee Rehab Center before he could set out. Poor Jim. I hugged and kissed him, we spoke for a few minutes, I yawned and said, "I'm going to bed."

Laughing, Jim said, "Oh, great, I haven't seen you for a month and you're going to bed?" But he kissed me again and bade me sleep well.

Saturday morning arrived. Grady came at around ten-thirty as the wedding was scheduled for eleven. I explained to Grady about Gary advising that he vest in Sadie's presence. So, he brought his vestments into my bedroom and put them on. I have no idea if this made any difference. Sadie didn't seem to care much one way or the other. She was completely relaxed during the ceremony.

"Ready?" said my father. He turned his head towards me and I could hear the smile in his voice.

"Ready," I said. Walking with Sadie at heel, I took Daddy's arm, and we walked into the living room.

"Who gives this woman to be married to this man," intoned Grady.

"Frances and I do," and Daddy placed my right hand in Jim's and then faded back to sit with my mother.

"Please kneel," said Grady as the ceremony drew to a close. I knelt on the needlepoint kneeler that I had especially chosen. It depicted Jesus performing his first miracle, that of turning water into wine. This was a miracle. Just two and a half years after I felt that life was not worth living, I was marrying the man I loved, and I was poised to move forward into a new life. As I knelt, I discovered that Sadie had been lying quietly with her chin resting on the kneeler the entire time. With my right hand in Jim's left and my left hand resting on Sadie's head, Grady blessed our marriage.

Telling us to turn around and face our friends and family, Grady said, "Ladies and gentlemen, Mr. and Mrs. James T. Martin." We were husband and wife.

"I'm so happy for you," said my mother as she hugged me. And then we were separated by well-wishers as the reception moved into full swing.

As Jim and I drove away from my home, I gleefully ripped off my hot pantyhose and stuck my feet out of the car window. We whooped and laughed. "I could have murdered that photographer!" began Jim.

"Oh, God, I know. Wasn't she a pain? I was halfway expecting her to tell me to move my pinky finger a quarter of an inch to the right or something," I continued.

"And the way she kept trying to get different shots of the damn cake," said Jim. "All I wanted to do was dig in and eat the thing."

"Oh, my gosh," I responded. "You know, I never did get a piece of that cake, Guess I'll just have to wait until our first anniversary."

"What do you mean?" asked Jim.

"Oh, it's a tradition," I replied. "My mother will put a part of the cake in the freezer. Then, on our first anniversary, we can eat it."

"Oh, okay, another one of those southern traditions?" quipped Jim.

We drove to Wheeler Wildlife Preserve that afternoon and spent the night in the lodge overlooking the lake. We had champagne. We made love. We showered together and then we slept.

Pop, went the cork of the champagne bottle the next morning. "What a thing to wake up to," I laughed as Jim poured the bubbling wine into my glass. We propped ourselves up in bed and drank two glasses of champagne each while we watched the sun rise over the lake.

Later, after a brunch in the lodge, we continued north towards Tennessee. Somehow, I had forgotten my "get away bag," as my mother called it. It was packed with my toiletries and the nightgown that I was supposed to have worn on Jim's and my first night as a married couple. It made absolutely no difference to us. I'm quite sure I wouldn't have bothered with the nightgown even if I had it with me. My parents had put the suitcase on a bus Sunday morning, so our first stop, before going on to our apartment in Smyrna, was the Nashville Greyhound station.

After we collected the suitcase, Jim suggested that we go out to dinner. As we entered the restaurant, a waiter said, "You can't bring that dog in here." I waited for Jim to come to my defense and explain it to the waiter. This was what southern gentlemen did. They took care of any unpleasantness. But Jim said not one word.

"Um, she's a Seeing Eye dog," I began tentatively. That made no impression whatsoever on the waiter.

"Take her outside at once and tie her up," he commanded.

Glancing in Jim's direction for courage which, incidentally, you don't have to see in order to receive, I said in a much stronger voice, "No, she's a Seeing Eye dog. You have to let me in with her." Then I rummaged in my purse for the legislation handbook that they had given me at The Seeing Eye. Handing it to Jim I said, "Show him the page for Tennessee. Taking the booklet, Jim found the correct page and handed it to the waiter. The waiter read it and relented. We were allowed into the restaurant after all.

After an otherwise uneventful dinner, Jim and I finally arrived at our apartment in Smyrna. The next day, I went to work at The Tennessee Rehab Center. In the space of five days, I had brought my first Seeing Eye dog home, gotten married, moved to a new home in a new state, defended myself to a waiter who didn't know the law, and started a new job. I didn't do things by halves, oh no.

21 | a life together

THOSE WERE HEADY DAYS. Could there be anything better for someone fresh from the ivory tower than starting a brand new program? While I had been at The Seeing Eye, Jim had been scouring Murfreesboro and Nashville for just the right environments to teach his students. We drove to all the places he had picked out and he showed me the routes he was planning to teach.

Meantime, I was getting to select the equipment for the blind rehab program. We had the kitchen remodeled. I set up a large open area as a living room and dining room. I wrote the curricula for all of the areas in which I would be teaching.

We traded in Jim's car for a pickup truck. We started looking for a house to rent. We wanted a place with land where we could have animals and grow a garden. We finally found an old farmhouse in Beech Grove, Tennessee. We rented six acres that were part of a sixty-five acre farm. The house had been built before the civil war and there was a small cabin of sorts behind the house which had been slave quarters.

Beech Grove was in central Tennessee, in the foothills of the Cumberland Plateau. As the Appalachian Mountains peter out, the Cumberland Plateau begins. It runs from northeast to southwest, finally ending in Alabama. All along its length, the plateau is characterized by ridges that split off from the main body like long fingers. Where these fingers split away from the main body there are steep valleys called hollows. Our house was in one of these hollows.

We drove down the dirt road, crossed the bridge over the small stream and arrived at our new home. "Hey, you never did carry me over the threshold of our apartment. Want to do it now?" Without a single word, Jim picked me up, threw me over his shoulder in a fireman's carry and walked into the house. Laughing hysterically, I said, "That's not exactly what I had in mind."

"Well, I carried you over the threshold. That's what I was supposed to do, right?" quipped Jim.

"Oh, you," I replied. "You know that's not what I meant." And together we walked around our new home. The house was in the shape of an L. Across the front, from left to right, were a living room, another room which later became my computer room, and the bedroom. Behind the bedroom were the bathroom, dining room, and kitchen which formed the L. The bathroom, utility room, and pantry had evidently been enclosed from what had once been porches. The result was that the only way into the bathroom was either through the bedroom or the dining room. The kitchen, dining room, my soon-to-be computer room, and living room all opened onto an L-shaped back porch. It was easy to imagine that this back porch had been the hub of life for the house. We put two rocking chairs on the back porch and spent many an hour there, either relaxing or working.

The house had neither central air conditioning nor heating. The twelve-foot ceilings helped keep us from getting too hot in the summer. There was a large LP gas heater in the kitchen and a small LP gas heater in the bathroom. There was also a wood stove in the living room.

"Let's get a goat," said Jim one morning.

"Fine," I replied. How does one get a goat?" We ended up

with not one, but two goats. Sara was the doe and we named her kid Bucky.

"Wrap your thumb and index finger around the top of her teat," began Jim. He was teaching me to milk Sara. "Then tighten your fingers in a sort of downward progression."

"Like this?" I asked. "Nothing's happening. What am I doing wrong?"

"Okay, also pull gently down as you tighten your fingers."

"Ah, I get it," I said, as the first stream of milk zinged into the galvanized tin pail.

By this time, my father had started having trouble with his arthritis. No longer able to handle his heavy rototiller, he gave it to us. After tilling an area behind the house for a garden, Jim said, "We need to figure out some way for you to keep the rows straight when you plant seeds." We hammered in stakes at both ends of each row and strung clothesline from stake to stake. Then we planted our garden.

"What do you think about getting some chickens?" asked Jim.

"Sure, let's get some chickens," I replied. That's how a box of thirty mixed sex chicks came to live with us. My mother was a representative for the clothing manufacturer, Doncaster. She had some huge wardrobe boxes and we used one of them for the chicks. We placed the box in the utility room, filled it with straw and strung a light over the box to keep the chicks warm. When Jim judged they were large enough to live outside, we simply opened the door of the utility room and all thirty chicks trooped outside.

"Hey," I called to Jim. "The straw in this box is full of droppings. Won't that be great fertilizer for the garden?"

"Yep," replied Jim. "That's what I was thinking too. Can you pick up the box?"

"Sure, I'll give it a try." That's how I came to be elbow deep in chicken shit. When I lifted the box, it promptly disintegrated. I just sat down on the floor and laughed. "I, um, think I'm going to need some help here."

When Jim came into the utility room and saw my predicament, he burst out laughing as well. Somehow we got the mess out of the house and into the garden.

By the next summer the bounty began to roll in. We canned green beans and tomatoes. We froze corn and peas. I stuffed yellow squash with spinach in a concoction that my mother had taught me to make and froze them. We bought a freezer.

We dropped onions into pantyhose, tied knots in the pantyhose, dropped in the next onion and continued until the pantyhose were full. We hung them in the utility room. Whenever I needed an onion, I'd just grab a pair of scissors and cut the next one off. We also kept bushels of potatoes in the utility room.

We gave away tomatoes, cucumbers, zucchini, and squash. We gave away eggs, oh did we give away eggs. The blind rehab center was on the fourth floor of the Tennessee Rehab Center. During the months of July and August, people from all over the fourth floor came by to see what we were giving away. One job placement specialist told me that we had kept them in vegetables and eggs for two months running.

As the chickens matured, the roosters became aggressive towards each other. Jim said, "We'll have to begin killing the roosters before too long." This involved, first, fasting the rooster for twenty four hours. After that, Jim would grasp the rooster by his feet and swing him, upside down, like a pendulum to make him dizzy so that he would hold still while Jim used a hatchet to chop off his head.

"Want to do the next one?" Jim asked.

"What?" I replied. "What, you want me to chop off the next chicken's head?" This seemed about as inane a suggestion as I have heard yet.

"Well sure, why not?" Come on, if you could hammer in the nails when we were fixing up the chicken coop, you can do this."

"Yes, but nails are already dead. I mean, if I miss or only partially hit the target, well, that would be terrible." I have no idea why Jim seemed so keen that I should behead the next chicken.

"Look," he said, "I'll partially hammer in two long nails in this piece of wood. I'll put the chicken's neck between the nails. Then you can easily feel where the nails are and aim in between them."

After Jim nailed the nails in the board, we practiced. After a few dry runs, all of which resulted in my burying the hatchet exactly where it needed to go, I agreed to give it a try for real. So, I did it. I chopped off a chicken's head. And, yes, by the way, they do run around with their heads cut off.

In the end, we had about fifteen hens and two roosters. The roosters were of different breeds, and they didn't seem aggressive towards each other.

Iris was the next to join the family. She was a thirtyish-pound dog that looked like a fox. She had a triumphant plume of a tail that curled up over her back. She also liked killing chickens. When she killed the second chicken, Jim tied the dead bird around her neck and left it there for two days. That cured her. She never went after another chicken.

The last two creatures to join us were two heifers. They were both pregnant, so, when they calved, we doubled our bovine population.

Following a medical appointment in Birmingham, my father drove me back to Tennessee. Rather than turning around and going home, he spent the night with us. He slept on a pull out bed in the living room.

"I know this house has a funky layout," I said, as I smoothed the blanket on the bed. "The only way into the bathroom from here is through our bedroom. If you need the bathroom in the night, just come on through. Well, it's either that or go out onto the back porch and come into the bathroom from there."

"Where's your broom," said my father from the back porch as I entered the kitchen the next morning.

I took the broom from the pantry and took it out to him. "Here you go," I said, puzzled.

"It's this damn rooster. He keeps coming up on the porch." Whack, went the broom and the rooster squawked and took off in a whirl of feathers and indignation. While the two roosters weren't aggressive towards each other, the red one in particular, could be aggressive towards people. My father was no stranger to aggressive roosters. He had grown up on a farm in Mississippi. It was really quite shocking to see my father go after a rooster with a broom.

Pulling myself together I asked, "How did you sleep?"

"Oh, fine," he replied. "I started to go the long way to the bathroom rather than come through your bedroom. But once I was out on the porch I thought, what the heck? So, I just took a whiz off your back porch."

In complete amazement now I said, "You did? You actually peed off our back porch? That's extraordinary." This was a side of my father that I had only occasionally glimpsed. He was getting a kick out of my astonishment. My mental image of my father was that of a serious, taciturn, and dignified man. And here he was, being downright playful.

22 | on the rocks

WE STILL HAD JOB OPENINGS at the Tennessee Rehab Center. About four months after Jim and I started working there, a friend who was a couple of semesters behind us at Western Michigan came to look over the place and to consider whether he wanted to apply for a job. Chuck came along with a friend, Doug. In an effort to impress them, Jim and I decided to show them some of the sights. Beech Grove was about sixty miles from the town of Sewanee, Tennessee. And Sewanee is the home of the University of the South, where I attained my bachelor's degree in English. The college is located on a ten thousand acre domain. It straddles the Cumberland Plateau and is absolutely gorgeous. There are several spots from which you can look down across the valleys below. I thought a hike from Morgan's Steep down to Bridal Veil Falls might be a good hike for the four of us.

"Wow," said Chuck, as he looked out across the valley towards Cowan and Winchester.

"Yeah, it's impressive isn't it."

"So, which way is the trail," said Jim.

"It's down here and then to the right. Can you see it?" I replied.

Jim moved forward out onto the limestone shelf and turned right. "Yep," he called back, it's right here. We all trooped after him and began our hike. It was about a mile to the falls. The Cumberland Plateau is riddled with caves and underground rivers. This particular river emerged from the side of the mountain, fell and tumbled down about a hundred feet and then went back underground.

"Wow, this is spectacular," said Jim as we approached the falls. We all simply stood there, taking it in. We were standing on the edge of the mountain, right above the spot where the river emerged and looking down on the cascading water.

"Look, over here," began Chuck. "If we walk out across this little spit of land, over to that spot over there, we'll be able to look back at the falls."

"Sounds like a plan," replied Jim. "And look, when we get out there, the sun will be behind us and I'll just bet there will be rainbows in the water."

The spit of land was a sort of land bridge. There was a wash in the side of the mountain to the right of the falls. The rock fall had left a small bridge of land over the wash. This land bridge went out to a larger flat area which was our goal. You could say we were chasing rainbows.

At that point in our relationship, Jim and I had not done much hiking together. And, since I had only had Sadie for a few months, we had done even less hiking as a threesome. What we've learned since is that it's much better if I go first. That way, Jim can see what's ahead and warn me about things like drop-offs. However, at this point, we had not learned those lessons. Chuck was in front, followed by Doug, then Jim, with me bringing up the rear.

It had rained recently and the ground was fairly slick with mud in spots. It was one of those spots on which I placed my foot. One moment, there was ground beneath my foot. The next moment I was falling.

I hit the rocks. I landed hard, taking the impact on my heels, butt, and the back of my head. Although I knew that I could be falling a hundred feet, I didn't tense. I was completely relaxed when I hit the ground and that's probably why I wasn't injured. But Jim was a different story. He, seeing me begin to fall out of the corner of his eye, turned and tried to grab me. The result is that he summersaulted over the edge and landed on the right side of his head. When the dust settled, I was lying on my back with my feet below my head at about a forty-five degree angle. Jim was on top of me. He was lying across me with his head at my ankles and his feet at my shoulders. He was unconscious.

Jim was choking. My emergency medical technician training snapped into action. Reaching into his mouth, I scooped out the mucous and cleared his airway. Then my concern was to stabilize his head. I knew, only too well, that this was a prime candidate situation for a spinal cord injury. At that precise moment, my right leg went into what rock climbers call, the sewing machine knee. It began to jerk uncontrollably. I took a deep breath and willed my rebellious leg to be still.

Jim moaned. As he began to regain consciousness, his hand moved up to my throat and began to tighten. Jim tells me he has no memory of this. But much later, it became the running joke that he was trying to choke me in retaliation for my having dragged him over the cliff.

My instinct was to try to keep Jim still. However, once he regained consciousness this was impossible. He got to his feet and looked up. Shaking his head he said, over and over again, "We fell from up there?"

When I had been a student at Sewanee (yes, the school does go by the name of the town), I had helped start a technical terrain-rescue team. Several of us who were rock climbers decided that we needed to be better prepared to help people who got in trouble climbing. Rock climbing was becoming enormously popular and people who knew only the basics about climbing were getting in trouble. We arranged that an emergency medical technician class be taught at the school. There were about ten of us who became certified. Rather than being certified as ambulance EMTs we were certified as

Rescue EMTs. Chuck went back to campus to get help and it was this very group that came to help us.

"Sue, is that you? What the hell are you doing down here," said Doug Cameron as the rescue team arrived. Doug had been in that very first EMT class with me all those years ago.

"Hi, Doug," I said. "I know, this is a hell of a note isn't it?" Then the rescue team got to work. They strapped Jim to a long spine board and carried him out.

"Sue, are you injured at all?" asked Doug.

"I don't think so," I replied. "I hit my head pretty hard but, aside from seeing stars, I think I'm okay." Doug examined me anyway. He checked the dilation of my pupils and said, "I don't know, your pupillary dilation isn't the same in both eyes."

"That's because one of them is a prosthesis. I promise, I'm okay."

"All right then," said Doug. "Can you walk out?"

"Yes, I think so, but I'm not sure I can work Sadie. She's got a pretty strong pull that I don't think I'm up to dealing with." Sadie had fallen off the cliff with us. Aside from a scratch on her muzzle she seemed perfectly fine. So, I took off her harness and Doug instructed one of the other EMTs to walk out with us. The walk seemed to take forever. Finally, we arrived back on campus. They loaded us into an ambulance and took us to the Sewanee hospital.

While the Sewanee hospital was adequate, it was not equipped for all emergencies. Jim's X-rays showed some irregularities in his thoracic vertebrae. Though he told them he had congenital scoliosis they felt he needed a higher level of care than they could provide. The doctor came out to tell me they were going to send Jim to a large medical center in Chattanooga. Chuck and Doug and I discussed the logistics of what to do next. I asked Chuck to drive our truck to Chattanooga, and he agreed.

"Can I ride with him," I asked as the next crew of EMTs took over.

"No, said one of them. It's about an hour drive to Chattanooga from Sewanee. I did not want to be separated from Jim for that long.

"Here," I said to Chuck as I handed him Sadie's leash. "Take her with you." Taking a deep breath, I just got in the ambulance. Once I was there and settled, the EMTs relented.

"Will you call Jack and let him know what's happened?" said Jim as they took him into the emergency room at Erlanger Hospital in Chattanooga.

Jack is Jim's eldest brother. He lives in a fairly small town. "Sure, I'll try to get his number from directory assistance," I replied. It turned out that there were six John Martins listed in that small town. On the fourth try, a woman answered the phone. "Is this John, I mean, Jack Martin's residence?"

"Yes," said the woman hesitantly. "Who is this?"

"Oh, Donna?" I asked.

"Yes, who is this," she repeated.

I identified myself and she put Jack on the phone. After I told him what had happened I decided I should probably call my parents.

"Hello," said my father.

"Daddy," I replied, "Something pretty bad has happened. We were hiking at Sewanee and Jim and I fell. We're at the hospital in Chattanooga. They say that Jim might have a spinal injury."

After a long pause, my father replied, "This is not good. Do you have any other details?"

"No, they're examining him now. I think they're doing more X-rays. They took X-rays at the Sewanee hospital and sent us here."

"Okay," my father finally replied, "keep us posted.

23 | beyond the call

THEY ADMITTED JIM TO ERLANGER HOSPITAL. By this time it was getting very late. I was exhausted. But I was also covered in mud. There was a window seat in Jim's room and the nurses said I could sleep there.

"Is there any way I can get my jeans and sweater washed?" I began. The nurses were fabulous. They took my clothes away to be laundered. They gave me a hospital gown and a basin of warm water so that I could wash the worst of the mud off. Then I went to sleep. But I didn't sleep long. Every other hour, a nurse came in the room, awakened Jim and asked him some questions. This is standard operating procedure when someone sustains a concussion. I had been through the same thing twice, once when I fell from my horse and once when I hit my head on rocks when my kayak flipped over. Although Jim had no problems with the questions, What is your name? and What's the date?, he had a heck of a time with the Do you know where you are? question. By the time he got that answer down pat, "Erlanger Hospital in Chattanooga," he never ever forgot it. To this day, when the question of our whereabouts comes up, one of us still may answer, "Erlanger Hospital, Chattanooga."

With the arrival of the dawn, I began a crash course in independent living. Yes, okay, I had lived on my own in

Michigan and now in Tennessee. I had earned a graduate degree. I had a job. But this was a very different kettle of fish. I knew nothing of the layout of this hospital. I was completely on my own. We were stranded in Chattanooga with no transportation. We had no idea when Jim would be discharged or how we'd get home when he was. While they had agreed that Jim had no injury to his spine they were taking all of the precautions which indicated that he was not out of the woods yet.

I pulled on my clean jeans and sweater, harnessed Sadie, and went out to the nurses' station. "Yes, how can I help you?"

"Hi," I began. "I need to take my dog outside and then I need to see about getting something to eat."

The nurse described how to get to the cafeteria. She said there was a door to the outside just beyond the cafeteria. I set out. Everything went well at first. Soon, however, the route the nurse had described ceased to match reality. The hallway that was supposed to be on the left just wasn't there. I stopped. Thinking back over what the nurse had said, I just couldn't figure out where I had gone wrong. I was completely alone. Where were all of the people that usually seemed to be scurrying around in hospitals? Should I go back and start over? Should I keep going in hopes of finding someone who could help me? Why couldn't just one thing go right? I resisted the urge to sit down on the floor and cry. Thinking back to Oscar and my drop off lesson, I took a deep breath and moved forward with renewed resolve. At last, I heard voices in front of me.

I was moving into one of those open places that all hospitals seem to have. After asking directions, I finally smelled the aroma of bacon and coffee. Passing by the cafeteria, I reached down to touch Sadie's nose when she stopped. Sure enough, she was pointing her nose right at the push bar of the door to the outside. Relieved, I exited the hospital.

When I came back in, I proceeded to the cafeteria and entered it. I froze. The place seemed to be the size of the average cargo hold. I listened carefully but couldn't hear anything that gave me any clue to the layout of the place. I stood there forever trying to decide how to proceed. Finally, a man approached and asked if I needed any help. Hugely relieved I said, "Yes, please. I'd like to get some breakfast and take it up to my husband's room.

"Okay," the man replied. Do you want to take my arm or something?"

"No," I replied, "Just lead the way and I'll tell my dog to follow you."

When we arrived at the cafeteria line, the man asked if I knew what I wanted. "Well, just a regular breakfast, maybe some eggs and toast, and, I don't know, grits or hash browns or something?"

He filled a plate for me, placed it on a tray and then said, "Here, I'll carry this for you. Where would you like to go?"

"I had hoped that I could take it back up to my husband's room, but that's pretty far away," I replied. Thinking that the man probably worked in the kitchen I said, "I'd really appreciate your help. Are you sure you have time to walk with me? It's pretty far away," I repeated

"No problem," said the man. "Which unit is your husband on?"

I told him the unit and we set out. This was a gift. In a new environment, one of the dangers of trying to figure things out yourself is that a guide dog can learn an incorrect route and repeat it. Being able to go directly from the cafeteria to Jim's room meant that Sadie could learn the proper route and be less likely to repeat the false turns that I had made on my first attempt to locate the cafeteria. The route on which I followed my savior was far more direct than the route I had taken earlier. I praised Sadie at each turn and each elevator call button.

When we arrived at Jim's unit the man said, "What's your husband's room number?"

"I have no idea," I replied. "If you follow me, Sadie will show us his room."

"This is my husband, Jim," I said as we entered the room.

The man shook Jim's hand and said, "Hi, I'm Dr. Abramson. I'm a pathologist here at the hospital."

"Oh, I thought . . . well, never mind what I thought," I said. "My name is Sue and this is Sadie. I can't tell you how much I appreciate your help."

"I'm just happy I could help you out. Jim, may I borrow your tray for Sue's breakfast?"

"Yeah, sure," Jim answered. Dr. Abramson lowered the tray and rolled it over to the window seat. He then placed my breakfast on the tray.

"Okay, here you go. You do this by the clock, right?" And he told me where everything was on the plate.

"Thank you so much, Dr. Abramson, I can't tell you how much I appreciate your help." And he took his leave.

With a good breakfast in me life looked a little better. "That was really nice of him, wasn't it?" I said to Jim. But the gratitude I felt went way beyond, "nice." A little while later I went out to the nurses' station and asked them if there was some kind of recognition that the hospital gave to employees who went above and beyond. It turned out there was such a thing. Without giving details, I simply said, I want to recommend that Dr. Abramson receive that recognition. There was a moment of silence caused, I can only guess, by the fervor in my voice. Then the nurses said that they would see to it.

I started to turn away and then hesitated. "You know," I began, "I need to recommend that you folks receive that recognition too. What you did for me last night, you know, washing my clothes, bringing me the basin of warm water so I could wash off the mud . . . I guess I was sort of preoccupied and I didn't thank you properly. Can you do that? Can you recommend yourselves as well as Dr. Abramson for that award?"

The nurse smiled, "Yes, we'll take care of it."

By the next afternoon, they began making noises about sending Jim home. "Wait a minute," I said. Apart from the fact that we were stranded with no transportation, this was a very bad idea. Jim had started bleeding from the right side of his nose and from his right ear. "He's bleeding," I said, "You can't send him home like this."

The time had come to ask for help. "Mama," I began, "I think I need your help. Jim's bleeding and they're talking about sending him home. This is just nuts. He's bleeding from his right ear."

"Okay, honey, we'll come. We wanted to from the start but didn't want to, well, never mind, we're on the way."

A couple of hours later, they were there. In his quiet yet authoritative voice, my father asked to see Jim's doctor. When the man entered the room, my father introduced himself. "Hello, I'm Dr. Wiygul, Jim's father." This was the first time that either of my parents indicated that they had taken Jim as their son, that he was part of the family. There were to be many more demonstrations of this attitude in the years to come. My father went on to point out that, with the bleeding, Jim could not possibly be sent home. After listening to my father's concerns, the doctor agreed to do more X-rays. That's when they discovered the skull fracture. Jim had fractured his skull just behind his right ear.

"Are you okay," asked my father. I had swayed slightly while standing at Jim's bedside.

"Yeah," I replied. "Why?"

"You look a little unsteady on your feet." Daddy then did an informal neurological examination. "I think we'd better get you checked out," he said. In the emergency room the resident was clearly intimidated by my father's quiet authority. "Retired," said Daddy after introducing himself. This seemed to put the other man at his ease and he began his examination.

"Your pupillary dilation is uneven," he began.

Wow, this was the second time in a few days that a medical professional did not recognize my prosthesis. With a nod to the ocularist who had given me such a good match, I said, "I know, my left eye is a prosthesis," I told him. There turned out to be nothing at all wrong with me but it was good to have that confirmed.

A couple of days later, when Jim's bleeding had stopped and they felt that he was medically stable, we went home. My parents had been staying in a nearby hotel and it was they who drove us back to Beech Grove. When Jim was settled in the living room, my mother said, "Are you sure you're going to be all right? We really don't mind staying if you'd like for us to."

"No, I appreciate the offer, but I think we'll be fine."

I had a need, a deep need, to be alone with Jim in our own home. We had been through an ordeal. I simply wanted to be alone together, to just be.

24 | maine things considered

WE HAD A GOOD YEAR AND A HALF or so at The Tennessee Rehab Center. I really enjoyed the folks with whom I worked. Jim flourished. Chuck, the friend who had been with us on the trip to Bridal Veil Falls and another O&M instructor joined the staff. But Jim had been the first O&M instructor at the center and was the de facto leader of the group.

We loved our house and land. We loved having the animals and growing our vegetables. Starting a new rehab center was very rewarding. But there were things about the Tennessee Rehab Center that were not so wonderful. It was a rehab center for all sorts of disabilities. Of the two hundred or so residents, about two-thirds of them had mental or emotional disabilities. Given the population it was not surprising that the center put a big emphasis on behavior modification. For the most part, we ignored the imperatives to use various behavior modification techniques on our students. There were even some jokes about it among the blind rehab teachers. Many were the times that the answer to some question was, "Let's run a baseline!" We were supposed to measure behaviors, do some behavior mod intervention and then measure the behavior again to see if the intervention had been effective.

The most hilarious situation concerned a young man

who was congenitally blind. Sometimes, folks who are blind from birth develop mannerisms. The most common one is simply a rocking motion, either of the head or the upper body. One theory goes that, lacking visual stimulation, young children who are blind stimulate themselves with repetitive motions. Another theory is that the mannerisms are somehow comforting. Unless a teacher or parent works with the child to curtail these mannerisms, they can become lifetime habits.

This young man had a habit of stimulating his genitals and always seemed to be walking around with an impressive erection. The psychologists called us into a meeting to discuss what they wanted us to do. First, we were to do no intervention but just get a baseline count of how many erections the young man had in a given hour. Once we had the baseline, we were to intervene each time we saw an erection. We were just supposed to tell the young man to stop. This was to go on for a week, at which time we would run another baseline.

I could barely contain myself until Jim and I were alone. Then I broke into hysterical laughter. "Yeah, right, what am I supposed to do," I chortled. "Here, let me just have a feel of your penis, what, like every five minutes or something?"

The thing that got us looking for other jobs however, concerned tension between the blind rehab staff and the recreation staff. The recreation staff treated those of us with blindness in a very patronizing way. A meeting was called in which we were supposed to lay out our concerns and come to some kind of understanding. Before the meeting, the head of the blind rehab department called us together. "Now this is the way you're going to behave," she began.

"Whoa, whoa," I blurted. "You don't get to tell me how I'm going to behave. Besides that, how are we supposed to work out our differences if we can't be honest."

This was one of those situations in which not being able to read body language was a definite disadvantage. Laying his hand on my knee under the table, Jim whispered, "Leave it."

Later he told me that the director looked furious, as though she would quite like to 'Snatch me baldheaded,' as they say in the South. This was not the first disagreement I had with the director, but I promised myself that I was going to try to make it my last.

Something about the state of Maine has always fascinated me. Having never been there before I'm not sure where the fascination came from. I had applied for a job in Maine during our internship but there was just the one opening and we both needed jobs. A classmate, John, got that job and now he's director of the statewide Division for the Blind and Visually Impaired. I called Beth, the lady with whom I had interviewed a couple of years before.

"Hi, Beth, it's Sue Martin. You might not remember, but . . ."

"Oh, I remember you all right," interrupted Beth. "How are you? Where are you?"

I explained that we had been working in Tennessee for the past two years but were ready to move on.

"We saw in the JVIB that you have an opening for a rehab teacher in Rockland. Do you know if the state has any openings for O&M instructors?"

In the world of blind rehab in Maine, all of the rehab teachers were employed by the private agency while the O&M instructors were employed by the state.

Beth was silent for several seconds. Then she said, "Let me check on something and call you back."

It was several days later when Beth returned my call. "Okay, here's what we've done. "There was an opening for an O&M instructor in Bangor. We've taken that position, turned it into a position with our agency, and moved it to Rockland, where the rehab teaching position is open. Do you think the two of you would be interested?"

"Yes," I replied. "That sounds like it has potential. What happens next?"

Neither Jim nor I had ever set foot in Maine so we made plans. We bought our tickets and arrived in snowy mid-January. I loved it. Jim didn't care one way or the other. For him, having grown up in Michigan, snow is just what you have in the winter.

After our interviews, we climbed into our rented car and drove north. The jobs were in Rockland which is about half way up the coast of Maine on the way to Canada. We spent a couple of days in the area and just looked around. Everything about the place fascinated me. I loved the snow. I loved the accent of the locals. I was ready to go. Jim, as was his want, was more circumspect. "So, what do you think," I asked, back in the farm house in Tennessee.

"Well, let's make a list," said Jim. So, we sat down at the kitchen table and made a list of pros and cons.

"So," began the director of the Maine Center for the Blind, "will you be joining us?"

"Yes," I replied. "I think we've decided to come work for you."

We gave the Tennessee Rehab Center a month's notice and began our preparations. We couldn't afford to pay a moving company so we moved ourselves. We packed our belongings. We rented a twenty four foot U-Haul truck.

"I can't really see the pickup truck from the driver's seat," said Jim. Jim was going to pull our truck behind the U-Haul truck. Pondering the dilemma, he came up with a solution. "You have two rigid canes, right?"

"Yes, but how will those . . ."

So, he duck-taped the two canes horizontally to the back of the cab window. Then he tied a bright red bandana to each of the canes. It must have looked pretty bizarre, but it seemed to do the trick.

We had gotten a cat at some point during our time in Tennessee. The reason for the cat was purely utilitarian. It was her job to keep the field mouse population in check. Since my dog's name was Sadie, we named the cat Hawkins. Hawkins was quite feral and self-sufficient. The only time she was ever in the house, and the only time we ever fed her was when she had kittens. As soon as the kittens were old enough to go outside they took up the feral lifestyle. They kept down the mouse population, not only for us, but for our two neighbors. We had asked the neighbors about the kittens and they both wanted us to just leave them. They could clearly take care of themselves.

The plan was to put Hawkins in the back of the pickup truck which had a cap. We placed a foam pad in the truck, covered it with an old bedspread and put Hawkins' food, water, and a litter box in the truck. The only problem was that we couldn't find Hawkins. "She's probably off hunting somewhere," said Jim.

"What should we do?" I asked.

"Here," said Jim, "Why don't we take this little guy instead?" Jim scooped up the black and white kitten and showed him to me.

"Okay," I began, "That works. What should we name him?"

Jim thought for a moment and said, quite definitely, "Holstein."

"Holstein?" I asked. "Why Holstein?"

"Because he's black and white and looks like a Holstein cow. Or he would if he was about twenty times larger."

Laughing, I agreed and Holstein went into the back of the truck. Iris, the dog who looked like a fox, went into the cab of the U-Haul with Jim and they set out.

For reasons that are lost in time, I flew to Maine while Jim drove. I spent three days staying in an independent living apartment at The Maine Center for the Blind in Portland before Jim arrived. We both stayed in the apartment for a few more days, doing orientation tasks and filling out paperwork.

With those tasks completed we headed for Rockland, picking up our friend John on the way. He had agreed to help us unpack and get things squared away in our new house. Following the directions we had been given, we pulled up to the rental house. Jim unlocked the door and we went in. After taking a tour of the house, I ventured, "It's pretty small," which was an understatement. The house was tiny. The rooms were tiny. I honestly didn't know how we were going to be able to get all of our stuff in this house. I had a sinking feeling about this whole thing. Giving myself a mental reprimand, I said, "Okay, let's figure out where things are going to go before we begin. As we brought furniture into the house my feelings sank lower and lower. The freezer was the last item and it presented us with quite a dilemma. Not only was the house small, its layout made it seem even smaller. This particular hallway just dead ended and didn't seem to have any purpose. So, we stuck the freezer at the end of that hall.

Once the house was in some semblance of order, we all loaded into the pickup truck and went to a local super market. On the way home from the store, Jim said, "Hey, let's stop at this convenience store. They have pizza. There's not a snowball's chance you'll be able to cook anything tonight." The store was called the No Eye Deer. When we asked, the proprietor told us that people kept asking him what he was going to call his store, and he had "no idea." So that became the store's name.

That night I got our bed made. We pulled out the couch, which then filled almost the entire living room. I had to scramble over the thing to make it up, as there wasn't enough room to walk around it. As I crawled in bed that night, not even Jim's embrace did much to comfort me.

Jim drove John back to Lewiston on Sunday. On Monday, we went to our office for the first time.

"What's this," I thought to myself, "Same song second verse?"

They had us crammed into a corner of the office.

Thus began our life in Maine.

25 | a drive for perfection

OUR FIRST HOUSE IN MAINE WAS ON CLARK ISLAND road in St. George, a few miles south of Rockland, where the office was located. It was within sight and sound of the ocean. I have auditory memories of the mournful sound of the foghorn. Oddly, at least to me, I also have a strong auditory memory of Robert J. Lurtsema's morning show, Morning Pro Musica. It was broadcast each morning, at six o'clock while we were usually up and stirring, getting ready for work. He always began the program with recorded bird song. I can hear the sound to this day. I can also hear his lugubrious voice and the long pauses in his commentary.

Clark Island was owned by a family, possibly named Clark, we never knew. There was only one home on the island and it was rarely occupied so we had free run of the island most of the time. We'd walk to the end of the road, past the Craignair Inn, and so onto the island. Sometimes we'd walk on the trails of the island and sometimes we'd go down to the shore and boulder hop. I'd turn Sadie loose and she'd spend most of the time in the water. Then we'd swing by the old quarry, throw a stick for her to fetch a few times to get the salt water out of her fur before heading home.

Rockland, at that time, was primarily a fishing village, with tourism taking over in the summer. It's about two hours

Down East of the New Hampshire border. The term, 'Down East,' actually refers to traveling in a northeasterly direction. It came from the days of sailing ships. The prevailing winds blow in a northeasterly direction. When a ship sails before the wind, in other words, with the wind coming over the stern, it is moving downwind. Hence the term, 'Down East.'

In Tennessee, our students came to us and lived in a dorm during their training. The jobs in Maine were itinerant. We had to go to our student's homes, schools, or workplaces and teach there. The first thing I had to do was hire a driver. Unfortunately, the agency offered only minimum wage to this person I would spend more waking hours with than my husband.

The first ad I placed in the Rockland newspaper drew only one response. He was a man in his twenties. The only problem was that his tires rendered his truck unsafe. What to do? "I feel kind of stuck," I said to Jim. "I mean I don't seem to have a whole lot of choice here."

"The guy seems nice enough," Jim replied. "What do you want to do? Should we buy him tires?" That's what we ended up doing. The guy never showed up for work again after he got the tires. The next driver I hired tried to seduce me. When I refused, he got in his car and left, taking my computer with him and leaving me stranded in a town thirty miles from home.

We had left Tennessee in late February. The glorious southern spring was just beginning. Maine was to be locked in snow, ice, and freezing temperatures for another month. I began to learn about snow. And what I learned was not good. If I walked anywhere at all with Sadie, her legs and belly got coated with sand and salt. I had to constantly wash gloves and mittens because they got coated with the same stuff whenever I opened a car door. But this continual snow and cold hit Jim hardest. He had grown up with this stuff. And he had so enjoyed winters in the south by contrast.

Our lives in that first house we rented hadn't started out very well. And things didn't get better. I grew so weary of having to squeeze around the furniture. The kitchen and what passed for the dining room were particularly tedious. We never did get the box springs up the narrow steep staircase to the second floor bedroom. We had to store them in the barn and just put the mattress directly on the bed frame. There was a tiny closet in the bedroom and that was the only closet on the second floor. We had to buy a clothes rack and put it in the second bedroom in order to have enough room to hang our clothes. With that and a long table in the second bedroom it was just about full and required the same squeezing around as the dining room and kitchen.

As a child I had been prone to car sickness. It seemed to have gotten better as I grew older but it again emerged as a problem when I started driving considerable distances to see my clients. And then there was Sadie. She broke out in something like hives every time she got in deep snow.

"Oh, this is just great," I began. "My job requires that I drive long distances and I get car sick every time I do. And my dog seems to be allergic to snow."

"Hmm," Jim replied vaguely.

Both of us were in some degree of depression. The days were short and dark. The nights were long and darker. Mainers seemed reserved and almost aloof. And we both started getting sick. This has happened to us every time we've moved to a new state. It's like we don't have the immunities for the local bugs. While we both got sick I began a chronic period of trouble with my sinuses that only ended when I had surgery several years later.

Those problems were trifling when compared to what I had been doing in my drive for perfection. When I was eighteen years old I became bulimic. I was much older than most people when they get sucked into this trap. As a teenager in the sixties and seventies there was a ton of peer pressure to be thin. Twiggy was "in," fat was "out." I started to be aware of my weight at the age of fourteen or so. Seems that as soon as the awareness came to me I promptly began to gain weight.

I tried weight watchers. That was no good. I tried more exercise. That didn't work either. Finally, after a particularly large meal I did it. I just thrust my fingers down my throat and threw up.

Wow, this was cool. This was marvelous. I could eat all I wanted and never have to face the consequences. I felt powerful. Every time I purged I felt powerful. And I felt secretive. Power, control, and secrecy, those are what bulimia meant to me. It was the secrecy that tripped me up in Maine. It became much harder for me to find places where I could purge. Our house was so small that we seemed to be on top of each other constantly. The only restroom in the office was one with stalls and there always seemed to be another person in it. And there was no predictability about what kind of rest room I'd find when I was on the road.

Jim and I started arguing. Having never seen my parents have so much as a serious disagreement, I was not prepared for this development. Our arguments seemed to me to be heading our marriage for a divorce. I entered therapy with a psychologist named Paul.

It was through Paul that we escaped the horrid house we had rented. His wife's parents owned a "barn." I put that in quotation marks because it only looked like a barn. Inside, it was amazing. The living room measured forty by forty feet and had a cathedral ceiling. It had a window measuring seventeen by twenty-two feet facing out across a field and pond to a grove of trees and the ocean. It was an amazing space. And it had just become vacant.

With no hesitation we broke our lease, packed up and

moved. Our housing troubles were relieved but my bulimia was getting out of control. We moved into the barn in the autumn. That Thanksgiving we had a houseful. Most of the folks who worked in blind rehab were not from Maine. We established a tradition of inviting all of our coworkers over for Thanksgiving. That year we had a blizzard on Thanksgiving day. Consequently, everyone stayed overnight. After the huge Thanksgiving meal I watched desperately for a chance to purge. It just didn't come. With fifteen people in the house I just couldn't find a time to sneak away and throw up. I felt desperate and trapped. By the time everyone could leave I was feeling terrified of what my life had become.

That Saturday night I couldn't sleep. I kept going over the feelings of being trapped that I had when I couldn't purge. I was getting sucked back into the whirlpool. Paul had made me promise him that if I ever thought of harming myself I would contact him before I did anything. That's the only thing that got me safely through the weekend. Early Monday morning I called Paul's office and made an appointment.

"Paul, you have probably saved my life. You know that, right?" I said. Ushering me into his office, Paul asked me to sit down. "The only reason I'm here is because you made me promise you that I'd talk to you before I did anything to harm myself."

Getting up from his chair Paul came and sat beside me on the couch. He simply said, "Tell me."

I tried. I tried to tell him this last secret. I couldn't do it. Telling Paul that I was bulimic would change everything. There would be no going back. I felt as I did before I pulled the trigger. But this time I would be doing something to pull myself out of the whirlpool, not something that would commit me to full emersion in it. In some desperation I simply said, "I'm bulimic."

"Hi, come on in," said Paul when Jim got to his office an

hour later. "I'm checking Sue into the psychiatric unit at Penn Bay. It's all arranged. All you have to do is take her over there."

"Okay, but . . . " Jim was clearly baffled but, having gone through the ordeal of telling the truth to Paul, I just couldn't do it again. We held hands in silence as Jim drove the few miles to the hospital. After I had gotten checked in and shown to a room Jim asked me again to tell him what was up. "I can't do it right now. I'm safe here. I'll be okay. I'll tell you tomorrow, okay?"

"Okay, I love you," and he took his leave.

The next morning Jim brought me some clothes. There were only five or six patients on the psychiatric unit. Both patients and mental health workers wore street clothes. During my five days there I learned to tell the truth. I was finally able to be honest about my bulimia with Jim.

"I'm bulimic," I began on the third morning of my hospitalization.

"You're what?" replied Jim. I was incredulous. I had to explain the whole thing to Jim. I had to tell him what bulimia was and what I had been doing for almost thirteen years.

"Oh, that explains . . . ," Jim paused, "well, that explains a lot of stuff." We talked on for the better part of an hour, and, then, Jim hugged me and headed to work.

They had never had someone who was blind on the psychiatric unit, and it was a time of learning on both sides of the desk. There was talking therapy of course, but we did all sorts of other things as well.

One exercise was a group session in which we were to relate to each other something of which we were proud. They gave us advance notice of this activity so I asked Jim to bring in my goalball and one of the trophies I had won in a goalball tournament.

"And I scored the winning goal," I concluded. What a reaction. Both patients and staff began asking me all sorts of questions. The entire group went out in the hallway so that I could demonstrate throwing and blocking. I was amazed. I had told these people the truth. They knew my ugly secrets. They knew that I had attempted to kill myself. They knew I was bulimic. Yet they accepted me, even appeared to like me. I hugged this experience to me as I left the hospital a few days later.

THUJA OCCIDENTALIS

northern white cedar

PART THREE

RECOVERY

~~~~~

We cannot change the past,
but we can change our attitude toward it.

Uproot guilt and plant forgiveness.
Tear out arrogance and seed humility.
Exchange love for hate—thereby, making the
present comfortable and the future promising.

Maya Angelou

26 | two clients, one goal

George

I MADE MY WAY UP THE SNOWY PATH and knocked on George's door for the first time. He was a quiet, reserved man in his mid-eighties. He lived in an old farmhouse on a large farm in Dexter.

George led me through his kitchen and dining room into his living room. He had a hard time hearing me speak. After a couple of false starts, I was able to get the tone and volume of my voice just right and we began our visit. Included in the referral information was a notation that George was having trouble identifying his medicines, one of which was for his heart condition. When I asked, he recited each medication, told me how he identified it, what it was for, and when he took it. A little confused by his adeptness at what was supposed to be a difficult task, I asked George to do that again. Again, in his quiet way, he gave me all of the particulars on his medicines. So, out the window went the plans I had made for George's first lesson.

I sat back and we chatted for a little while. I felt like a bull in a china shop, with George speaking in his reserved manner and me having to bellow back at him so that he could hear me.

In the course of our conversation, I noted several tasks around the house which could be made accessible. I showed him large-print materials such as a calendar and address book, gave him a pad of bold lined paper and some bold markers, and asked if he would like a large-print check register. He declined all of these, at first saying very quietly that he supposed he could get along. After a little contemplation, George allowed that some of these items might be helpful but turned down the check register saying he didn't write checks. He told me he knew how much money he had, where it was supposed to go, and therefore had no need to write a check.

As I began to know George better and gained an understanding of what he wanted to be able to do around the house, our work together proceeded. I marked his appliances and thermostat and he allowed that this, too, might be helpful. Explaining that he could have operator assisted telephoning at no charge brought about the same reaction. I was beginning to wonder what, if anything, would really interest George.

Gordon

I reached into the car for my bag. Throwing it over my shoulder I walked up the sidewalk and knocked on the door. "Hello, my name is Sue Martin," I began.

"Ah, great," replied Gordon. "Please, come in. This is my wife, Christine. I've been waiting for your help for several months. Come on in and let's get started."

Coming to work with Gordon was an adventure. I never knew what to expect when I walked in the door. He'd always have a project. One month we'd work on his genealogy program. The next month saw us creating a letterhead which he could use for stationery in his snail mail correspondence. Then we'd be off and running to find a stock quote web site which would work properly with his screen reader.

Each new thing we discovered delighted Gordon and he was never stingy in showing his delight. When people ask me to tell them some of the greatest stories of my work I always tell the story of when Gordon received his first email from a family member. I don't recall, at the moment, who sent that first one but it absolutely thrilled Gordon.

The other great moment was when I placed Gordon's large keyboard before him. It was an IntelliTools keyboard. These keyboards come with standard overlays which can be inserted. You can also create custom overlays. This is what my assistant, Cindy, and I did for Gordon. We used vibrant colors of high contrast to create the overlay. I started to explain the overlay but quickly realized there was no need. With a spreading smile Gordon just began to type away.

George

I settled in my usual chair at George's. I asked him if he had liked to read when he could see and he told me that he did a fair amount of reading. I told him about talking books. He politely thanked me and declined. He said that his only real interest was in gardening and selling his vegetables. Aha, I thought. Now we were getting somewhere. Here was something in which George showed some real interest. I told him that was great and I could help him figure out a way to still have his garden come spring. He simply said no, he didn't think that would be possible. I put the gardening on the back burner until springtime and went on to low vision.

George's macular degeneration was pretty advanced and he had a hard time seeing even the largest size practice materials. He brought home a tiny, very strong hand held magnifier from his low vision exam. It was a real struggle for him to use this magnifier but then I've seldom met anyone as determined as George. One morning when I arrived at his house he announced that he had read the obituaries with his magnifier. I was astounded. I knew that with his level of visual functioning, this was an accomplishment of great perseverance and patience. I had George try to use the magnifier to read directions on all sorts of things in the kitchen. He could read a few things if the print was large and of good contrast. Unfortunately, some food items have their directions in yellow on a clear background or blue on black. The magnifier just wouldn't do in all of these situations, so I brought George a Voxcom. George or a helper could record a message on the magnetic strip of a small card. It might be the name of a spice or a reminder of the ratio of water to rice and how long to cook them. A rubber band kept the recording with the container, ready to play back in the small Voxcom gadget.

Aside from gardening, and it was still midwinter, it was with the Voxcom that I saw the first bit of emotion from George. He thought that device was so slick. We recorded a bunch of labels and directions for various items around the kitchen and George said that his daughters would help him with the rest of the labeling. The next time I came to see George he had prepared gingerbread for me using the recorded directions on a Voxcom card.

Gordon

Wondering what awaited me I opened the door into Gordon and Christine's kitchen and called a greeting. Once we were settled in the living room, where Gordon kept his computer, I had a surprise. Instead of having a task or project in mind Gordon, for the first time, asked me what kinds of things I taught to my other clients. A couple of months earlier I had worked with a woman in Rockland who was a minister. She needed access to the Bible. I had several versions of the Bible on CD but they needed to be broken down into books and labeled properly so that they could be easily retrieved. This turned out to be a monumental task. I related the story of my labors with the Bible to Gordon and he immediately declared that he wanted a copy too.

I copied the disks containing the Bible to Gordon's computer and we were off and running. Gordon would recall a snippet of a passage or a certain story from the Old Testament and we'd go look it up and read it. Then Gordon would recite some poem or other that he had learned in Sunday school. His memory for these rhymes was prodigious and he kept us entertained for hours.

One of the more memorable projects I worked on with Gordon involved his quest for knowledge and understanding of classical music. Gordon wanted to play music CD's on his computer while pausing and moving around amongst the tracks. I explained to him the keystroke for pausing is CTRL+p.

During a morning session, shortly after he had taken his diuretic he sat straight up, held one finger in the air, and with a big grin, announced to the world, "It's control pee time!"

George

As the snow began to melt, I pondered George's situation. Although George remained quiet and reserved, I had seen a couple of glimpses of his humor and pride—like when he brought out the gingerbread he had made. I asked him about gardening again. Again, he politely told me that he didn't think he'd have a garden this year. I asked what he would be doing now if he were going to have a garden. He told me he would be reading seed catalogs, ordering his seeds, and starting seedlings in his basement or a greenhouse. On my next visit, I brought George a loaner closed circuit television to see if it would work for him. I showed him all the functions of the machine and left.

When I returned in two weeks, George was transformed. He was reading absolutely everything with the CCTV. His life was coming back to life. He had ordered his seeds from the catalog and asked me if I could teach him to hammer nails so that he could build his greenhouse. By the next visit, George had his seedlings started in his greenhouse and was getting his tractor ready to cultivate his garden. George was off and running.

We ordered George his own closed circuit television. After I delivered it in late June, I didn't see George until early August. He led me into the dining room where he kept his CCTV and told me to wait. He disappeared into the kitchen and when he returned he presented me with five perfect cucumbers. He then patted the CCTV affectionately and said, "Your program has made my life worth living again".

Gordon

Ecce quam bonum. See that which is good. So says the seal of the University of the South, my alma mater. I've never known anyone who embodied that sentiment more than Gordon. Gordon was able to see the good in everything. While I might have been the teacher, there is no doubt that I learned as much from Gordon as he learned from me. When his family called to tell me of Gordon's death I had powerful mixed emotions. I began to cry. But I also began to smile. Gordon will live on in my vivid remembrance of the time that we spent together.

~~~

In graduate school I had been sorely disappointed upon learning that I would be working primarily with seniors, many of them with other disabilities in addition to blindness.

Working with George and Gordon was not only a humbling education in my chosen field, it was also a transformative experience for me as a teacher and as a human being. Who was I to dismiss someone, anyone, just because of age or disability. My life and attitudes were becoming a tapestry full of texture and rich hues. I realized that I deeply wanted my clients, many in their seventies and eighties, to experience the balance of their lives in the fullness they so richly deserved. Teaching them the skills and providing them with the tools to do this was enormously rewarding.

27 | at what price

I HAD BEEN ATTENDING OVEREATERS ANONYMOUS meetings for months. I had tried every community resource available but I could not break free of bulimia. Determined not to repeat another brush with depression and thoughts of suicide I sought a residential treatment center.

I arrived at Bramley Heath in New Orleans in mid-May. "Hello, my name is," I have no memory of my therapist's real name so I'll just call her Linda, "My name is Linda. I'll be your therapist while you're here at Bramley Heath."

Shaking the woman's hand I said, "Nice to meet you." Linda showed me around the facility. We agreed on the best place for me to take Sadie outside at relief times. I met some of the other residents.

The next morning my two months in hell began. There was a structure to each day and each day was full of group and individual therapy sessions. The various therapists led these sessions. Most of them were in recovery from an eating disorder of one sort or another themselves.

At meal times, we had to weigh and measure everything we ate. Four ounces of protein, two or three cups of vegetables, one cup of fruit, I don't remember exactly but it was something like that. Then two therapy sessions in the morning, two in the afternoon, and one after the evening meal.

About a week after I got there, my therapist called me into her office. "We have decided that you cannot have your dog with you in therapy sessions."

"What?" I began. "Look you knew I was going to be bringing her. You told me it was no problem. And now you're going back on your word? I can't believe this. You can't do this." By now I was standing and glaring at Linda. I was actually shaking.

"Calm down and sit down," said Linda. When I was once again seated she began, "We have decided that the other patients' interactions with you are going to be different if you always have your dog with you."

"Well that's not my problem, is it? If someone sees me differently just because I'm blind and I have a dog, seems to me that's their problem, not mine." We continued to argue. Finally Linda called the hospital director. I'm going to call her Alex.

"What's the problem," said Alex as she entered Linda's office.

I'll tell you what the problem is," I began. "You people knew I was bringing my dog. You said it would be no problem. And now you're going back on your word. Look, I don't mind using my cane. I have good cane skills. But that's not the issue. I simply cannot leave Sadie in my room all day. That's not how guide dog teams work. She's trained to work for me. If I don't work her for two months that's going to cause some serious problems with our working relationship."

I pulled a wadded up napkin out of my pocket and heaved it in the general direction of the trashcan. "You missed," said Alex mildly.

"Good," I said as I glared at her. "This is totally unacceptable. If this is the only condition under which you will provide treatment to me I'll just leave." A long silence followed.

"If you leave now, we will consider it against medical advice and you'll be on the hook for the ten or so thousand dollars that your time here has already cost."

I gaped. I was trapped. I was helpless.

"Why don't you go process this for a while," began Linda.

"Process this?" I began. "What the hell does that mean. Look, don't give me your psycho-babble. Speak English why don't you."

Trying to soothe me, Alex said, "What Linda means is why don't you go away and just think about what we're proposing. Calm down and think it over. Then we can talk about it tomorrow."

Back in my room I seethed. This was an impossible situation. All I wanted from these people was treatment. Why did they have to impose some pseudo social psychology bullshit on me? And we could not pay the bill that I had already run up. But the main reason I took the course of action I did was because I was there to break my bulimic behavior.

"All right," I started, back in Linda's office the next day. "Here's what I'm willing to do. I will leave Sadie in my room but not all day every day. And you have to call The Seeing Eye and speak with a training professional in my presence. You have to agree, before we call the school, that you will abide by their decision on this."

Once again, Linda called Alex. What, was this woman incapable of independent thought? "All right," said Alex, "We'll do that, we'll call the school. But we'll do it, just the two of us, Linda and me."

"No way," I retorted. You've already shown that you're not people of your word. I know good and well what the school's reaction to this is going to be. I want no opportunity for you to come back to me and lie about what the school says."

"We were thinking that, if you were not in the room, we wouldn't have to break your anonymity." That thought had certainly occurred to me as well.

"Yes, you carp on about how we're all anonymous here don't you. I'm not wild about it myself, believe me. But I simply do not trust you."

And so the call was made. As I expected, the school did not go along with their plans. The trainer did not like it one bit. He finally agreed that I could leave Sadie in my room for one therapy session in the morning and one in the afternoon. They had to give me a radio to play while Sadie was alone and they were not to deviate from this schedule.

A few days later Alex called me into her office. What now I thought.

"I'm afraid I have some really bad, and sad, news."

I just looked at her.

"Linda committed suicide last night."

I gaped, speechless, at the hospital director. I couldn't say anything. I couldn't say anything at all for a full five minutes. "I, I'm so sorry. . . " I trailed off. I sat down. I simply could not imagine this woman's grief. More to the point, I could only too well imagine what had been going through Linda's mind. Here was a woman, in recovery as was I, considered stable enough to be employed as a therapist to help others with eating disorders, and look what had happened. If anything was sufficient to drive home the fact that I was dealing with a life threatening situation, this was it. I left Alex's office with my head down. I had to make this work, I simply had to.

I really did try to participate in the various therapy sessions. I thought my success depended on it. But mostly I found myself thinking things like, 'This is stupid,' and, 'What does this have to do with bulimia?' Even with a radio playing to distract her Sadie still barked when she was alone. I'd be sitting in one of the therapy sessions, trying to concentrate, trying to see how whatever we were doing or talking about was going to help me in my recovery efforts, and I'd hear

Sadie bark. I'd cringe as I heard her aggressive sounding bark, knowing I could do nothing to correct her. It was a terrible feeling of helplessness.

Most of the other women were participating in yoga and calesthenics classes, but I wasn't allowed to do either of those things. I kept asking, and they kept telling me I wasn't ready. Why?! Why wasn't I ready, I kept wondering. I usually walked a couple of miles outside each day. There was a circular route that many of us walked together.

One morning, I was told I wasn't allowed to walk two miles a day any longer. I have to admit that I lost my temper. "You make me leave my dog alone for two hours a day and now you're not even going to let me work her? This is bullshit. You're taking away everything that defines us as a team. Why are you doing this?"

When all the dust settled they came out with the truth. The truth is I was losing weight, much more weight than they had wanted or expected me to lose. So, that's why they kept adding food to my meal plan. I didn't care how much they adjusted the plan, I flatly refused to shorten my walks. In equal parts desperation and defiance, I harnessed Sadie and went for my walk, tacitly daring them to challenge me. They didn't.

"We want you to see a neurologist," began the woman who had taken Linda's place.

"What for," I demanded.

"We think there might be some neurological damage from the gunshot." I thought this another really stupid idea. I was there for treatment for an eating disorder. I had already had neurological tests, and I was perfectly fine.

"Whatever," I said. I was tired of fighting. So, they did some neurological tests, which showed me to be perfectly normal.

There was one exercise that had a profound effect on me. It was called "stringing." They measured different parts of my body with strings, which they then laid out on the floor. The idea was to objectify a person's body: how large the wrists, ankles, waist, hips, pelvis, etc. actually were. The theory was that when we looked in a mirror, habit had taught us to see ourselves as fat. They asked if I thought there was a way that they could do this exercise so that it would work for me. I told them to use white string and lay it out on a dark carpet. Even if I had gotten no visual input from this exercise it would have been effective.

"Wow," I said. I was crawling around on the carpet examining the size of the loops of string. "Am I really that tiny?" I'll never forget examining the loop of string that represented my wrist. I began to have a different, and more realistic, body image.

That place began my recovery from the eating disorder. But God did I have battle scars. As I walked out the door of that benighted place the freedom—both from the tyranny of bulimia and from the place itself—filled me with joy.

I was going home. I was going home to Jim.

Going through that hell served only one purpose. I never, never as long as I lived, wanted to have to go through that again. That alone was enough to insure that I maintained an honest relationship with food.

28 | bones of contention

BEING BACK HOME WAS HEAVEN. **Being back with Jim was heaven.** For the first few months I was amazed, over and over again, at how free I felt. I had more energy and more time in which to use that energy. In this new found freedom I became willing, no eager, to try new and different things.

It was mid-summer. Rather than sleeping upstairs where the only small windows faced south, we rearranged the living room, pulled out the sofa and used that as our bed. In the mornings, we'd fix coffee, prop ourselves up on the sofa bed and watch the sun rise. In my absence Jim had gotten permission from the folks who owned the barn to plant a huge garden in what had been a sheep pen. Goodness, the vegetables he produced were wonderful. For the next two months I enjoyed cooking the squash, zucchini, eggplant, beans and everything else he brought in. When we had too much for ourselves we gave it away to the folks who owned the land. When we had too much for us, the land owners and our friends, Jim began to sell to the Belfast food co-op and at the Belfast farmer's market.

The only problem I had was Sadie. Even following the school's instructions while at Bramley Heath had left her free to bark to her heart's content during those hours when I had to leave her alone. She barked at everyone, including myself, Jim, and even my supervisor. Her bark sounded very aggressive and it began to alarm me. I finally called the school and asked for help. Peggy came to Maine in September. We met at a fast food restaurant in Bath. As I waited for Peggy to enter the restaurant I began to fear that Sadie would be perfectly behaved, Peggy would ask why the heck I had called for help and immediately depart. The moment Peggy saw me and approached the table Sadie gave one of her aggressive sounding barks. After shaking my hand Peggy said, "Ah, yes, we have a problem here."

Peggy stayed for two days. She gave me all sorts of strategies for dealing with Sadie's aggressive barking, none of which made any real difference.

Shortly before I left for Bramley Heath I had a new prosthetic eye made. Over the years I had lost tissue pressure in the socket of my left eye. This is normal but the result is that a prosthetic eye eventually becomes a bad fit. My first prosthesis had not been custom made. The ocularist in Birmingham had been able to find a good match from his stock. But the eye had begun to rotate in the socket without my knowledge with the result that I appeared to be looking at my left ear. A few times the thing just fell out. It was time to have a custom prosthesis made.

This is done, not by a physician, but by an ocularist who is a craftsman and an artist. We went to the Mass Eye and Ear Infirmary to have the eye made. On the first day they injected a putty-like substance into the socket. When it had become firm they shaped the outside surface, matching it as closely as possible to the shape of my right eye. Then they sent us away for the night. The next morning, the ocularist had my new eye ready. He first inserted it into the socket and asked me to look in all directions. Satisfied with the movement of the eye he asked how it felt. I told him it felt fine. Then he removed it and began to paint it. It was like sitting for a portrait.

When he was done, the ocularist put the eye back in the socket and turned to Jim. "What do you think?"

"I think it looks great," said Jim. "It fills the socket much, much better, really nice job."

The ocularist wasn't so sure though. He had me move into several different places in the room so that he could compare my eyes in different lighting. "No, I don't think it's quite right," he finally announced. We discussed it and he concluded that the eye needed to be repainted. "It will be fine for the time being but I know I can get the color closer to your right eye. And there won't be any further charge. It's my mistake so we'll repaint it for free."

There simply hadn't been time to get this done before I headed to Bramley Heath, so it wasn't until I returned to Maine that Jim and I were able to go to Mass Eye and Ear. My eye had been duly repainted. Then the ocularist told us to go out for lunch and the eye would be ready in a couple of hours' time. When we returned we were sitting in the waiting room when a woman walked in with a child. Sadie growled at the child. I corrected her. She growled at me. I got up, went out in the hallway and took off her harness. "That's it," I said to Jim when he joined me. "She's retired as of this moment. This is all Bramley Heath's fault. It's all their damn fault."

When we got back to Maine I called the school and told them of my decision to retire Sadie. I spoke with the director of training for quite a long time. I had been hoping to retire Sadie but keep her as a pet. Barking and growling however, are easily passed from one dog to another. "It won't be fair to your new dog," concluded the director of training. This made things even worse. I knew I was making the correct decision to retire Sadie but now I had a whole new set of problems. I had to come to terms with letting her go completely. I had to find her a new home.

I was just sitting there after hanging up the phone when

Jim came in with the mail. "Here's a letter from Bramley Heath," he said.

Looking up, I said, "What the hell does that place want with me now?"

"What's wrong?" he said.

"What's wrong is that I can't keep Sadie. I just spoke to Seeing Eye and I'm going to have to find Sadie a new home. I can't keep her."

Sitting down, Jim said, "Why not?" I explained the problem. When I finished I asked Jim to read whatever Bramley Heath had sent.

Jim opened the envelope and read the letter in silence. Then he said, "They're inviting you to a reunion in Thomaston next month."

"They're what?" I spluttered. Placing my head in my hands I shook it slowly. Then I finally let loose with all of the anger that had been simmering inside me. "I hate that place, no way am I going to a reunion, or anything else for that matter, that has anything to do with the place."

Then I turned my attention back to the problem at hand.

I talked to our veterinarian.

I was still seeing Paul, the psychologist, on an infrequent basis. I talked to him.

I put out the word in the office. Paul came through first. He knew a colleague who was willing to take Sadie.

On a Sunday afternoon, I packed up Sadie's bowls, toys, leash and grooming equipment. Placing all of this, along with Sadie, in the truck Jim and I drove to Paul's colleague's home in Camden. "I hope it works out," I said, as we drove away.

"Okay," I said to Jim, "let's go riding."

Putting the truck in gear Jim headed for our friend Vicki's farm. Vickie's day job was as a nurse educator. I had met her when I did a presentation to her nursing students on how someone who is blind and who is also diabetic can measure blood sugar and draw up insulin. Vickie's real passion, however, was breeding and training her Morgan horses on her farm in Union. I and occasionally Jim would go trail riding with her. Knowing it was going to be wrenching, letting Sadie go, I had called Vickie and asked if we could come riding that Sunday afternoon.

Jim and I drove in silence, each of us absorbed in our own thoughts. I was glad when we arrived at Vickie's and Jim drew the truck to a stop in the stable yard. As we emerged from the truck Vickie called a greeting.

"Sue, I've got Charm groomed and ready for you."

"Oh, great," I replied. "I love that mare. Who are you putting Jim on today?"

"My husband's stallion," replied Vickie.

"Stallion?" questioned Jim apprehensively.

Vickie laughed. "Don't worry Jim, he's a push-button horse. You'll feel like you're sitting in an easy chair."

Chuckling, Jim and I entered the barn and saddled the two horses we found cross tied in the corridor. Leading both horses into the stable yard we prepared to mount up.

"Ready?" called Vickie.

"Just about," I called back. Checking the girth of my saddle to make sure it was tight enough, I mounted up and we headed off into the woods. Vickie was first, I was next, and Jim brought up the rear. Apart from riding with Vickie I had only ridden once since becoming blind. That was with my friend, Joanne, someone with whom I used to fox hunt. Joanne had invited me to come riding with her only a few months after my suicide attempt. I had been ecstatic to learn that blindness presented no real barriers to horseback riding. My balance and communication with the horse was not at all impaired by my blindness.

Knowing that I had just given Sadie away Vickie went out of her way to make the ride fun and challenging. Two hours later, when we got back to the farm, I dismounted. Going riding had done the trick. However briefly, it had given me something else to think about instead of the feelings of failure in those first few hours of life without Sadie.

We turned the three horses out into the pasture and returned to the barn to clean our tack. I was using my German made jumping saddle that I had had since I was fourteen. I loved that saddle. I went into a sort of trance as I ran my hands lovingly over the familiar contours of the leather, making sure I got every inch of it cleaned and oiled. Finally, we headed home.

Two days later Paul's colleague called and asked if she could give Sadie back to us. She said that Sadie was just too much dog for her to handle.

Sadie proved too much dog for the woman and she called three days later to ask us to take Sadie back.

A little voice in my head had told me not to close the door on the other places at which I had put out enquiries. I went to our vet again. To my immense relief one of the kennel workers said that she would love to have Sadie come to live on her farm in Appleton. The farm was on fourteen acres and included a pond. The lady had an elderly Golden Retriever and was looking for a new dog to come and live with them. Hugely relieved I delivered Sadie to the woman the next day. As fate would have it, Jim and I had a trip planned to Michigan the very next day. Jim had kept an eye on job openings in Michigan and there was one in Gaylord. The reason for the trip was for me to interview for this job although we were also looking forward to visiting with friends. The only thing I remember about that job interview is that, at the end of it, they told me, in essence, "Don't call us, we'll call you," which didn't bode well for my chances of getting the job.

One thing that happened on that trip provided a crucial turning point. We were staying with Paul Ponchillia and his wife, Sue. Paul invited us to a goalball practice that took place on the second evening that we were in Kalamazoo. Goalball practices, at that point, took place in a totally different place from where I had learned to play all those years ago. I walked, sighted guide, into the gym with Jim. I was dressed in sweats, ready to play. Paul, however, had other ideas. "Hey Sue," Paul called. Jim and I walked over to where Paul was putting on knee and elbow pads.

"Here," said Paul. And he handed me Dinah's leash.

Taking the leash I said, "What, what do you want me to do with Dinah?"

"I want you to walk with her. I want you to take a walk with her," he replied.

"You want me to what?" I stammered. This was extraordinary. When Paul allowed me to walk with Dinah in the hotel all those years ago, it was different. That was a protected and enclosed environment. This was completely different. This was real business.

"But," I stammered, "But I don't even know where we are. This is a completely different place than the place where I learned to play goalball. I have no idea what it's like out there."

"No problem," Paul replied laconically. "Just go out the door and hang a right. Follow that sidewalk until you hit the street. Take a left and go, just go."

Hesitantly, I took Dinah's leash. "Are you sure?" I asked.

"Yes, I'm sure. Now get out of here so we can get this practice started."

In some wonderment I took Dinah's leash. I placed it over my left wrist and picked up Dinah's harness. Making the now familiar forward movement with my hand I said, "Dinah, forward." And she moved out. She moved out fast but with a gentle pull . I went with her. "Dinah, right," I commanded as we left the gym. Dinah turned right. We advanced quickly and, boom, she stopped smartly at the street. Reaching forward with my right foot I confirmed that we were at the down-curb. "Dinah, left," I commanded. She swung left and off we went down the sidewalk.

By now I was far more familiar with working a dog than I had been back in that Chicago hotel. I reveled in Dinah's gentle pull. With mounting appreciation I came to a halt with her at each street crossing. In the third block I heard the jingle of tags on a dog's collar. Someone was out jogging with a dog. I tensed. This was a situation in which Sadie always growled or barked. Dinah took no apparent notice of the approaching jogger who greeted me as he passed. This was what I had been missing. This was the way it should be.

29 | her name is quoddy

S SOON AS WE GOT HOME I filled out my application for
a return trip to The Seeing Eye. I was ready to go train
with a new dog as soon as I possibly could. November
passed. The second week in December I called the school.

"Hello Ms. Pursley," I began, "This is Sue Martin."
I opened my mouth to ask the question but Ms. Pursley
forestalled me.

"Ah, I'm so glad you called," she began. "You're on my
list of people to call today. Can you be here for the January
class? I know it's short notice but . . . "

This time I forestalled her. "Of course I can. When does
the class begin?"

"You'll need to fly down on January second. Can you be
ready to do that?"

Thinking fast, I calculated what needed doing and in
what timeframe it had to be done. "Yes, I think I can do that."

~~~

"Hello, my name is Drew Gibbon. I'll be your instructor.
Welcome back. Here, take my arm and I'll show you to your
room." Everything was exactly the same as it had been three
years ago. We were still to address each other by surname.

There were still three instructors, each with six students. None of that would change until I went back for my third dog.

"I'm thinking of a shepherd for you," Drew said. "Will you be okay with that?"

In my mind I flashed back to an incident in my childhood. A couple of friends and I were riding our ponies. As it was summer we were all riding bareback wearing shorts and no shoes. We had just come out on the road after a rollicking gallop on a woods trail. Feeling hot and thirsty we decided to take a shortcut off of Winward Drive that came out near one of my friend's houses. Then we could water the ponies, let them cool off, and get something to drink ourselves.

So, off we went. As we passed the first house on the left on Winward Drive a huge German Shepherd came rushing at us. He bit me on my left foot and then went for my pony. The pony completely lost her head, took the bit in her teeth and flew down the middle of the road. Winward was a dead end road. As she came into the woods at the end of the road she swerved to the left. I sailed off and crashed into a thorny blackberry patch.

Pulling myself back from the memory I hesitated. However, having had such a time with Sadie, a Lab, I took a deep breath and said, "Okay, a shepherd would be fine."

"Her name is Quoddy," said Drew as he handed me her leash. "She's black and tan with a silver streak down the center of her back." Quoddy was a very gentle dog and my gentle father developed a special relationship with her. He used to lovingly run his fingers down the silver streak on her back. The first time he did this he related to me a Hindu legend of how the God Shiva ran his fingers down the back of a chipmunk to comfort the little creature, "And that's how chipmunks got the stripes down their backs," he concluded.

Quoddy was exactly the right dog for me after the tumultuous years with Sadie. She was quiet and dignified. Her work, though not brilliant, was steady and consistent. When I brought Quoddy home and we began our lives together we had some startling discoveries. When out in public with Sadie I always had to have a bit of my attention on her. When seated at a restaurant table, for example, I had to have a foot firmly planted on the leash at all times. Sadie rarely settled and sat still in such situations. With Quoddy I could more fully focus on whatever we were doing, whatever that might be. Sadie had been so much dog that she completely overshadowed little Iris, the dog that looked like a fox. With Sadie gone Iris' true nature came out. We started calling her the hyperactive little snit.

I think it was February when the call came from the Michigan Commission for the Blind. Having dismissed any possibility of getting that job in Gaylord I was stunned. In truth I had quite settled into our lives in Maine and I think I would have been content to stay there. "But you won't have a job," I said to Jim.

"Yes," he replied, "But you'll be making a lot more money than you're making here." That was true enough. We went through the same routine that we had gone through in Tennessee. We wrote down all of the pros and cons.

I felt uneasy about this move. True, things hadn't exactly started out well in Maine. Justified or not, Maine was the place I associated with the whole bulimia thing. But I was coming into my own as a teacher. I was in recovery from my eating disorder. Jim really wanted to go home though, and he'd been looking for a way to get back to Michigan since we left graduate school.

His desire for home overcame my reluctance.

We decided to move to Michigan.

30 | you can't push a string

IF YOU'RE EVER IN A CROWD OF STRANGERS, at a convention for example, and you see people holding up their left hand, palm out, and pointing to places on their hand, it's a good bet they're trying to describe where something is located on the lower peninsula of Michigan, for Michigan is comprised of two peninsulas, the lower and the upper. The peninsulas are connected by the five-mile-long Mackinaw Bridge. The upper peninsula connects to Wisconsin on its western border and Canada on its eastern border. Well, it would connect to Canada if not for the St. Mary's River, which flows from Lake Superior into Lake Huron. The town to which we moved, Gaylord (pronounced "Gay-lerd") would be just above the middle knuckle of the middle finger of that same left hand.

My office was right in the middle of this small town. For the first time I could easily walk to stores and restaurants. It was summertime and the weather was wonderful. The autonomy of being able to decide to up and go to lunch wherever I pleased or just go for a walk on the tree-shaded streets was great.

With this new-found autonomy I was able to work with Quoddy as I had never worked with Sadie. We explored together. We got lost and found together. Our relationship became deeper and more intimate than my relationship with Sadie ever was. Quoddy's deliberate steady work habits took a while to get used to. The first problem that appeared was a hesitation at the end of a street crossing. I have no memory of doing this, but I must have corrected Quoddy at some point when she failed to stop at an up-curb. I had to be something of a cheerleader with Quoddy. If I ever needed to correct her, I had to do it gently and quietly. In fact, after our first year together, I controlled Quoddy almost entirely with my voice.

As we drew near the up-curb or ramp at the end of street crossings I encouraged Quoddy with my voice. Occasionally I used a forced pull. To accomplish this maneuver I took the leash in my right hand and pulled, quite gently, straight up until she began to move forward. Every time I reached the sidewalk I praised Quoddy lavishly. Gradually her street crossings became good and solid.

One problem of long standing found a new solution while we were in Michigan. I had been having problems with migraines for several years. I remember only one migraine in the years before I became blind. When they really began to bother me was when we lived in Tennessee. There are zillions of theories about what causes migraines and I've pretty much given up on figuring it out.

"Jim," I began, "I've got a migraine again. I'm just so sick of this; I'm sick of being sick."

"Why don't you call your doctor," replied Jim, reasonably, and I did so.

After listening to my symptoms the doctor told me to go to the emergency room. He called ahead to let them know I was coming and told them to give me a shot of Demerol and Phenergan. Jim took me in to the Gaylord hospital and they gave me the shot. It was a miracle. I lay quite still while I felt the pain leave me.

The next time I had a migraine, I went to the ER alone, telling Jim I wanted to take control of my pain management. Eventually, I would go to the Gaylord hospital by myself without telling Jim anything about it. I didn't become a full-fledged drug addict overnight but these behaviors that characterized my active years of bulimia began to creep back into my life. The secrecy of budding substance abuse, and the sideways thinking that accompanied it, reminded me of Bramley Heath all over again. And simply thinking of Bramley Heath brought back my resentment at the way they had treated me.

It was true that the place had done its job as far as getting me into recovery from bulimia. For many months that was all that mattered. As time passed, as I got used to living a life free from bulimia, the ecstasy of being in recovery faded. Instead of being content with being in recovery I dwelled with resentment over the way Bramley Heath had treated me and the loss of my Sadie dog.

Then there was my childhood of sweetness and light. It had left me ill prepared to deal with such conflict. I could just hear my father's disapproval of my desire for vengeance on Bramley Heath. I could hear him saying, "You're whining. You've got that whining tone in your voice that I don't like to hear."

I had simply never learned to deal with anger and resentment. The thoughts festered and grew. I began to fantasize about getting revenge on Bramley Heath. I dreamed of suing the place for the loss of my dog. I kept thinking that Sadie's early retirement was all their fault. And what kind of place would employ a counselor who was so depressed that she would take her own life, right when I was supposed to be in her care? The place clearly had problems.

During the course of one particularly restless night I slipped in and out of uneasy dreams. Jim and I had had, of course, many discussions of the situation over many months. We had, in truth, just about talked it to death. I sensed his frustration but there was nobody else for me to talk to. Somehow on this evening, in my dreams, my father, Jim, and

I were in St. Mary's Episcopal Church in Birmingham. Daddy was wearing a crown and carrying a palm branch. Then we were singing the hymn "For All the Saints." With the sound of the hymn in my mind, "And when the strife is fierce, the warfare long, Steals on the ear the distant triumph song," I finally relaxed.

Eventually, I fell into a deep welcomed sleep.

"Is there an Episcopal church here," I began the next morning. Although I wasn't exactly ready to turn everything over to a God of whom I wasn't sure, at least my dream provided me with a course of action, however vague. I had grown up steeped in the liturgy, rituals, and music of the Episcopal Church. Although not a regular church-goer and not even entirely sure of whatever faith I might or might not possess, the church was still familiar. The more I thought about it the better I liked the idea of speaking to a minister. I needed someone besides Jim, someone who could bring fresh perspective to this thing, because I was clearly stuck.

"Yes," replied Jim. It's called St. Andrews. We've driven by there a bunch of times."

As soon as I got to work I called directory assistance and got the number for St. Andrews. "Hello, my name is Sue Martin," I began. "May I please speak to the rector?"

"You are. My name is Pete. How can I help you?"

Well here was a new one. Growing up, and at Sewanee for that matter, Episcopal ministers were always addressed by their title and surname. Adjusting my mind to the concept of addressing a minister by his first name, I began. "Well, I grew up in the Episcopal Church in Alabama. I've never been to St. Andrews but I'm really struggling to deal with some stuff that happened to me recently. Can I . . . would it be okay for me to come and talk with you?"

"Of course it would. Would you like to come right now?"

"Yes, yes, that would be great. I know the church is within

walking distance of my office. I'm blind and I'll be coming down there with my Seeing Eye dog. Keeping that in mind, can you give me directions?" Pete gave me excellent directions and we hung up.

"Hello," he called. "Hang a left at the next driveway you come to. I've been keeping an eye out for you." Shaking hands, Pete ushered me into his office. "Would you like something to drink? I've got coffee, Coke, or water." Handing me a glass of water, he sat down.

"Now, tell me what's happening?"

Pete listened in silence as I explained about having an eating disorder. As I told my story I felt the resentment and anger welling up inside all over again. I told him of my decision to seek treatment at Bramley Heath. I told him about speaking with the director of training at Seeing Eye and the compromise of leaving Sadie alone for one hour each morning and one hour each afternoon.

"But the barking and growling that started then, well, I was just never able to correct it. That's why I had to retire her. It was because of that, because of what they made me do at Bramley Heath. I want to make them pay for ruining Sadie, to pay for what they did."

When I came to the end of my story Pete came over and sat down on the floor in front of me. He talked, I listened.

Pete explained, "Bramley Heath isn't the problem. You've got to let go of this anger before it destroys you."

And then, after a good minute or so, I heard the compassion and caring in his voice. "Please."

"But how," I almost wept. "I can't quit thinking about it. And the more I think about it the more pissed off I get."

What Pete then said to me that afternoon as he sat on the floor was quite simple. "You can't push a string."

That afternoon was the first of many hours I would spend with Pete, as we would work through my reaction to the situation. You can't push a string. In my mind's eye I pictured pushing at the end of that piece of string with my finger. It offered no resistance. It couldn't be pushed. Could it be true? Could I possibly be able to choose the way I reacted to the events around me? Like a piece of string? As we continued to talk it through it suddenly sank in. I had been feeling like being a string was the same as being a wimp. I realized that it was the opposite. By choosing how I reacted to people and situations around me I would be dealing from a position of strength.

Gradually Pete helped me see the situation differently. My anger and thirst for revenge were harming no one except me. As long as I nursed my feelings of resentment I would remain mired in bitterness. It was over and done with. I needed to move on. There was no way I could be a loving wife, no way I could be an effective professional, with this bitter resentment festering inside me.

Gradually, I began to let it go. In letting go of such anger I could begin to heal. What mattered was that I had taken the first step towards a more healthy reaction to anger.

31 | back in the saddle

ALL THE WHILE I WAS LEARNING TO MANAGE ANGER life was going on.

Michigan is a big state and my territory was vast when compared to Maine. At least I didn't have to hire a driver. Until Jim got a job he could fill that role. We had loads of fun traveling together.

We spent a memorable few days in Paradise, a small town on the shore of Lake Superior. After working with clients for a few days, we took some time off and explored. We hiked in the woods. We went to Tahquamenon Falls State Park and walked down a zillion stairs to the bottom of the falls. We swam in Lake Superior. That was when we discovered a very "unshepherdly" trait in Quoddy. The dog was a German Shepherd. Shepherds aren't supposed to like the water. The first time we swam I didn't even take off her harness. I put her at down and told her to rest. Then we waded out into the lake. Everything was fine until I went under. She immediately sprang into action. She ran to the water and flung herself in, harness and all. She came out to, "Save," me. It was hilarious. This dog clearly had some kind of identity crisis. She loved the water all her life and got into it whenever possible.

Three of Jim's siblings lived in Michigan, and, for the first time, we were able to spend holidays and special occasions with his family. Jim's brother Carl and his wife, Shirley, lived outside of Detroit. Shirley stabled her horse, Riff Raff, at a place that had an indoor arena.

We spent that Labor Day weekend with Carl and Shirley. "Would you like to go riding?" Shirley asked on Sunday morning.

"That would be great!" I replied. This was just what I had been hoping for. I hadn't been in the saddle since we left Maine. I pulled on my jeans and the boots that I had thrown hopefully in my bag before we left Gaylord.

As we emerged from the car I took in the familiar sounds and smells. We entered the cool dimness of the stable and Shirley led us down a corridor to Riff Raff's stall. Snagging a halter from a hook on the wall she entered the stall and haltered the horse. As Riff Raff approached the open stall door I reached up and ran my hands down his face breathing in the treasured scent of horse, hay, and manure.

"Can I help you groom him?" I asked.

When Shirley got Riff Raff cross-tied in the corridor she showed me where she kept her brushes and I began. I took my time, wanting to savor the experience. Jim, holding Quoddy's leash, Carl, and Shirley were leaning against the wall chatting and watching me work. After currying Riff Raff I switched to a soft brush and went over him again. I brushed out his mane and tail and asked Shirley if she had a hoof pick.

"There you go," I said to the horse when I had finished, "now you're all handsome and ready to take on the world."

Stepping to Riff Raff's head I dug a carrot out of my pocket and offered it to him from the flat of my palm. I stroked his velvety nose as he crunched the carrot contentedly.

"Let's get him saddled," said Shirley, as she returned from the tack room with her saddle. Handing over Riff Raff's bridle, she asked, "Want to bridle him?"

After buckling the girth, Shirley turned to me. "Here you

go," I said, handing over the reins. Shirley then led the way to the indoor arena with Riff Raff's shoes ringing on the concrete with each step. Taking Quoddy's leash from Jim, I picked up the harness, and we followed.

Shirley directed us to some elevated seats at one end of the arena and we all settled down to watch. I listened to the sound of each gait as Shirley exercised Riff Raff. The thud of hooves at a walk, the faster two beat rhythm of a trot, and the three beat rhythm of a canter.

After about twenty minutes Shirley approached and asked if I'd like to ride. I lit up, and handing Quoddy's leash to Jim, I made my way down to the arena. I was excited. Since that day long ago, when I had first realized that I could take direction from light, that tiny patch of light perception had remained stable. Through long experience I had learned that I could never fully depend on what I perceived visually. I could, however, sometimes pick up little pieces of visual information that might be useful. I had noticed the row of skylights running down the center of the ceiling and thought I'd be able to maintain my orientation by glancing up at the ceiling as I rode. When Shirley asked how I wanted to do this I explained about the skylights. I mounted up and headed off.

After walking once around the perimeter of the ring to get a feel of the place I moved out at a sitting trot. It felt great. Then I took Riff Raff into a smaller circle and got him on the bit. This was wonderful. This was amazing. I moved as one with the horse. I didn't need to see his neck to know that it was arched, his face perpendicular to the ground.

From a sitting trot I moved the horse out and began posting, slipping my right hand down to insure that I was rising with the forward movement of the outside leg as we made ever widening circles.

Then I realized that I was keeping track of where, in the arena I was, not so much by looking up at the skylights, but by the kenesthetics that my first O&M instructor, Oscar, had taught me about so long ago. With complete confidence I moved Riff Raff out into a nice collected canter, bringing him back to a trot at the place where I imagined the letter C would be were I in the dressage ring.

Later, as Jim and I sat together in the back seat of the car, I rested my head on his shoulder. "That was wonderful," I murmured contentedly.

"It was pretty wonderful, watching you out there doing something that you're so good at, something that you clearly love."

I hesitated but then I said, "We're going to have horses one day, aren't we?"

Jim laughed. "I'd say that's a big ten-four, good buddy, as you southerners would say."

Jim got a part time job, also with state government, as a vocational rehab counselor." He worked three days a week which meant I had to get a driver for the first time. It was even more difficult than it had been in Maine because the state paid nothing. All I could offer was a state car and a free lunch. As we moved into the fall it felt like summer vacation was over. The fun ended and work felt grueling.

The snow in Gaylord began in late October or early November. Gaylord sits at the highest elevation of the northern lower peninsula. Storms came, from west to east, across Lake Michigan. They dumped snow on the west coast of Michigan, gathered strength as they moved inland and dumped more snow when they hit Gaylord. This lake effect snow was almost constant. The only variation from the three or four inches of snow per day was when we got twelve or fifteen inches instead. It was fairly exhausting just keeping up with it, keeping the porch and the walkway out to where we parked our truck shoveled and clear of snow. As I heaved another shovel full of snow off the path, I thought longingly of our summer adventures.

The call from a friend in Maine came in late November. They had established a brand new orientation and mobility position in Ellsworth. And the rehab teaching position in Bangor was vacant. Ellsworth is where the entire world hangs a right to go out to Mount Desert Island, Bar Harbor, and Acadia National Park. Bangor is about thirty five miles inland.

As we discussed our options Jim told me that, in coming back to Michigan, he had been trying to come back to a time rather than a place.

The time was the 70s and the place was a homesteading farm in Bangor, Michigan. He had moved to the farm as part of a class at Western Michigan University on homesteading. On the farm Jim learned how to grow and harvest food using organic techniques. He learned animal husbandry. He learned about slaughtering cows and pigs, which is the reason he eats neither beef nor pork. But mostly he found himself in the company of like-minded folk. The counter-cultural nature of the farm appealed to him. Living in concert with nature rather than imposing himself on it appealed to him.

It was thus difficult for me to be objective about the decision to move back to Maine. I was excited but I tried not to let the excitement overcome my objectivity. There was a little fear as well. Moving across the country is never easy. There are always unknowns . . . the biggest being how Jim would handle leaving his beloved state, Michigan.

It was the last week of January when we headed out for Maine.

32 | a question of wheels

FOR ME, THE MOVE TO MAINE FELT LIKE COMING HOME. The place appealed to my senses, all of them. I loved the aroma of Balsam Fir and Northern White Cedar. There was the smell of something dusky, almost certainly a heath, either Mountain Laurel or Rhododendron. The first time I caught the aroma of white cedar in Maine I was transported back to childhood. I had attended a summer camp, Camp Nakanawa, in the Tennessee mountains, for many years. The camp used Old Town wood and canvas canoes, the ribs of which were crafted of white cedar. The aroma brought back to me those glorious years of summer camp, when I had been so happy, where I had won medals and trophies, where I had been deemed a girl of sterling character, earning my silver letter twice. And now here I was face to face with the source of that aroma that awakened so many memories. What a joy to discover the fissured silky bark, so distinctive that it's unmistakable, the lacey fan shaped leaves, just as distinctive.

There was the ocean. The only similarity between the ocean and a lake is that they are both bodies of water. There the similarity ends. The heaving unpredictable waves of the ocean feel wild and free. Who knew where this water came from? Who knew what exotic shores it had seen?

As winter gave way to spring the Black Capped Chickadees

greeted the day. As spring moved into summer the loons, with their primal, haunting call, came to nearby Chimo Pond. In the height of summer came the hermit thrush with its musical flute-like call. It took being away from Maine for a time and then coming back for me to appreciate all of these things.

It was completely different for Jim. Although we had tried to be rational about this move it was more complicated than that rational list of pros and cons we had made. For Jim, Michigan was still home. But we had gone back there and it hadn't worked. The move back to Maine felt like a failure to him. Jim settled into a funk that lasted over two years.

After six months in that first rented house the owners began making noises about selling it. We had no intention of buying it so we looked around for another house to rent.

"You know," Jim said, "We could move anywhere really. Do you want to look for something on the water?"

"What," I replied, "Like something on Chimo Pond or Green Lake?"

"Well, no," he hesitated, "I was thinking of something on the ocean."

I hesitated in my turn and, then, agreeing, I said, "Okay then, let's look for something on the ocean." Keenly aware of Jim's discontent, I readily agreed. I was so pleased that he was showing an interest, so pleased that he had an opinion, that I kept my reservations to myself.

Jim called the realty company and made an appointment to see the house the next weekend. "Hello," said the realtor. "My name is Dick. What a beautiful dog," he added, as I came around the truck with Quoddy. We introduced ourselves. I stopped. I listened to the waves as they rolled in on the shore. Although the house still lay between me and the bay I could feel the expanse. I could feel the wide open freedom drawing me towards it.

Walking down to the house, Dick said, "It's a million

dollar view, isn't it?" He unlocked the door and we entered a sort of entrance hall. "When this house was built it was intended to be a seasonal cottage. Where we're standing right now, this room and the bathroom beyond, just there, were originally part of the porch." We turned left into the kitchen. Dick continued, "I'm not sure why but there's a gas cooktop and oven as well as an electric."

The rest of the house was one open room. There was a fireplace opposite a bay window that overlooked the bay. Upstairs there were two bedrooms and another bathroom. None of the rooms were large. We went back downstairs and Dick opened the glass door onto the front porch. It took my breath away. It was spectacular. From the broad expanse of the bay small waves ran up onto the rocky shore.

"Here," said Dick, "Come down here." We descended eight or ten steps from the porch, crossed fifteen feet of lawn and began down a much longer flight of steps that ended at a small dock.

Later, when we were back in the house, Dick asked if we were interested in renting it.

I began, "The ad in the paper said, No pets. It doesn't matter about Quoddy of course but we have another dog. Her name is Iris. She's in the truck if you'd like to meet her." Thankfully, the realtor was completely enchanted by little Iris and said we could rent the house.

"What do you think?" Jim began.

"Well," I said, "The whole thing depends on transportation doesn't it?"

Ah yes, transportation, it's an endless issue for someone who doesn't drive who wants to live off the beaten path.

I asked around the Bangor office while Jim asked around the Ellsworth office. That's how I met Mike and Genevieve. Mike was a professor at the University of Maine and Genevieve taught at an elementary school in Bangor. They agreed that I could ride with them into town each morning.

"Okay," I said to Jim, "That's half the battle. Let me see if I can work out transportation home now." There were two other individuals that someone in the Ellsworth office had mentioned. Ralph and Jackie both worked at the Bangor Mental Health Institute, BMHI. Both agreed that I could accompany them home in the afternoons and come into town with them on days when I couldn't catch a ride with Mike and Genevieve.

"Let's do it," I said, when I called Jim at his office. He agreed and we moved to the house on Frenchman's Bay.

From everywhere in the house there was the sound of the ocean. We became intimately familiar with its moods. There was the gentle lapping of the summer ocean. There were the wild crashing waves of windy days and storms.

On weekends we'd sit on the front porch and drink our morning coffee. Many were the times that Jim looked up and said, "There's a whale," or, "The bald eagle is back."

We lived in a stunningly beautiful place. But there was ever Jim's discontent. He spoke of Michigan often, even though we had been there done that and it hadn't worked out. Whenever Jim went into one of his funks and started talking about Michigan I just clammed up. I felt guilty for liking Maine. I didn't know what to say, I felt guilty, and I clammed up.

This was the constant background rumbling that accompanied the beginning of our life back in Maine. Despite those rumblings we got on with things. Sometimes life just goes on and you have to go with it, and sometimes that's not a bad thing.

33 | wheel life stories

BETWEEN MY NEW FRIENDS, MY PAID DRIVER, AND TAXIS I patched together a system of transportation that worked pretty well.

On days when I caught a cab to BMHI to meet Ralph or Jackie, I had the driver drop me at the emergency room entrance. Entering the hospital through a door near the ER I could easily get to Ralph's office or the library where I met Jackie. I began to notice that when I gave my destination to cab drivers they sometimes became quite rigid and refused to enter into conversation. I mentioned this to Jackie one day and she burst out laughing.

"What's so funny," I began.

"Well, think about it," Jackie said. "A woman gets in a cab and asks to be taken to the emergency room of a mental health hospital. They probably think . . . "

I joined in the laughter. "Oh, oh my gosh. You don't think they assume that . . . "

"Well, yes," said Jackie, "They probably think you're going to check yourself in or something." And then Jackie broke into another fit of laughter. "a long time ago the hospital used to pay people who brought patients into the ER." She was almost incoherent as she continued, "Have any of the cab drivers gotten out to see if they can collect a fee?"

I received a referral from the medical director of BMHI. Dr. Wilson called, explaining that they had just admitted a woman whose visual impairment was due to head trauma. "I understand that, in cases like this, in cases where there is trauma, the sooner intervention can begin the better the chances that the patient can learn to use remaining vision."

"Yes," I agreed with Dr. Wilson. "Let me juggle my schedule. May I call you back?" I asked. He agreed and gave me his direct number. I called back and offered to see his patient on Thursday.

I'll call the patient Fran. "Fran, this is Ms. Martin," Said Dr. Wilson as I entered his office.

"What?" bellowed Fran loudly. Completely unprepared to be yelled at I took a step back.

Seeing my reaction Dr. Wilson said, "This is another effect of the head trauma. Fran is unable to modulate her voice." Gathering my wits I began. I sat down before Fran. I told her that I would be doing some tests on her vision and asked if it was okay if I touched the back of her head. With my hand resting gently on Fran's head I brought a pen light into and out of her visual field. Feeling her head move with the movement of the light I knew I had something to work with.

I said to Dr. Wilson, "Yes, I think I can work with Fran." I outlined a program of vision stimulation and agreed to begin the next week.

Dr. Wilson walked me out to the car where my driver waited. It was a brisk day. As I arrived at the car I turned and reached out to shake Dr. Wilson's hand just as a gust of wind hit us. I grabbed his tie instead of his hand. We had a good laugh and I went on my way.

"You're not going to believe what happened," I began as Ralph and I drove home that afternoon. I told Ralph the story of grabbing Dr. Wilson's tie instead of his hand.

"You know what," said Ralph, "Dr. Wilson lives in Bar

Harbor. I'll bet he'd be willing to give you a ride home when plans A and B fall through."

So, Dr. Wilson had become plan C.

Getting into Dr. Wilson's car, I reached for the seatbelt. What I found was a ragged end of nylon. The seatbelt had been cut somehow. "What happened," I asked.

"I'm not entirely sure," he replied. "I always lock my car, well, okay, I usually remember to lock my car," he said. "I'm thinking an employee may have done it because of the state shutdown you know." Maine was having fiscal problems and there had been a partial shutdown of state services for the past two weeks. "It's odd though," he continued, "If the car was unlocked you'd think whoever it was would have done something, anything, besides just cutting the seatbelt." The discussion of disgruntled employees, cut seatbelts, and the fact that Dr. Wilson wasn't responsible for the layoffs carried us all the way to Ellsworth.

A couple of months later, during the ride to Ellsworth, Dr. Wilson told me that he had discovered who cut the seatbelt. He spoke in a voice devoid of emotion. This was odd because we had discussed the cut seatbelt many times and his efforts to discover the culprit, but that's just how Dr. Wilson was, taciturn.

"So, how'd you discover who did it?" I asked.

"Well, it was when the car was parked on a street in Bar Harbor. I had left my dog, you know, the Golden Retriever, in the car. I looked up just in time to see her eating through the driver side seat belt. So, now we have a matched set."

He spoke so matter-of-factly that it took me a minute to get it. He was making a joke. Most of the times that I rode with Dr. Wilson it was in the afternoon. It was during one of my rare trips with him in the morning that I finally got him laughing. I had just returned from a conference. One of the presentations I attended was given by a woman named Judy.

"So, this lady was asked by the CDC to do research on the level of awareness of sexually transmitted diseases on the part of teenagers with visual impairments. They wanted to compare awareness in that population with awareness in the general population," I said. "The results of the research showed a much lower awareness on the part of folks with visual impairments," I paused.

"So, what happened next?" Dr. Wilson prompted.

"The CDC asked this woman to develop training in the awareness of sexually transmitted diseases aimed at teens who have visual impairments," I said. "Since most folks who are legally blind have some degree of usable vision, Judy decided to exploit that. She got male genital models in all sorts of colors, and then got condoms in all sorts of contrasting colors. So, she's got all of these genital models in her carry on as she went through airport security. The guy at security said, 'Are you here on business or pleasure?' and he unzipped the bag."

I stopped.

Suddenly, Dr. Wilson exploded in laughter. He laughed and laughed and even pounded the steering wheel. When he finally stopped laughing, he turned to me. "People think I'm a stick in the mud because I'm quiet, so they almost never tell me stories like that one."

He chuckled again.

The scariest transportation related episode occurred when Hurricane Bob was working its way up the Atlantic seaboard. The day it was supposed to come ashore in the Frenchman's Bay area Jim and I headed out to our respective jobs making each other promise to keep an eye on the weather. The storm was not supposed to hit until evening so we thought we'd be okay to go ahead and go to work. I walked into my second client's house at a little past noon. He had Maine Public Radio playing. "Repeating, all offices of Maine State Government closed at noon due to the approach of Hurricane Bob." I stopped in my tracks, thinking.

"Damn," I said to Steve, my client. "I'm riding with my friend Ralph who works at BMHI. I've got to get over there right now." My driver and I unceremoniously turned right around and left. I was terrified. What if Ralph had left without me?

Then I thought of Jim. Where had he been going today? "Damn," I said again, to my driver. "Jim's out on Little Cranberry today," referring to a small island to which Jim traveled by mail boat.

"Just wait for a second while I run in and see if Ralph is still here," I said to my driver. Ripping off my seatbelt, I got Quoddy out of the back seat and almost ran into the hospital. Rounding the corner I discovered the door to the finance department to be wide open. I ran in, calling Ralph's name as I did.

With perfect composure, Ralph said, "I'm right here waiting for you."

"Oh, thank goodness," I began.

Surprised at my consternation Ralph said, "You didn't think I would leave you did you?"

His calm voice brought me up short. Of course Ralph wouldn't have left me. What had I been thinking. "Well, no," I began. "I was just panicking I guess." I took a deep breath. It was okay. "I'll go tell my driver that everything is all right," I said, a bit sheepishly.

On the drive back to Ellsworth, Ralph questioned our storm preparedness. "No, I don't need to stop anywhere. We have plenty of batteries for flashlights. We'll be fine.

Arriving home at around one-thirty, I found the house deserted. Uneasily I thought of Jim, Little Cranberry, and the mail boat. Feeling a little desperate I called a neighbor. "Do you think he'll be able to get home," I concluded, after telling the neighbor of Jim's whereabouts.

"Yes," calm down," the neighbor began. "Just look outside," she continued. I took the cordless phone out on the front porch.

Feeling sheepish once more, I got the point. "It doesn't really feel stormy yet," I said. "I mean it's windy and overcast but it doesn't feel stormy yet."

"Exactly," soothed my neighbor. "The mail boat will get him home just fine. Now just call again if there's anything else you need."

Jim arrived at around four o'clock. We lost power shortly after that. Hurricane Bob hit at around seven, which coincided with high tide. We sat together on the window seat of our second floor bedroom and watched. Jim said, "Wow," over and over again as we watched the twenty five foot rollers hit the shore. While, "Wow," was the only word he uttered, he packed a lot of emotion into that one word.

Even through the closed windows the roaring of the wind and the waves was impressive. "I want to go outside," I said to Jim. "I want to feel it as well as hear it."

"Okay, let's do it," Jim agreed. We went downstairs to the glass door onto the front porch. The house faced east and the storm was coming in from the northeast. The wind was buffeting the door. Placing my hand on the door I felt it shutter as a gust slammed into it.

"Maybe this isn't such a grand idea," I murmured.

"Come on," said Jim, "Let's go out the other door. The other door opened onto the south side of the house so it was a little sheltered. We went outside. We stood still, we listened, Jim watched, we both experienced the hurricane. We stood on the porch for a long time. I had no inclination to leave the shelter of the porch. We said not a word. In truth, we wouldn't have been able to hear each other if we had spoken.

Back in the house at last we both gasped. "Wow," this time we both said it together. Having experienced the hurricane first hand, up close and personal, we hunkered down to wait it out. We snuggled under the covers. Quoddy sighed. Iris turned in several circles before settling down. The wind roared. The waves crashed. We slept.

34 | with extended arms

DURING A MORNING TRIP INTO BANGOR Genevieve said, "Are you interested in joining the AAUW?"

"I don't know," I replied, "What is it?"

"Oh, it's the American Association of University Women. The Ellsworth chapter meets this week and the meeting is just around the corner at Deborah Cravey's house. She's originally from Alabama so you'll have that in common with her."

"Okay, sure," I replied. "When's the meeting?"

That's how I found myself entering Deborah and Madison's house for the first time. Shaking my hand, Deborah said, "Hi, I'm Deborah. I understand that you're originally from Alabama, Birmingham, right?"

"Yes, I'm originally from Birmingham, you?"

"I grew up in south Alabama, but my husband, Madison, did his internship at Lloyd Noland Hospital in Birmingham."

I gaped, "Lloyd Noland, really? My father worked there for forty years!"

"Yes, really," Deborah said. "Madison is an ophthalmologist here in Ellsworth now, but we lived in Birmingham during his internship."

I was reeling. This was going almost too fast for me to keep up. "Get outta here," I began. "If your husband is an ophthalmologist he had to have done his ophthalmology rotation under my father. Daddy headed up the department of ophthalmology at Lloyd Noland, like, forever!"

That was the beginning. Later, even when separated by years and miles, whenever we got together with Madison and Deborah it would be as though no time at all had passed.

I don't remember the topic of that first AAUW meeting but it was my first foray into the community. I do recall that someone at that first meeting told me of a woman named Masha who lived just up the road. The person told me that Masha had been a braille transcriptionist at one time. I didn't pay much attention. I get that kind of thing all the time, My uncle trains guide dogs, or, My cousin's best friend's fiancé teaches braille . . . It's as though, when they first meet me, people cast about for anything and anyone to do with blindness to use as a topic of conversation. I usually go with the flow and hope that, as they get to know me, people will realize that blindness is just part of who I am and that I have other, far-reaching interests.

I had reason to recall this conversation a couple of months later. All services for blind children in Maine are coordinated through Catholic Charities. I learned from one of the teachers of visually impaired children, TVIs, that they were desperately seeking someone who could custom translate braille. It had taken me several months to learn the entire braille code including all of the two hundred-plus contractions. I thought of a blind child going through the same process. Where would such a child get materials that contained only the contractions he had already learned but also contained fully spelled out words that contained contractions he hadn't yet learned? I called Deborah.

"Yes, her name is Masha," Deborah told me after I had explained the situation. "She and her husband, Walter, are both fascinating folks. Good luck getting Masha away from her loom. She's really into spinning and weaving these days. And Walter, he used to work for Kodak as an optical physicist or, an optical something or other. Tyler and Elizabeth have both gone on walks with Walter to learn about mushrooms. He's a well-known mycologist.

"Wow, okay, do you think Marcia would mind if I called her to talk about her taking up braille transcription again," I asked.

"Oh, I think it's a grand idea," Deborah replied. "But her name is Masha, like mash with an 'a' on the end."

That's how I met Masha. I got her number from directory assistance and placed the call. She was totally agreeable to chatting about braille transcription and invited me to come over at once. "Hey Jim," I called. "I'm going to go over to Masha Litten's house to talk about her doing braille transcription again. What do you think the best way to find her driveway is?"

Jim considered for a moment and then said, "Okay, you'll be walking south on Seal Point Road. Quoddy will show you Route 204. Go ahead and cross 204 and take your alignment from the far side. If you cross straight over Seal Point, you should hit their driveway."

So, I harnessed up and set off. The Litton's driveway was very long. There was absolutely nothing to let me know if I was in their driveway or not. Eventually I came to a house. Quoddy took me to the corner of the house, down a few steps, and stopped at a door. Without looking for a doorbell, you never know where those things are, I simply knocked on the glass of the door.

A petite woman answered the door. "Hi, you must be Sue," she spoke warmly. "Come on in. She led me into the most amazing home. We walked up a few stairs into a den. Something about the feel of the room put me in mind of a fire in a stone fireplace, dark wood, leather upholstery, and books. The ceiling soared two stories above us. Crossing the den, we mounted a few more stairs to a level containing a kitchen and sort of sun room with a dining table. The entire wall was glass. Then Masha led me out, onto the most amazing deck I've ever seen. It was huge. And it hung out over the bay. Crossing to the railing I looked down on the waves as they rushed in and crashed on the rocks.

"Sue," said Masha, yanking me back to reality, "This is my husband, Walter."

I crossed the deck and shook hands with Walter. I felt, I'm not sure how to describe it, I felt a lively intellect. I felt a keen inquiring mind. "Welcome to our home," he said, simply. I was intrigued by the pair of them. They both seemed ageless to me. Though not young or even middle aged, somehow, 'elderly,' just didn't fit.

Catching my attention, Quoddy whined. She was looking down at the waves and whining. "Do you mind," I began, "Do you mind if I let my dog loose? She loves the water, and she's just dying to go down there and investigate."

"Oh, certainly," replied Masha, and continuing she added, "I didn't know that German Shepherds liked the water."

"I know; she's maybe having some kind of identity crisis." Then I said, "Watch," as I took off Quoddy's harness and leash. Quoddy bolted for the stairs down from the deck. In a moment she was right there below us. I listened as she happily splashed about in the water.

After a few minutes Masha said, "What's she doing? She went right out there in the water and dove her head under. Then she came up with a rock in her mouth. And look, she's brought it back up to the shore and dropped it. What's she doing?"

"Just watch," I said. Quoddy performed the ritual that Jim and I had come to know so well. After dropping the first rock on the shore she went back, dove her head under and came up with another one. Splashing to shore, she deposited the second rock beside the first. Then back to the water she went to do it all over again.

"We've decided that, lacking a proper sheep to herd, Quoddy is herding rocks," I told them.

"That's extraordinary," Walter murmured.

I knew that Quoddy would be perfectly safe so I turned to Masha. "So, you were a certified braillist?" I began.

"Oh, yes," she replied. "But I haven't done it for years now. I'm much more involved with my spinning and weaving." She hesitated, and said, "Would you like to see my loom?"

"Oh, yes," I replied, "I'd love to." Showing me to a narrow flight of stairs, Masha and I climbed to an upstairs room.

"Here, sit down here on this bench," said Masha. I sat and examined the loom in front of me. Handing me a flat piece of wood around which the spun wool was wrapped Masha said, "Here, this is the shuttle. It carries the yarn or thread through the shed. Here, feel back along the parallel threads. They're called the warp. See how they're separated, some are higher than others. The space in between is called the shed and you pass the shuttle through the shed.

Feeling the open space between the warp threads, I passed the shuttle, from right to left, through the space. "Okay, what do I do next?" I asked. Next, Masha showed me how the beater is used to insure uniform snugness of the threads.

"The next thing you need to do is use the treadles to change the shed," began Masha. I had to push back from the loom a bit and duck down so I could feel the treadles. Once I had my feet on them and was sitting straight again Masha directed me to feel the warp threads as I worked the treadles. The lower threads changed places with the upper threads. "Now run the shuttle back through the shed," said Masha. This time I passed the shuttle through the shed from left to right.

"Of course there's more to it," said Masha, "But that's the general idea."

"So, if the parallel threads are the warp the horizontal threads are the woof?" I asked.

"Yes," Masha replied, "Woof is an older term. These days it's called the weft."

I examined the completed part of Masha's weaving. "What a marvelous texture," I said.

"This is a satin weave," Masha began. I asked Masha how she had gotten into spinning and weaving. As she told her story she showed me samples of her weaving, using them to illustrate her story. I was fascinated and listened intently as she spoke.

Eventually, Masha said, "But it's not my weaving you've come to talk about. Tell me about the brailling."

After I had explained the need for someone who could do custom brailling, Masha agreed to begin braille transcription again. I gave her my brailler and a pile of braille paper and she was off.

35 | if you can't beat 'em

THE NEXT SATURDAY MORNING, as we sat on the front porch drinking our coffee and watching the bay, Jim said, "What do you want to do this weekend?"

"I don't know. What do you fancy?"

Looking over at Mount Desert Island, Jim mused, "I'd kind of like to go over to MDI, you know, go hiking or something, but the tourists will be out in swarms. The place will be mobbed."

It was true. During the summer months and the months of autumn color traffic could be a nightmare. Most residents muttered and complained, but just put up with it. My view was that the area needed the revenue, so what was the point of complaining?

"You know," I said, "All of those tourists just might have a point."

I remained at the top of the steps descending to the yard. Slowly, I turned my head, gazing over the water towards the island.

Eventually, Jim said, "What point do the tourists have?"

I didn't answer. I was still looking at Mount Desert and thinking of the carriage trails, the hiking trails, the lakes, the mountains, all of it.

Eventually, Jim admitted, "I see what you mean. Maybe

they do have a point."

Turning around I said, "Do you want to go to the island today?"

Retrieving my coffee cup from the porch railing I sat down. Silently sipping from the cup I thought about the island. There are fifty-eight miles of carriage trails. These are wide smooth gravel roads used by walkers, bicyclists, horseback riders, and in the winter, cross country skiers. There are hiking trails to suit any fancy. Many climb to the top of the various mountains on the island. Some take the hiker deep into the woods, along dancing streams beneath towering trees. The lakes are clear and cold. Everywhere is the ocean. You can drive to it. You can hike to it. You can hear the crashing waves as you ascend the mountains.

Jim spoke, "What about a hike?"

"Sounds good, carriage trail or real hike?"

Jim thought for a moment and said, "Let's do a little of both. We can park at Jordon Pond House, take the carriage trail to that trail up Penobscot Mountain."

"Sounds good," I replied. "Want to have lunch at Jordon Pond House?"

"Yep, let's get going."

With NPR on the radio we set out. It was midmorning when we found a parking place in the overflow lot at Jordon Pond House. I harnessed Quoddy and Jim snapped a leash on little Iris. We took the short trail to the main parking lot, crossed it and entered the woods.

As we gained the carriage trail we moved out. The carriage trails require almost no thought or concentration. "Hey, before we do the trail up Penobscot Mountain can we just go along the carriage trail for a bit?" "I wanted to feel the open grandure of standing high above Jordon Pond, of looking across the pond to the silhouettes of The Bubbles, two mountains at the north end of the pond. I wanted to hear the waves of the pond far below as they lapped the shore.

"Okay, sure," Jim agreed and, side by side, we set out. We greeted the other hikers and bicyclists as they passed. Stopping at a point high above the pond I drank in the experience. Jim took a couple of pictures and then said, "Ready?" I agreed and we headed back in the direction we had come. Taking a right on an intersecting carriage trail we made our way to the hiking trail up the mountain.

The trail was rough and I stumbled repeatedly. I was getting frustrated but I didn't want to ruin the day so I said nothing. It was when I almost fell that Jim had an idea. Looking around he left the trail, went into the woods, and brought out a long smooth branch of cedar. "Here, let me break off these twigs and you can use this as a staff." Gratefully I took the branch, hefted it and experimented with it, reaching out to probe the trail in front of me. When I was ready we set out again.

The stick made all the difference. Much more sure of my footing we ascended Penobscot Mountain. At the top we rested. Taking the water bottle out of the backpack we passed it between us. Jim poured some water in the plastic bowl we had brought for the dogs. We sat companionably and agreed that the tourists indeed did have a point. That's the great thing about MDI. If you make the decision to just deal with the traffic it's all worth it. We had only passed two groups of hikers once we started up the mountain trail. Even in midsummer on the coast of Maine it's still possible to get away from it all.

When we were ready we headed back down the mountain. Back on the carriage trail we rejoined the walkers and bicyclists. It was the oddest thing. For the first time I felt a sort of camaraderie with the people that we passed. Other walkers greeted us and complimented the dogs. The bicyclists politely let us know of their presence by saying, "On your left," as they aproached us from behind. When we came to the outflow point of the pond we turned left and walked along the rocky shore to the sweeping lawn up to Jordon Pond House. Then we walked up the grassy slope to the restaurant.

By this time it was one o'clock and there was a waiting line to be seated. Built in the 1870s Jordon Pond House has traditions of long standing. It is most famous for tea and popovers. "Here you go," said the young woman as she placed the basket of piping hot popovers on the table. "Now, what else can I bring you?"

"We're fine for now," Jim replied. Each of us took a steaming popover from the basket. Cutting mine open I slathered it with butter and strawberry preserves. Then I closed it up and waited for the butter to melt. Once I judged it was ready I bit into the light as air pastry.

"Yum," I said. "I think I want the crabmeat and havarti quiche today. You?" Jim opted for the salmon and we placed our orders.

Back in the car we joined Car Talk on NPR and headed home. "Let's get some fish for later," Jim said as we approached Ellsworth on Route 3. There was a truck parked on the right side of the road that sold seafood. Pulling off the road we got out of the car and walked up the few steps to the inside of the truck.

"Hello," began the woman in the truck. "What can I get for you today?" After some deliberation and discussion we purchased an Atlantic Salmon fillet.

That was the beginning of the building of our traditions. One day of the weekend we'd do stuff that needed doing around the house. The other day of the weekend we'd do something fun. Depending on the time of year we'd either hike or ski, Go on a whale watch or simply out to dinner. Our adventures usually took us to MDI but sometimes we'd go further downeast to Schoodic Mountain or, in the other direction, to Blue Hill, Castine, or even as far as the Camden

Hills.

In the beginning Jim's and my reality was far apart. My reality was the joy I felt listening to the water of the bay from everywhere in our house. It was the feel of the openness of the bay drawing me towards it. It was the clients who were learning to be independent through my teaching. It was the community of the people who came into my life one by one.

At first Jim's reality was far from mine. Gradually the feelings of failure engendered by leaving Michigan eased. As we built our new traditions together our realities merged.

When deciding what we wanted to do for fun each weekend we'd begin by figuring out whether we wanted to play tourist or do something more obscure that only native Mainers would know about. When deciding what kind of hike we wanted to take our shorthand became "real hike" or "carriage trail." The truck on the side of the road that sold seafood became, simply, the Fish Lady. It was these traditions that started making a difference for Jim. He still spoke of Michigan but less frequently.

We settled into our lives in Maine.

36 | winter on the coast

FOR THE REST OF THE SUMMER we continued to build our traditions. The months of August and September are the busiest as far as the tourists are concerned. Instead of eschewing Bar Harbor during those months we learned to revel in the hustle and bustle. When the cruise ships began anchoring in Bar Harbor, it felt like Mardi Gras. Passengers came ashore by the score. In the space of one block you could hear three or four different languages.

The fall foliage in Maine peaks between mid-September and mid-October. During peak leaf season, there are multiple cruise ships docked along the coast and the roads seem filled with tour buses. And then it's all over. The next thing that happens is November. The month of November in Maine is grim. The trees have lost all of their leaves. It's too early for snow. Jim's description of November in Maine? "Rain, drizzle, and fog, oh, my!"

"We need to join the YMCA or something," began Jim on one rainy November morning. We were both missing the weekend adventures of the summer and fall.

I sat up, "Okay, let's do it. I'd love to start swimming again." So, we joined the Y. Jim usually lifted weights or used the aerobic machines like the stationary bicycle or rowing machine. I lifted weights sometimes but mostly I swam. I love the water. What can I say, I'm a Pisces? There's something hypnotizing about swimming. I'd settle into a steady free style and just swim.

On days when I had only paperwork to do I started staying at home to do it. Then the migratory birds began to settle on the bay. The sound that the birds make is magical and almost indescribable. It's a symphony of whistles, squeaks, and calls. It's completely different from the quacking or honking sounds made by ducks or geese when flying. Even through the closed bay window where I had my desk I could hear it. When I think of winter on Frenchman's Bay it's the sound of the migratory birds that I remember . . . a sound interrupted only occasionally by the low thrum of the diesel engines of the scallop boats moving across the bay. I loved those days of working at home. Jim would make sure I had plenty of wood for the fireplace before he left for work, and I'd keep the fire going all day.

We waited for snow. Snow on the Maine coast is persnickety if you happen to enjoy cross-country skiing. Snow usually moves across the state from west to east or moves up the coast in a northeasterly direction. The ocean is much warmer than the land, and, often, the snow turns to sleet or rain as it approaches the coast. The most annoying pattern for the snow is when it snows several inches of nice light snow, turns into sleet mixed with rain, and then freezes solid. The result is something like concrete, slippery but dangerous concrete.

For most of November and December the snow was no good for skiing. It ended up as the slushy or concrete variety. Finally, in January, the conditions were perfect. We were waiting for our friend, Chuck, to arrive. Chuck worked for one of the west coast guide dog schools and was in Maine to evaluate someone who had applied for a dog at his school.

"Hey Jim," I called from the kitchen. "I've got this soup and everything ready for Chuck but if he doesn't get here soon it's going to be too late to go skiing on MDI."

"I know," said Jim. "He said he'd be here an hour ago. Look, I'm going to go ahead and put the skis in the truck." I had given Jim new skis for Christmas. He was going to use his new ones and Chuck was going to use his old ones.

"Sounds good," I replied. "When you get the skis and poles in the truck come back in and I'll have your soup ready." As we sat at the table eating our soup Jim asked what I was going to feed Chuck. "I don't know," I'll give him a sandwich or something." When Chuck finally pulled in the driveway we unceremoniously stuffed him in the truck, handed him a peanut butter and jelly sandwich, and set off. During the drive to the island we caught up with each other's doings of the past couple of years. As we drove over the causeway, Jim said, "So, where do you want to go?"

"Oh, Jordan Pond House for sure," I answered. "Let's do that loop that begins with the long, gradual downhill to the stream." Jim agreed, and we headed in that direction. There were only two cars in the unplowed main parking lot. We pulled across and stopped near the woods.

"Here you go, Chuck," said Jim, handing Chuck his old skis. He disentangled my skis and handed them over. After snapping my boots into the toe holds I pulled on my gloves and got my wrists settled in the straps of my poles.

"Okay, everybody ready?" asked Jim. "Let's go." We had to go up a very slight hill into the woods and then along a path to the carriage trail.

I got there first. As Jim came out of the woods I said, "Any tracks?" While cross country ski trails in Acadia National Park are not professionally groomed enough people ski there to keep the trails pretty well defined.

"Yep, about two feet to your left," Jim instructed. Stepping in that direction I felt the first track.

"Left or right?" I called.

"Right," Jim called back. We had done this so often that we had a sort of shorthand. Feeling further left with my left ski I found the parallel track and settled both skis firmly in the tracks. When Jim and Chuck were ready we set off. We went about thirty yards on this carriage trail and then took a left. This was the beginning of a long gradual downhill slope that I loved. Insuring I had my skis in the tracks I whooped and set off.

At first I took long graceful gliding strides, using my poles to propel me forward. As my speed reached the critical point where propulsion was no longer necessary I put my skis together, leaned forward, and began to fly. The wind whipped through my hair. Along with the sound of my skis flying over the snow came the sound of the stream below and to my right. Both of us ran along our appointed courses, free and joyful.

I knew I was going to pass the place where we needed to turn right but I didn't care. I never wanted to stop. When I reached the bottom of the hill I turned and headed back up to the intersecting carriage trail. Jim and Chuck were there waiting for me. The next part was short but tricky. "How do you want to do this," asked Jim. "Want me to go ahead and call you when I'm down or do you want me to ski behind you and tell you when to turn."

Considering the alternatives I said, "Behind me I think. That way you'll be closer the whole way and I'll be able to hear you more easily."

"Okay, go for it. The snow is pretty uniform along here, no tracks to really follow. I'll stay close behind you." I set off more slowly. This part was steeper and I knew I'd be flying again soon. The tricky part was the ninety degree turn to the left halfway down. I picked up speed.

"Left," called Jim. I angled my right ski to the left and leaned into it. "Okay, good," Jim called. "Now straighten up and go for it!" I did, and arrived breathless at the bottom of the hill.

Chuck had never seen us ski together. As he joined us he said, "You guys are incredible. It's like you're reading each other's minds. You make it look so easy. Sue, have you ever thought of skiing competitively?"

"No, not really," I replied. "It's so much fun, I wouldn't want to mess things up by having a training schedule or a real coach or anything like that."

We moved out again. As we crossed a bridge the stream was now on our left. We skied three abreast and talked as we moved along the carriage trail. "You guys don't know how lucky you are to live here," began Chuck. "I don't think I've heard the sound of a free flowing stream since I moved to California." We asked Chuck about his work for the guide dog school. He told us about all of the travel that he was doing. It was his job to fly all over the country and evaluate applicants to his school. "Oh, yes, the travel has its good aspects but it's getting a little old. I'm actually thinking of switching jobs at the school. I want to learn to train guide dogs."

By now we had reached the long uphill part of the trail. Talk ceased as we worked our way up the hill. Arriving slightly winded at the intersecting trail that would take us back to Jordan Pond House we rested. When we set off again we reached the part of the trail where Penobscot Mountain rose steeply on our left and dropped steeply on our right. I paused for a few minutes to take in the wide open space to my right. Then I set off again. There was one more nice little downhill part of the trail which took us to the Jordan Pond outflow stream. Then it was back up the hill to the parking lot. Divesting ourselves of skis and poles, we threw the lot in the back of the truck and headed home to a fire and hot soup.

37 | the competitive urge

HUCK'S COMMENT ABOUT COMPETING as a cross country skier kindled a spark. I contacted the United States Association of Blind Athletes, USABA, and inquired about upcoming competitions. It was too late for winter sports but the annual USABA summer games were on the horizon. That particular year the summer games were rolled into the National Games for Disabled Athletes.

"Jim," I began tentatively. "Think I could compete in the National Games next summer?"

"What, like in goalball or something?"

"Well, that's what I was thinking. But the problem is that there aren't enough women players in Maine to form a strong team."

During goalball practices around the state I usually had to play with the men. At tournament times we managed to put together a women's team but none of the other women wanted to compete at the National level.

"Why don't you swim."

Startled I looked at Jim and said, "There's an idea. I never thought of swimming." Swimming was just something I did. I had never swum competitively, never been coached, never even thought of swimming as a sport in which I could compete. "I like that Idea," I said, after some reflection.

"Well, you're good. I've watched you, and you're a good swimmer. Why not?"

Why not, indeed! I began swimming in earnest. There was no question about which stroke I should use. While I played around with backstroke and breaststroke, the crawl was my forte. I needed to decide at which distances I should compete.

Finding the swimming instructor beside the pool at the Y, I said, "Hey, John, I'm thinking of competing in swimming events this coming summer. What do you think?

"It's a great idea. Freestyle, I assume?"

"Yep, that's what I was thinking. Can you help me figure out which distances I'm best at?"

"I've watched you swim for the past several months. You'd do well at the longer distances, but I've never seen you go all out at shorter distances. This is a twenty-five meter pool. The shortest distance in competition is usually fifty meters. Go ahead, give it a shot. Go all out to the other end of the pool and back."

At slower speeds I could glide to the wall of the pool and make a graceful turn. Swimming as fast as I could, though, meant that I fairly slammed into the wall at the end of the second lap. "You okay," asked John.

"Yeah, I'm fine. It's going to take some practice, approaching turns when I'm swimming as fast as I can."

"Aside from that, I think you could compete well at the shorter distances." We settled on the events: 50, 100, and 1,600 meters, the longest of the events.

There was one other decision I had to make. Since I was thirty-five years old, I could compete in the open class *or* the masters. My original idea was to compete as a master in all of the events, but John encouraged me to choose the open class for the fifty-meter event. "It's your best distance," he said. "It would be way more prestigious to medal in the open class."

I swam. Gradually my turns at faster speeds became

smoother. I bought my plane ticket. Then my shoulders began to hurt. After describing the pain to John he said, "It's because you're crossing over the midline of your body at the top of each stroke." I tried changing my stroke but it all fell apart. I could only swim well if I just swam. Thinking about the placement of my arm at the top of each stroke slowed me down so much that it just didn't work. I decided to continue swimming the way I was rather than trying to do it correctly.

One morning, as I woke up, I groaned in pain. "What's wrong," asked Jim.

"It's my shoulders. They're killing me, both of them."

"Why don't you go ahead and take a shower? That usually helps doesn't it?" I just lay there. I knew that a hot shower would help but the hardest part was getting out of bed. I had to use the muscles in my shoulders to sit up and that first movement each morning was agony.

Each morning I lay there thinking that I just couldn't do it. I was so close. The games were just two weeks away. How could I quit? I had worked so hard to get here. I had raised money by speaking to civic organizations. I just couldn't quit.

"I've got to see a doctor," I said the next morning. "The pain always subsides to a dull roar once I'm up and have had a shower. But I think I've got to find out if going ahead with training and competition is going to do irreparable damage.

"Good idea," said Jim. He helped me find an orthopedist in Bangor who specialized in sports medicine and I made an appointment.

"What's the verdict?" asked Jim when I called him after seeing the doctor.

"He did X-rays and said there's nothing structurally wrong. It's all muscle and tendon damage. He doesn't think it's going to hurt for me to go ahead with the competition. He gave me a prescription for some pain medicine and told me to use ice after each practice and each event in the competition."

"So, you're going to go ahead with it?" asked Jim.

"Yep, I can do it. I've got an appointment with him for the week after I get home."

Ten days later I arrived at Hofstra University along with over three thousand other athletes. I registered for my events, was assigned a room in a dorm, and given a key. My first event, the sixteen hundred meter was that evening. I hadn't run into any of my friends by the time of the event so I had to loop Quoddy's leash around one of the bleachers and leave her alone. At the sound of the buzzer I dove in and began to swim. I was out of Quoddy's sight on the starting block. As I swam into her line of vision she barked. I made my turn at the end of the first lap and headed back. As I left Quoddy's line of sight she barked again. I almost choked with laughter. The event involved thirty-two laps and Quoddy barked once during each and every one of them.

I won the event. By then several friends had arrived and were there to cheer as the gold medal was placed around my neck. We all went out for a celebratory beer, and I fell in bed exhausted but thrilled.

I was awakened just before midnight by the coach of the Colorado women's goalball team. After introducing himself he said, "Look, I know you came to the games to swim. But Dr. Ponchillia says you're a pretty good goalball player. The problem is that we only brought three women for our goalball team and one of them is injured and can't play. We can't mount a team unless we have three players to start the tournament. You'd only have to play in one game and after that we can complete the tournament with only two players. Will you help us out? Will you play in the first game?"

By now I was wide awake. "Well," I began, "I can do that. As long as the game isn't during one of my swimming events."

"It isn't, I've already checked. Your other two events are day after tomorrow and the goalball competition begins tomorrow." The next morning found me using a magic marker to draw the number 3 on the back of the shirt that was given to me when I registered. I had never played any position other than right wing. But the team had a right wing and they asked me to play left wing instead. I didn't really have a horse in this race so I agreed. Completely relaxed I began the first game.

It was the best I had ever played. I scored goal after goal. I blocked everything that came in my direction. We won easily. The coach said, "I can't thank you enough. We can carry on from here." I was having a blast so I offered to play in the rest of the games that day. He agreed and I played in three or four more games. For the first time I played center. I was good at that too. We won every single game that day. It was easily the best goalball I had ever played.

The next day I took gold in the one hundred meter swim in the master class and silver in the fifty meter open class. Amazed, exhausted, and triumphant I returned to Maine.

38 | paying the price

When the dust settled I had to deal with my shoulders. I kept my appointment with the sports medicine doctor. He prescribed more pain pills and referred me to a physical therapist. It took no time at all before I was referring to Rob, the PT, as a physical terrorist. After doing an evaluation he recommended that I see him three times a week. Every Monday Wednesday and Friday I arrived at 3:30 and was ready for Jackie or Ralph to pick me up at 4:15.

Each therapy session began with me lying on a heating pad with other heating pads draped over my shoulders. In the beginning I could only do very gentle isometrics. Rob showed me how to use a doorjamb for resistance and press very gently with my arms in different positions. At the end of the exercises he had me lie down again and his assistant iced my shoulders. I had to do the exercises at home as well. Gradually the pain eased.

"From one to ten?" questioned Rob as I arrived for our next session. He asked this every time. I had to give him an estimate of my level of pain on a scale of one to ten with ten being the worst pain. When I started using numbers of one and two the next phase began.

"Okay, now that we've reduced your pain to a manageable level, the next step is to build up your muscles. We've got to do it in such a way that these muscles here," and he ran his hands over the top and front of my arms, "Are balanced by these," he indicated my triceps and the muscles down my side. I was reminded of my work, years before, with Oscar, my orientation and mobility instructor. Both Oscar and Rob took the time to explain, not just how to do something, but why it was done in a certain way.

During the long hours that I patiently and methodically did the exercises to repair the damage to my shoulders I thought about competition. What drove me to compete? Where did this desire, this urge, to compete come from?

Well, it was no different, really, than the everyday struggles of life. It was the same desire that led me to strive for excellence in everything. And working through any pain resulting from this drive for excellence was just part and parcel of the deal.

Then the letter from the USABA arrived. Jim read it to me that night. In amazement he read the last line, "On the basis of your performance at the National Games for Disabled Athletes, you are invited to try out for the 1992 Paralympic goalball team." I gazed at him in shock. Neither of us spoke for several minutes.

"Read that last line again," I said. He read it again.

Then he withdrew several other sheets of paper from the envelope. After a few minutes he said, "This is a spreadsheet of stats from the National Games." He looked at it for a few more minutes and said, "They've invited twelve people to try out. And look at this, you had the seventh-best performance of the lot."

When I woke up the next morning I felt excited without quite knowing why. Then I remembered the letter. Jim was still asleep so I woke him up gently by snuggling in his arms. "What do you think?" I whispered.

"Hmm...," he said sleepily. "What do I think about what?"

"The letter," I whispered.

"What letter?" I was trying to decide whether to grab the glass of water on the headboard and dump it on his head when he laughed. "I think it's exciting. Are you going to do it?"

"I really want to, but before I decide I want to make sure that I'm not going to screw up my shoulders again. I'm not at all keen on going through this physical terrorism again."

"Good point. When's your next appointment with Rob?"

"Tomorrow," I said. "I'll ask him then." We lay there for a little longer, listening to the waves washing ashore and thinking about this new adventure. After a while I said, "Do we have any videos of me, well, of anybody really, playing goalball? I need to explain it to Rob and it seems like a video would be the easiest way.

That night we hunted through every video we owned but found nothing useful. "I'll just have to take my goalball with me tomorrow and show him how it's played," I concluded.

"So, what do you think?" I asked Rob. I had just shown him how to throw and block.

"This is pretty exciting," he began. "I think you could do it but it's going to take some work. It's going to mean a shift in our approach here. What we've been doing so far, well, I've been working towards simply getting you to the point where you can do what you want to without injury. You know, the things we talked about in the beginning, cross country skiing, hiking with your dog, that kind of stuff. If you do this I recommend that you begin some real weight training. We can do most of it here but at some point you'll need to join the Y or a health club."

When I got home I told Jim of my conversation with Rob. "I don't know anything about weight training," I said. "Can you help me with that part?"

"Sure, it would be fun to do that together. What about goalball practice though. There aren't enough real practices in the state to equip you for something like Paralympic level competition."

I mulled that one over for a few minutes. "If you're going to help me with the weight training why don't you just become my coach? You're a good player and if we play against each other without you wearing a blindfold, well, I think that would work."

So, Jim became my coach. I began fundraising. I got permission to practice in the gym of the local elementary school. We joined a health club.

"If you're going to be doing weight training and regular goalball practice you're going to need to gain some weight," said Jim, a few weeks later. "Why don't you try that Ensure stuff?" I tried it. I hated it. I began to find places all across my territory that made milkshakes with real milk and real ice cream.

The next trick was to find a team to play with at the trials. I asked Paul Ponchillia for help. Paul played at the International level and knew players and coaches from all over the country. After many phone calls it was arranged. I would play with the Pennsylvania team at the Paralympic trials in Indianapolis.

39 | the trials

THE TIME CAME FOR THE PARALYMPIC TRIALS. I flew
to Kalamazoo and spent the night with Vicki who
had been my teammate the very first time I played
goalball. The next morning we headed for Indianapolis with
the rest of the Michigan team. It was evening when we arrived.
There was time only to register, receive the obligatory t-shirt,
locate our dorm room and hit the sack.

The next morning I met the Pennsylvania coach, Diane.
"Let me introduce you to the folks you'll be playing with," she
began. "This is Ellen McMahon and this is Maggie Ostrowski."

We shook hands and went into a huddle. "What position
do you usually play," Diane asked.

"I've played right wing mostly but I can play any position.
I so appreciate you letting me play with you, it doesn't really
matter." It turned out that Ellen and Maggie were flexible too
so we switched around, all of us playing in all three positions.
Diane secured half an hour in the smaller gym so that we
could get the feel of playing together. By the time of our first
game we were ready.

"Ball in play," called the referee, and we were off.

Once again I experienced the eerie silence of a gymnasium
filled with people. Once again I felt all eyes upon me as I dove,
blocked, passed, and threw. With disappointment I heard

the single shrill blast of the whistle if my throw went out of bounds. In elation I heard the two blasts of the whistle when my team scored.

Maggie, Ellen, and I played well together. Having just met them I nonetheless knew that we were all in this for the same purpose, to show to the Paralympic coach that we were good and should be chosen for the team. . When I played center I was careful to pass off the ball when I blocked it so that they could have a chance at scoring. When I played left or right wing they did the same, passing the ball off so that those of us playing wing could have the same chance.

"Okay," began Diane, as we gathered after the first game. "You did well, really well. Ellen, are you okay after taking that throw in your stomach?"

"I'd just as soon have taken it somewhere else," Ellen replied, "but, yeah, I'm okay."

"Maggie, that was a beautiful score, the one you slipped by their left wing. I swear they never even knew it was coming." Diane continued to analyze our performance, making suggestions for the next game. "You know, you'll be up against that woman who plays head games next, right? Don't let her casual 'Got it' bother you. I've watched her and I can tell you that her tone of voice is total fabrication. When she says 'Got it' in that bored sort of voice, well, half the time she's wincing from taking a throw in the gut."

Diane continued to give us pointers and encouragement. Then she said, "Okay, you've got at least two hours before you play again. What do you want to do?"

"I'm going to take a walk," I announced. The others stayed in the gym to watch the next couple of games. While I was walking outside I analyzed my performance in the last game. While it wasn't my best I thought I had played well. What could I do better in the next game? Maybe I should retain the ball and throw more often. Perhaps I should try throwing down the sideline more often. What could I do to get the Paralympic coach to really notice me?

I played center in the next game. The very first throw from the other team hit my hip and bounced up and hung in the air for a second. I made a wild grab for it and missed. They scored. That first mistake was followed by others, none of them glaring, but I was rattled. Instead of the easy free grace with which I had played in the Nationals last year my playing took on an edge of desperation. Instead of play it felt like work.

On the last afternoon we sat in the bleachers to learn who had been chosen for the Paralympic team that would go to Barcelona. My name was not called. I blew the air out of my puffed cheeks and sighed. At first I felt disappointment. Then I started to analyze again. Surely I had played better than some who had been chosen. What was wrong with that coach? I nursed my hurt feelings all the way back to Kalamazoo.

The flight from Detroit to Boston was not full. I found myself seated alone in the center section. Folding the arm rests up and out of the way I laid down and slept. Hearing Quoddy whine, I awakened. I stroked her head and laid there thinking. Then I smiled and sat up. "Come here, sweet girl," I said to Quoddy. Placing her paws on my knees, she stood up and licked my chin. "You know what?" I said to her, cupping her chin in my hand. "I'm done with competition." Quoddy just looked at me.

I sat back, still smiling. The pressure of trying to prove myself to an International level coach had changed everything. With half of my mind on the game I had the other half on the coach who would decide my fate. She, the coach, had taken on more importance than the joy of playing the game. I had not played my best and I had not even enjoyed it very much. I was done with competition at that level.

By the time I walked up the jetway in Bangor to meet Jim I was smiling. "What's up?" said Jim. He knew I hadn't made the team. When I had spoken with him on the phone following the selection of the Paralympic players he had heard the anger and disappointment in my voice. Leaning in to kiss me he said, again, "What's up?"

"I'm done with International level competition. I didn't play well and it just wasn't fun," I said. Resting his arm over my shoulders, Jim gave me a hug. Then we walked out of the airport into the February afternoon.

The very next weekend the snow on MDI was perfect for cross country skiing. This time we did the loop around Eagle Lake. After snapping my boots into the toe holds we set out side by side, with long easy strides. "This is what I like," I said, turning to Jim. "This is what I'm good at. This is what I like. Just skiing for the joy of skiing."

Laughing, Jim said, "Come on, I'll race you to the bridge," and we took off. This kind of competition was all right by me. Making the slight turn to the right after the bridge I accidentally crossed my left ski over my right and went flying. All those months ago, when Chuck suggested that I compete in cross country skiing, I had told him I didn't want to do that because it would take the joy out of skiing.

I laughed and picked myself up. Back on my feet I set out with unconscious easy grace. Joy.

40 | clear as a bell

O N THE WORK FRONT there were some exciting
developments. Rehab teachers from all over the
state came together to develop a body of practice
for providing low vision services. Working with Pauline Beale,
an optometrist who was a specialist in low vision, and Karen
Cote, one of the true giants in the field of low vision, the
system began to take shape. When I worked at the Tennessee
Rehab Center, we needed someone on staff to teach students
to use their vision and low vision aids. I had turned to Steve
Erhnst. Steve was the supervisor of the low vision department
at the Southeastern Blind Rehab Center of the Department of
Veterans Affairs. I had worked, one on one, with Steve for two
weeks. That work allowed me to enter into the establishment
of the low vision program in Maine with gusto and confidence.

The first step was to determine if the client was a candidate
for low vision services. This could usually be done through an
interview. Indicators of possible success had almost nothing
to do with visual acuity or the client's ability to use his vision
going into a low vision intervention. A much better indicator of
success was a strong motivation to perform a specific task. The
person who lived alone and was responsible for reading mail,
paying bills, and following recipes was a better candidate than
the one who said, "I want to see better." The more specific the

goal the better the chances for success. Some clients feared that naming the task they really wanted to do would lead to failure. This is where good interview skills came in. If I thought there was something about which the client was holding back I'd work hard to tease it out.

Lillian was a good candidate. She lived alone in the remote town of Greenville near Moosehead Lake in the western mountains. She needed to read her mail, pay bills, and read packaging and directions in the kitchen. She wanted to continue her knitting and weekly bridge game with other residents of the apartment complex. "Hello, Lillian," I said when she opened her door to me. "It's good to see you again." This was my fourth visit with Lillian. During the first three I had marked her appliances and thermostat, helped her develop a plan for keeping her medications straight and determined that she was a good candidate for our low vision program. Settling in my usual chair I said, "Today I'm going to begin teaching you to use your vision better." Lillian knew that this was the plan, and she was eager to get started.

"The first thing we'll do in preparation for your low vision exam with the doctor is get you using your vision as well as you can. That way the doctor will have a better shot at prescribing just the right devices." Lillian had macular degeneration which causes problems with seeing straight ahead and in seeing fine detail. "Have you ever noticed that you can seem to see something out of the corner of your eye, but when you look straight at it you can't see it anymore?"

"Why, yes, dear," said Lillian. "It happens to me all the time. Why is that?"

"The problems you're having with your vision, the macular degeneration, well it has blanked out some of your straight ahead vision. So, the first thing we need to do is figure out where your remaining vision is. Does that make sense?"

"Yes, dear, it does. But how can you figure it out?"

Handing Lillian a piece of paper on which a clock face had been photocopied, minus the hands, I asked her if she could see the big dot in the middle.

"Yes, yes, I can see it," she assured me.

"Okay, what I want you to do is to try to point your eyes right at the dot. You may not be able to see the dot but that doesn't matter. Can you do that?"

"Well, would you just look at this," exclaimed Lillian. "You're absolutely right. When I look straight at where I know that dot is it disappears."

"Okay, good, that's what we expect; there's nothing wrong with that. Now, try to keep your eyes pointing right at that dot. Don't move them. Can you see any of the numbers around the face of the clock?"

I waited for Lillian to speak.

"This is so strange," she finally said. "I could swear that I see *10*, *11*, and *12* for a second, but when I try to see them more clearly they vanish. Why is that?"

This was good. I could work with this.

"It's perfectly natural to try to look straight at whatever you're trying to see. After all you've been doing that all your life. Now, because of those blanked out pieces of your vision, you need to learn to see things when you're not looking straight at them."

Taking the picture of the clock back, I handed Lillian another sheet of paper. There were single letters in 7M print spread all over the page. There were large spaces, both vertically and horizontally, between the letters. Moving directly in front of Lillian, I rested my hands gently on the back of the page. "Okay, Lillian," I began, "I want you to try pointing your eyes straight at the center of this piece of paper. Then I want you to tap the paper at each place where you can see some of the letters on the page."

I waited. "There's an *S* right here," said Lillian. "And a *Z* just here. And I think this is a *K*." I had my right hand resting gently on the upper right of the page, and I felt her taps all on my hand.

"Okay, well done," I said. "Now, let's begin learning to use your vision again."

I took out the 3M reading exercises taken from Dee Quillman's book *Low Vision Training Manual.* I also took out my braille version of the same exercise. Handing Lillian the print version of the exercise, I instructed her to open the booklet to the first page.

"In this first exercise you'll see that there are single letters printed on each line. As we progress the exercises will present words and sentences but these single letter exercises will help us get started. Are you ready?"

"Yes, dear, what do you want me to do?"

"From the work we just did, you'll be able to see things better if you point your eyes below and to the right of whatever it is you're trying to see. Go ahead and try it. Look just below and to the right of the upper-left-hand corner of the page."

When Lillian successfully identified the first letter I told her to keep her eyes still and slide the booklet to the left until the next letter came into view.

"When you have to view eccentrically it takes a lot more work to move and refocus your eyes so moving the print while maintaining your focus is much more effective."

Lillian worked hard that day and on all of our successive visits. I left her with materials so that she could practice on her own. "Think of it as being in training," I told her. "You're in training to read your mail and pay your bills. You're in training so that you can keep playing bridge every Wednesday. The more you train the easier it will be and the better you'll do," I concluded.

Lillian progressed through the entire 3M exercises but the 2M was just too small for her. It was time for her low vision exam.

"Hi, Dr. Beale," I said as we entered the exam room. "This is Lillian. Lillian, this is Dr. Beale, who's going to do the exam. Lillian seated herself in the exam chair, and I settled in my accustomed chair over to the side. Dr. Beale liked to have the rehab teachers at the exams because we could give her valuable information about the preparatory work we had done. At the end of the exam, Lillian declared that she was exhausted. But she was also elated. Using trial lenses and a hand held magnifier, she had just read one of her knitting patterns. Lillian picked out a frame for her new glasses and was issued an illuminated hand held magnifier and some reading glasses.

"What happens next dear?" said Lillian as we headed back north.

"Dr. Beale will ship your glasses to me next week," I began. "I'll bring them to you and then make sure you know how to use them properly."

"Well, that sounds just great," she replied. "You know, I have those reading glasses now. My bridge game is tomorrow. Would it be okay to use them?"

"Of course it would. You can compare using the glasses with regular playing cards and not using them with the large-print cards. That's a great idea. Then you can decide which way works best for you."

The next week I arrived with Lillian's glasses. "How did the bridge experiment work?" I asked her.

"Oh, my dear, it was a disaster," she opined. "I just couldn't keep the cards in focus so we switched back to the large-print playing cards."

Once we were settled at Lillian's kitchen table she produced the regular print cards and asked if we could start there. I had her put on the reading glasses and pick up one of the cards. With one hand resting gently on her head and the other on the back of the hand with which she held the playing card I immediately saw what the problem was.

"Bring the card closer to your face," I instructed her. "Keep coming, keep coming." When I knew that the card was closer to her face than the focal distance Dr. Beale had recommended I said, "Okay, now, move the card away from your face, slowly, slowly. Remember to look below and slightly to the right of the top left corner where the number and suit are located."

"There!" said Lillian in triumph. "There, that's just perfect. I can see it clear as a bell. How did you know what to do?" She placed the card back on the table and took off the glasses. Looking at me she said, "I worried all week long that these glasses weren't going to work. And you walk in the door and have everything working perfectly in about five minutes." Placing her hand on mine she simply said, "Thank you."

"You're welcome, Lillian. Are you ready to work with the illuminated hand-held magnifier?"

When Lillian answered in the affirmative, I asked her to get a package from the kitchen.

"Choose something that's in a box," I suggested. I wanted something with a rigid flat surface.

"Here's my box of cream of wheat. Will that do?"

"That's perfect," I told her. "When you use this magnifier you always want it placed firmly flat on the surface of whatever you're trying to see, like this. Then you move the whole thing, box and magnifier to your eye until things come into focus." Lillian read the directions on the box with only a little hesitation. The more we worked the better she did. After about twenty minutes I called a halt. "You're doing really, really well Lillian," I told her. "Rest your eyes now."

In the end, Lillian achieved all of her goals. Her determination, coupled with the specific tasks that she wanted to accomplish insured that she had the best shot at success. It was after my work with Lillian that I decided to submit a paper for a presentation at International AER. AER is short for the Association for the Education and Rehabilitation of the Blind and Visually Impaired. The conference that year was held in Los Angeles. The paper was accepted and I did my first presentation to an international audience the following July.

41 | log house, maine woods

THE PREVIOUS MARCH the realtor who owned our house
let us know that they were lowering the price and
beginning to more aggressively market it. Even the
lower price was way out of reach for us so we began to look
inland for a house that we could afford to buy.

We found the log house on ten acres in north Ellsworth.
We were both enchanted with it. Most of the downstairs was
one open room. The living room and dining area were beneath
a cathedral ceiling pierced by two huge skylights. The dining
room was adjacent a large kitchen with an island tiled in blue.
The kitchen counters were tiled in the same blue. A bedroom
and bathroom completed the downstairs. In the center of
the house was a wood stove on a brick hearth. The chimney
soared up through the cathedral ceiling. A flight of stairs rose
behind the chimney to a balcony overlooking the living room
and dining area. Off the balcony was a loft bedroom with the
ceiling sloping almost all the way down to the floor on either
side. There were two smaller skylights in the ceiling of the loft
bedroom.

We made an offer on the house and the cogs of purchasing
real estate went into motion.

When I was eight or nine my parents rented a horse
trailer and we took my pony to the farm in Mississippi. For

the entire week before we left for the farm I was full of excited anticipation. It was like a great dream coming true. I kept climbing the pecan tree in the front yard and coming to rest on what I called my thinking limb. I'd sit up there and think of all the fun Tony the Pony and I were going to have on the farm. That's exactly how I felt now, like something wonderful was about to happen.

Then we hit a snag. The water test showed high radon. At the time, the EPA had no guidelines for how much radon could be present in water. It did have guidelines for the amount of radon that was supposed to be safe in the air and the house passed the air test. The problem was that radon in water is released when the water is agitated, when you take a shower, flush the toilet, or use the washing machine. The owners of the house had been gone for almost two weeks when the tests were done so we didn't feel that the tests were valid.

"So, how do you get radon out of the water?" I asked Jim.

"I've been looking into it and it's going to be a problem," he began. "The cheapest and easiest way to do it is to run the water through a carbon filter. The radon gets trapped in the carbon and then you just have to change the filter every three months or so. The problem is that those carbon filter systems turn into a low level nuclear waste dump and have to be put in a basement or something."

"And since the house is on a slab, that won't work for us." I said.

"No, it won't." Continuing, he said, "There is this new method of filtering radon but it's really expensive.

It's a tank that holds about fifteen gallons of water. When the tank is full it's agitated for a few minutes and the radon gets released. Then it's vented out of a pipe that has to be higher than any opening in the house like a window. That's so the radon can't be drawn back into the house."

"Where the heck would we put such a thing?" I asked.

The house was really small. "I mean, how big is this thing?"

Eventually we worked it out. We found a company in Orington that was willing to install the radon purifier. We paid for the purifyer and its installation. The people who owned the house built an attached room off the back of the house to put the purifier in. We closed on our first house in early October.

Oh, did we love that house. We put our bed in the loft bed room. With the two skylights and the three big windows that faced south, it was like sleeping in a tree house. The glass doors in the living room opened onto a small deck, then there was an open area which was the closest thing we ever had to a yard. Aside from this open area the property was heavily wooded. The further from the road we got the rougher the terrain became. There were huge granite boulders that looked like a bear might den under them in the winter. There was a small stream that ran across the back of the property. Hanson's Landing Road ended at Branch Lake about half a mile from our driveway. We thought it was just about perfect.

What the house didn't have was storage space. There was no basement, no garage, nowhere to put things like lawn mowers, our canoe, roto tiller or anything. We had to put all of that into storage for the time being. "we've got to build a shed or something," said Jim one November morning.

"Okay," I replied. "do you know how to build a shed?" I asked hopefully. "Because I don't have a clue."

"No, not really," he said. "But I've stopped at Hammond Lumber Company a couple of times now and I think they have what we need." A couple of weeks later they delivered the materials and left them on two pallets in the driveway. "Hmmm," said Jim, over and over again as he walked around the materials on the two pallets.

"Hmmm, what?" I asked.

"I'm just wondering if we can actually do this ourselves."

"Hang on, let me go get the instructions." Jim spent the

next half hour or so walking around the materials with the instructions for assembling the shed in his hand. "Okay, so the trusses are already assembled and they're on the first pallet." He walked around muttering. "These must be the particle board flooring pieces." He walked and muttered some more. "Cinder blocks to put the main support beams on. Shingles. Nails . . . Okay, I think I understand how it goes together."

I was glad he thought he understood because I was still clueless. We spent our first Thanksgiving weekend building the shed in the rain, the drizzle, and the fog, oh my.

"Let's put it right over here," said Jim on Thanksgiving morning. The spot was about twenty or twenty-five feet away from the house on the other side of the driveway. "It's relatively flat," he continued. "We'll have to angle it a little to get it between the trees." We measured and placed the cinder blocks at each corner with another cinder block halfway along the sixteen foot length. Then we laid the heavy beams, making an eight by sixteen foot rectangle. We worked steadily in the drizzle and by the end of the day we had the shed framed up.

Exhausted we came inside and dried off. "I'm going to build a fire," said Jim.

"Sounds great," I replied. I know it's Thanksgiving and everything but I'm pooped. What do you want for dinner?" We ended up having peanut butter and jelly sandwiches in front of the wood stove and then we went to bed.

We got off to a great start the next morning by installing the first two pieces of flooring sideways. "Oh, shit," said Jim. "I see what we did now. They should have been horizontal and we put them in vertically."

"Should we rip them out and put them in properly?" I began.

"No way, They're just going to have to do the way they are. I'm not ripping anything out. But we'll do the other two pieces correctly. That'll just have to do."

By now I had hit my left index finger one too many times with my hammer. I've got it," I said triumphantly. Running in the house I grabbed my left ski glove which was heavily padded. It did the trick. I hit my finger plenty more times but the glove kept me from injuring my finger more than it already was.

It was when we were nailing the T111 sheets of plywood to the back of the shed that Jim accidentally hit me in the head with his hammer. He was tapping the edge of the plywood, trying to move it over an inch or so and the hammer slipped. "Oh, my God, are you okay?" he almost shouted. I dropped my own hammer and plunked down on the wet ground and just laughed. He had not hit me very hard but his reaction was over the top. He must have thought I was dilerious from the blow to my head since I just sat there and laughed and laughed. He knelt in front of me and took my face in his hands.

"Oh, there's one for the books!" I chortled. "How to murder your wife with a hammer and make it look like an accident." He sat down beside me and we leaned against the back wall of the shed. We just sat there listening to the rain dripping from the trees. First, one of us would laugh. Then the other would take up the laughter.

"Okay, let's get this finished," Jim said. By the end of the second day we had everything done except for putting the shingles on the roof. Once more we fell into bed, exhausted.

On Saturday morning we commenced a crash course in shingling a roof. For some reason the instructions for this part of the process weren't clear. I called Hammond Lumber. "The first course of shingles go on upside down," he began.

"Hold on," I said, "What's a course?"

Sighing, the man resigned himself to talking a bimbo through the process of shingling a roof. He gave me instructions for putting the first row of shingles on the roof. "Hang on," I said, "I'm just going to tell my husband what to do." I ran outside and related the information to Jim. Back inside I grabbed the phone. "Okay, what's next." It took several trips in and out of the house but we finally got the hang of it.

Jim was fine working from a ladder. Since our fall from the cliff in Tennessee he wasn't comfortable actually climbing up on the roof to nail in the upper courses of shingles so I did that part. By mid afternoon we were finally finished. We stepped back and looked at our masterpiece. We still had the one by four trim to do but it was essentially complete. We jumped in the truck, drove to the storage building and brought everything home. It took three trips to get it all but what a feeling of accomplishment. On Sunday we rested.

42 | ice and snow

WE HAD SNOW EARLY THAT YEAR. By the second week of December we had already received over a foot of snow when Jim and I made a delightful discovery. A fire road about a hundred yards from our house wound through the woods and ended at a summer camp, Camp Jordan. "Why do you think they plow this fire road?" mused Jim.

"Who knows," I replied, as I snapped my toes into the bindings of my skis. "Great for us though." If we had a heavy snow they plowed the road leaving snowbanks on either side. They didn't plow it all the way down to the ground though. For whatever reason they left several inches of snow which was perfect for skiing.

Just before the third weekend of December we got three more inches of snow. They wouldn't bother to plow that small amount of snow from the fire road and I knew the conditions would be perfect.

"Hey Jim," I called from the kitchen. "Do you want to go skiing?"

From the living room in front of the wood stove Jim said, "Nah, I feel like I'm coming down with a cold." Jim had mentioned that he had a tickle in his throat that morning and, though I was expecting it, I was disappointed. I continued to load the dish washer thinking regretfully that I was going to miss the opportunity to get out and ski this weekend.

"I really want to go skiing," I began. Then I thought, Well, why not? Why not just go skiing by myself? I put on my boots, got my gloves, put on my down vest and a head band and simply announced, "I'm going skiing."

"You're what?" said Jim. He turned to look at me just as I reached for Quoddy's harness. "You're going to go skiing by yourself?"

"Yes, I've got it all figured out. I'm going to walk down to the fire road and ski to the lake and back." I'll put Quoddy's collar bell on before we start out." I paused and said, "Okay?" It was a funny feeling. I had never done this before and, while I felt fairly confident, I didn't want to sound like I was asking permission.

"Taking a deep breath Jim said, "Okay, just be careful."

Exhilarated, I harnessed Quoddy, bundled my skis and poles together, and with them slung over my right shoulder I set out into the silent world. As I walked down to the road to Camp Jordan I took great lungfulls of air. An occasional breeze dislodged snow from the branches of the spruce and fir trees and it fell to the ground with a whisper. Quoddy turned into the fire road. I directed her to walk the fifteen or so yards into the woods and she stopped at the chain across the road. Unbuckling her harness and leash I hung them over one of the posts that held the chain. I ducked under the chain and got ready. Before setting out I called Quoddy to me, clipped on her collar bell, and told her to stay close. Of course this was meaningless to Quoddy but it felt like insurance. In truth, when we had skied the week before, she had stayed right behind me the whole time.

We set out. "Yo, dog!" I called. Quoddy was in front of me. I heard the bell on her collar but, for the first time, I realized that I could see her black back against the white snow as she trotted past. I could actually see her. I had to look down and to the right in order to do it but I could see her. "Come back here where you belong," I called. She did and we continued on our way. Then I thought, heck, if I can see her it would be better if she was in front of me. During the long flat stretch at the beginning I started trying to teach her to stay in front of me. I'd point my ski pole straight ahead, make encouraging noises and praise her when she moved out in front of me. It turned into a game.

We paused at the top of the steep hill and I caught my breath. "Okay, poopy dog, go-go-go-go!"

To my amazement she trotted out and I followed her. I could actually follow her visually. Wow! This was great. The downhill slope increased and I had to snowplow to keep from running over her. Then I crossed the tips of my skis and went flying. Quoddy ran to me and started trying to lick my face. "Stop it already," I said, covering my face as she tried to lick me. "It wasn't your fault. Stop!"

I just sat there in the snow and played with Quoddy for a few minutes.

"Come on goof ball," I said, climbing to my feet.

The rest of the trip to the edge of the lake was uneventful. The lake had started to freeze but there was still plenty of open water.

We turned and headed back up the long gradual slope. Poised at the top of the hill I looked down at the steep slope ahead of me. Again, I pointed my ski pole down the hill and told Quoddy to go-go-go. And she went. Full of amazement that I could do this I followed her visually. Wow, it was so much fun. When we got to the bottom I promptly turned around, calling Quoddy to come with me, and we went back up the hill. We came down together two more times before heading home.

"Jim," I called as I entered the house. "You're not going

to believe what I just did."

Jerking out of a doze in his recliner Jim said, "What, What did you just do?"

"I followed Quoddy visually. It was incredible. I've never tried to do it before because you've always been there to guide me. But, I don't know, on my own, I just tried it and it worked. It was so much fun!"

"Wow, that really is a surprise. That's really wonderful sweetie."

The next day I was ready to do it all over again. "I'm going skiing," I announced.

"Okay, just be careful," he said, just as he had said the day before.

When we got to the fire road I got everything ready and we set out. It didn't work. Today I could see absolutely nothing. What was going on. I knew Quoddy was right there in front of me because I could hear her collar bell but I could get no visual information at all. *What was going on?* Then it hit me. Yesterday had been overcast. Today was a bright clear day. The sun shining on the snow was washing everything out.

Oh, well, slightly disappointed I couldn't repeat the experience of yesterday, I skied to the lake and back not bothering to try to see anything. It was no problem to stay on the road because of my tracks from yesterday and the snowbanks on either side of the road.

When I entered the house Jim asked, "How was it?"

"Oh, it was all right. But I couldn't see anything like I could yesterday. It has to be because of the sun."

"Ah, yes, so you could see yesterday when it was overcast but not today when it was bright and sunny!" Continuing, Jim asked, "Could you ski okay?"

"Yep, it was fine, but it was a little disappointing. But you know what? Just discovering that I could do it visually was incredible. And next time it's an overcast day, well, now I know

I can do it whenever the conditions are right."

Jim got up and hugged me. "Never a dull moment with Miss Sue!"

We didn't get any more snow for a month. In early January we went into ten days of bone chilling weather. It got down in the minus 20's every night and didn't go above freezing during the day. The first weekend of this cold snap we walked down to Camp Jordan with our ice skates. Even before we got to the lake we could hear the booming. "Wow," said Jim, as we walked out onto the dock. "That's the loudest that booming sound has ever been."

We stood there for a few minutes just listening. "What do you think causes that again," I asked.

"When the lake freezes solid there's a space of air between the bottom of the ice and the surface of the water. Because Branch Lake is spring fed I think that causes the water to move beneath the ice. I guess the booming sounds come from when the lake bumps up against the bottom of the ice."

"Whatever, it's so eerie." At that precise moment Quoddy grabbed the laces of my skates, which were tied together, and dragged them a few feet back along the dock towards the shore. She dropped the skates and galloped all the way back to the shore. When she got there she sat down and just looked at us. We both burst out laughing. Almost incoherent I said, "It's like she's trying to tell me not to go out on the ice. Like the booming has her all freaked out and she's trying to prevent me from putting on my skates."

Controlling his laughter Jim said, "She's just playing, of course, but it does seem like Miss Dog is trying to tell you something."

We ended up not going skating that day. It had only been really cold for a few days and we just weren't sure about the ice. The cold weather continued for the next week and by the following weekend we judged that the ice would definitely be safe for skating. Instead of walking to the lake via Camp Jordan we left Quoddy and Iris at home and drove to the boat landing at the end of the road. Walking out on the ice, we took off our boots and put on our skates. Jim took off. He's a very good skater. I watched and listened to the sound of his skates as he zipped around.

The fun part about skating on the lake, at least for me, was that I could just go. There was nothing to run into so I could skate as fast and as far as I liked. I started out, a little wobbly at first, but once I got started I skated and skated.

"Sue," yelled Jim. "Head back in this direction." I turned and we skated towards each other. As he approached Jim started skating in circles around me. Then he skated straight at me. It all happened so fast. We both fell. The next thing I felt was the tip of one of Jim's skates stabbing into my ribs. It knocked the breath out of me.

"Are you okay?" I asked. Jim didn't say anything. "Are you okay," I repeated, crawling across the ice to his head.

"Yeah . . . " He stopped, waited a minute, and tried again. "Yeah, I hit my face on the ice." He was speaking very quietly. I waited for more.

Slowly he sat up. "I've never felt anything like that before. Talk about seeing stars."

I didn't know what to say so I waited.

Finally getting to his feet Jim said, "I've never broken a bone so I'm not sure, but something's wrong with my face. I'm going to have to go to the hospital. We made our way back to the car and headed for town.

"Hello," said the doctor as he entered the room. "You fell on the ice, right?" Then he added, "Oh, you went to Sewanee?" Jim was wearing my Sewanee sweat shirt that was too big for me.

"No, it's my wife's." Jim replied. "And yes, I fell on the ice and hit my face."

"Okay," said the doctor, when he came back in the room with Jim's X-rays. You've cracked the zygomatic bone just below your left eye." He pointed to the spot on the X-ray film. "There's nothing to be done about it except let it heal. There's a slight danger of injuring your optic nerve if the optic nerve gets into the crack and gets caught."

Jim digested the information and said, "How would I know? How would I know if the optic nerve got pinched in the crack?"

"It's most likely to happen when you're looking up. You'll experience diplopia, I mean . . . "

"I know what diplopia is," said Jim. "So, if I experience double vision what do I do?"

"I suggest that you contact your ophthalmologist or, if it's not during regular business hours come back here. If you want to put ice on it that might keep the swelling down and I'll write you a prescription for some pain medication."

Something stirred inside me. "You know, I've been having trouble with migraines. If oral medication doesn't work I end up in the emergency room and have to get a shot of Demerol and Phenergan. Could I try using oral narcotics instead?" After much discussion I walked out with a prescription for darvocet.

"I can't believe you just did that." We were back in the car and Jim was furious. "I have a broken bone in my face, and you somehow manipulate the doctor into giving you," he stressed the word *you*, "a prescription for narcotics! I can't believe you did that."

"Well, if it means I can avoid going to the emergency room the next time I have a migraine, won't it be worth it?"

"Oh, that's not the point. You are so damned manipulative." Shaking his head, he said, again, "I can't believe you did that."

43 | the sacred and profane

SINCE THAT FIRST TIME I RECEIVED A SHOT OF DEMEROL and Phenergan for a migraine when we lived in Michigan I had gone to the ER on several occasions. I did so responsibly for years. I was too busy living my life to allow the narcotics to take over. During the period of time when I was in so much pain with my shoulders leading up to and immediately following the National Games for Disabled Athletes, I took the oral pain medication as directed and only when I needed it. When I asked for those narcotics when Jim was in the ER with his facial fracture I crossed a line. I sought the narcotics for the feelings of bliss they provided, not for the relief of legitimate pain.

It all might have ended when the fifteen Darvocet prescribed by a doctor in the ER were gone.

My next doctor made a mistake. Instead of giving me a new prescription for a non-narcotic medicine I had been taking she prescribed a narcotic medicine with a similar name.

Wow, thirty Darvocet. How cool was this? I had thirty Darvocet and a year of refills. Demerol gave me a feeling of blissful oblivion. I floated away with no concerns about anything. I didn't even try to function. Darvocet, on the other hand, gave me a different feeling of bliss. I felt I could function just fine. In fact, I felt I could function better than usual. I felt powerful. Here came those feelings of power and control that bulimia had given me. And now, with my bottle of thirty Darvocet in hand, came the secrecy. I wasn't sure what Jim would say if he knew that my doctor had prescribed thirty Darvocet, but I didn't want to find out. It was my secret.

The previous winter I had taken a graduate course in psychology at the University of Maine. The course was taught by Geoff Thorpe. It met for three hours one afternoon per week. Coincidentally, Geoff lived on Phillips Lake just up the road from our house. My driver would drop me off at the university and Geoff took me home at the end of the class. It was about an hour's drive which gave us plenty of time to visit. On the way home one afternoon Geoff mentioned that he was going to choir practice that evening. I asked Geoff about the group with which he sang. That's how I learned of the Acadia Choral Society.

The Acadia Choral Society sang two concerts a year, one in December and one in May. As the summer passed I kept telling myself that I needed to call Shirley Smith, the director. Geoff had given me Shirley's phone number months ago. Finally, in August, I picked up the phone.

"Hi, Shirley, my name is Sue Martin. I took a class from Geoff Thorpe last winter. He told me all about the Acadia Choral Society. I'd like to see if I can sing with you this fall."

"Well sure," began Shirley. "Tell me about yourself. Tell me what experience you have." I told Shirley about singing in the choir at St. Mary's in Birmingham, singing with the elite Octette at summer camp, and singing with the Sewanee choir. "Well sure, we'd love to have you sing with us. We want to give the opportunity to anyone who is interested."

"Oh, great," I began. "Can you tell me a little bit about the music the group will be singing this semester?"

Shirley named the three works that would be on the program in December. I was already familiar with one of them, and I knew I'd be able to find recordings of the other two.

"There's one other thing," I began. "I'm blind and I haven't done this kind of singing since I became blind. But I'm sure I can do it. As long as I can get recordings of the works we're going to sing my husband can help me with the words. I'll just braille them out myself."

Then I held my breath.

After a minute Shirley said, "Do you by any chance work a guide dog? A German Shepherd guide dog?"

This was such an unexpected question that I was taken aback.

"Well, yes, yes, I work a guide dog, and yes, she's a shepherd."

"And did you recently move to north Ellsworth, somewhere near Winkumpaugh Road?"

Mystified, I said, "Yes, we bought a house on Hanson's Landing Road last October."

"Then I've seen you. I've seen you working your dog. I live in this neighborhood."

Shirley and I chatted for a bit more. She asked if I'd like to ride with her to choir rehearsals. I thanked her and told her that I'd be riding with Geoff.

The second Tuesday after Labor Day rehearsals began. The first thing Shirley did was pass out cassette tapes.

"You're singing soprano, right?" said Shirley, offering me one of the tapes. It turned out that Shirley made a recording for each section of the chorus. She'd play a professional recording of each work while playing the notes sung by each section on her digital keyboard. This was perfect for me. It made learning the music much easier.

I loved choir rehearsals. We didn't just learn the music and sing it, there was much more involved. Shirley taught us about the music during rehearsals. Sometimes she would bring in recordings of other works for comparison to the works we were singing. She taught us breathing exercises. She taught us that there is no long *A* in Latin.

"No, stop," said Shirley. "There is no long *a* in Latin." We had done it again. "It's not *kyri-a*," and she stressed the long *a* sound at the end, the way we had just sung it. "It's *kyri-eh*," she said, making a soft *e* sound at the end of the word.

The next time I was in the office, I had an idea. Photocopying the necessary letters from a large-print calendar, I made a little sign. When I was done, I had the words 'There is no *A* in Latin' on two pieces of paper. I took them home, stapled them to two pieces of cardboard, and stapled the cardboard to a small stick. In the end, it looked like the kind of sign protesters carry.

At the next choir rehearsal, I waited. Sure enough, when we sang the *Kyrie*, enough of us sang it with the long *a* for Shirley to stop us in exasperation. "Okay," she began.

Interrupting her I said, "Here Shirley, this might help," and I handed over my little sign. Laughing, she held up the sign and the entire chorus broke into laughter. For the rest of the rehearsals that little sign lay on the piano, ready for deployment should we forget how to pronounce *Kyrie*.

I really wanted to do my job, enjoy life in rural Maine, and participate with Acadia. The only problem was my headaches. They were making it very difficult. They were becoming regular and constant. The medication couldn't touch them.

~~~

"No wonder you're having headaches, your sinuses are a mess."

It was a month after the Acadia concerts and I was finally getting to the bottom of the cause of my head pain. It was Dr. Grant, an otolaryngologist who gave the verdict. "I want to do sinus surgery as soon as possible." The date for the surgery was set for the second week in January.

"Oh," I groaned.

"Hi sweetie," said Jim, getting up from the chair where he had been sitting. "How do you feel?"

"Like a truck ran over me. What's this thing under my nose?"

"It's to catch any blood that might drip out of your nose," said Jim.

"What?" I replied. "So, it's sort of like an oil drip pan under a car?" And we both laughed. "Ouch," I muttered and stopped laughing.

Over the next four days we got into a routine. Jim would bring Quoddy, harnessed, to my room each morning. She'd sniff her way right around the room, evidently checking for marauding aliens. Then she'd jump her front feet up on the bed, sniff me up and down, and then settle on a blanket on the floor to keep guard. After my first cup of dreadful hospital coffee Jim also began bringing me a good cup of coffee from the kiosk across from the hospital.

When the time came, Dr. Grant removed the gauze packing from my sinuses. I had been looking forward to this as I had been breathing through my mouth and sounding like Donald Duck every time I spoke. When he finished I said, "I still can't breathe through my nose."

"Yes, don't worry about that. I'll have the nurses use saline to irrigate your sinuses. Gradually they'll clear up. But, under no circumstances are you to blow your nose or try to force anything. It will clear on its own."

Two days later, armed with a new prescription for pain meds, and strict instructions from Dr. Grant to take them only as directed, Jim brought me home.

44 | the brattleboro retreat

THE FIRST WEEK AT HOME WASN'T PLEASANT. I brought home several bottles of sterile saline and irrigated my sinuses four times a day. I was still in a lot of pain and tried my best to take the narcotics only as directed. Gradually my sinuses opened up, a tiny bit at first, and only on one side. Even the ability to breathe a little bit through one side felt like a triumph. After a week I went back to work. After two weeks I went back to Dr. Grant for a follow up visit.

"Yes," he began. "Yes, this is much better. How is your pain?"

"I've been able to work for the past week and, while I still have some level of pain almost all the time, I think it's getting better. I've done pretty well at keeping at the recommended dosages of the narcotics."

"Okay, that's good," he said. "For the next two weeks I want you to just continue what you've been doing this last week. Do your job, you can start taking short walks with your dog but don't go climbing any mountains, okay?"

Laughing, I said, "Okay, sure. Sounds like a plan. When do you want to see me again?"

"I'd like you to come back in two more weeks. If everything is okay then I'll release you to your normal activities."

I managed to make the narcotics last until almost the end

of the next two weeks but I ran out a few days before my next appointment. I had a constant low level pain in my head for two full days leading up to the next time I saw Dr. Grant.

After examining me he said, "Things are looking really good. I'm pleased with how you've handled the irrigation. Everything looks clean and healthy in there. I don't think we need any further appointments. I'd like to see you in six months just to make sure everything is still good."

"Okay," I said slowly. "But, Dr. Grant, what about the pain. I'm out of the narcotics and my head still hurts." For good measure I added, "And sometimes the pain is still pretty bad."

"Ah," he said. "Ah, yes, I was afraid this was going to come up. We had to use those drugs. I'm not going to prescribe anymore narcotics for you. You're going to have to do without the drugs." He waited.

What had I been thinking? Of course the narcotics had to come to an end. Summoning up some bravado I said, "Okay then, I'll have to do without them."

In a few days the bravado was gone. I felt as though the medical establishment had deserted me. I had nowhere to turn, no one to ask for help. A few days later I gave in and called the local walk-in clinic and asked to speak to the doctor on duty.

"Hi, it's Sue Martin. I had surgery recently and find myself in more pain than I can deal with."

Silence on the other end of the line. I knew this wasn't going to work, but I was desperate enough to push on. "If I come in would you be willing to give me a shot of demerol?"

"Absolutely not," said the doctor. "I'm sorry, you're going to have to go back to whoever did your surgery if you're still in pain."

Disappointed, I hung up.

In the end I returned to Dr. Grant. I was pretty sure he wouldn't give me any more narcotics but something somewhere had to give. Jim came with me to the appointment. He knew I was really struggling. He wanted answers as much as I did.

"I spoke to an addiction doc on staff before you came in," began Dr. Grant.

Addiction? What was he talking about, I thought? Then it hit me like a ton of bricks. I was addicted to prescription narcotics. Damn.

Dazed, I tried to listen to what Dr. Grant said next.

"I didn't use any names of course but the doctor that I spoke to gave me some advice. You've had a perfect storm. First you have your migraines and then you've had the pain from your sinuses being in such a mess. You've been taking narcotics—a lot of narcotics—for a long time. I had to prescribe the medicine before and after your surgery, but now I think you're in rebound."

"What's rebound," Jim asked.

"It happens when you've been taking a medicine for a long time. Your body gets used to a certain level of intake and when that level isn't there the 'symptoms' the medicine is meant to relieve appear again. I suggest that you let me refer you to the Brattleboro Retreat. It's a rehab hospital in Vermont. It has a very good reputation and I think you should go there."

Damn, I thought. Not another rehab hospital. I said nothing.

It was Jim who spoke first. "Look Dr. Grant, Sue had a horrible experience at a rehab hospital when she got treatment for bulimia. I agree that treatment is necessary but there's no way I want her to go through what she went through at Bramley Heath. I mean, her therapist committed suicide while Sue was in her care for God's sake."

"Good heavens," said Dr. Grant, "I don't know anything about this Bramley Heath place but I assure you the Brattleboro Retreat is a top-notch place."

"If I go there," I said, "How long will I have to stay?"

"I don't know, they'll make that decision when you get there and they have a chance to evaluate you."

We left for the Brattleboro Retreat early the next Saturday. As we drove south on I95 I curled up on the seat with my head on Jim's leg. I had a horrible, horrible headache. I drifted in and out of wakefulness for the entire trip. Jim shook my shoulder when we got there. "Okay, sweetie," he said, "we're here."

Sitting up, I rubbed my eyes and said, "Okay, where's Quoddy's harness?"

Jim picked up the harness from the passenger side floor and handed it to me. With Quoddy harnessed we entered the building together.

I made one last attempt. "My head is absolutely killing me," I said. "Can you give me something for the pain?"

It was Jim who answered. "No, I know you're in pain, sweetie, but," he turned and addressed the doctor, "she's here because she's addicted to narcotics. I'm not surprised that she asked for them but please, please don't give her what she's asking for."

I was furious. I could tell that the doctor had been ready to give me a shot and Jim had ruined it all. We continued with the admission process, and I hardly spoke to Jim through the entire business. Placing my suitcase on the bed in my room, Jim said, "I know you're going to be safe now. I know you're mad at me, but I had to do what I did. I had to keep them from giving you any narcotics."

"Whatever," I said, brushing the tears from my eyes. "You have no idea what it's like, what it's like to be in constant pain. It never quits and now I'm stuck. It's never going to quit now."

I turned away and sat down on the bed with my head in my hands.

"I did what I did because I love you," Jim said. "I know they can help you here. I do love you, and I want you to get better, to get out from under the tyranny of narcotics."

Summoning up the last shred of decency I possessed, I said, "Okay, I know, you did the right thing."

After Jim left they went through my luggage with me, making sure I didn't have anything with which I could harm myself. My first room at The Brattleboro Retreat was just across the hall from the staff room. I was on suicide watch. The pain was relentless. I dragged myself out of my room four times a day to take Quoddy outside. Other than that I didn't leave the room. They brought meals to me. I would pick at whatever was on the tray and then lie back down pressing my head hard into the pillow. Twice a day they took my vitals. I quit asking for drugs after a day and a half. I thought I would die of the pain.

On the fourth day I awakened pain free. I sat up slowly and smiled. "Come here Miss Dog," I said to Quoddy. She jumped on the bed and began licking my face. I laughed and shook her head back and forth. She made her wookie sounds and the nurse poked his head in the door.

"Ah, you must be feeling better," he said. "My name is Matthew. We met yesterday but something tells me you don't remember it." He came in the room and took the chair next to the bed. We've all been worried about you and, of course, curious about your furry friend. What's her name?"

"This is Quoddy," I said. "I usually don't let her on the bed. Guess she's been worried about me too."

"Want to come out to the nurses station? You can meet some of the other patients and mental health workers."

"Yeah, sure," I answered. "But I feel kind of grubby. Can I take a shower first?" Matthew waited for me to get my toiletries and some clean clothes together and showed me to the communal bathroom. Later, feeling much better, I harnessed Quoddy and headed for the voices I could hear down the hall. I was introduced to six or seven patients, a couple of whom seemed to be sitting on the floor. The two mental health workers introduced themselves and I was invited to pull up a chair or a piece of the floor and sit down. Wanting to be close to Quoddy I settled myself on the floor.

Inevitably there were loads of questions about Quoddy. I took off her harness so that people could pet her. Rather than following her as she made the rounds I just unclipped her leash. In her gentle way she went from person to person getting her ears fondled or her back scratched. When she was done she settled regally by my side and crossed her paws.

Matthew joined us. "When you're ready you can begin to participate in the therapy we offer. We think it's important for you to go ahead and get started. Are you ready?"

"Sure," I replied. "What's the schedule like?" Matthew told me there was a group therapy in fifteen minutes. After that came lunch, an hour of down time and then some individual therapy.

"And at three o'clock most of us are going cross country skiing.," he concluded.

"Really?" I said in some surprise. "Can I join you? I love to ski"

"Of course," he replied. "We'll be out for about an hour. Will your dog come with you or stay here?" It was one thing to ski with Quoddy on the fire road at home. I knew the terrain intimately. This was a different matter. I had no idea of the proximity of roads or traffic so I decided she'd better stay in my room.

"I'll leave her in my room but she really does need some exercise. After lunch could someone show me somewhere that I can take her for a walk?"

"I'll do that," piped up Janice. She was one of the mental health workers. "I'm fascinated with Quoddy and I'd love to see how the two of you work together." Janice and I started walking together every day.

I eased into life at The Brattleboro Retreat. Staff and patients alike accepted me without making any assumptions of what I could or couldn't do due to blindness. Everything the staff asked me to do seemed reasonable and logical so I did it. We talked a lot about warning signs and sideways thinking. We talked about strategies for times when we might need to take narcotics. As I listened and learned I easily identified specific points over the past year where I had made bad choices. Instead of seeing my family , my friends, and coworkers as someone from whom I needed to hide my behavior I came to see them as my allies. Mostly, I learned to tell the truth. I learned to be truthful with myself and I learned to tell the truth to others.

Rather than feeling an adversarial relationship with the staff as I had felt at Bramley Heath, it seemed like we were all on the same team. Many an evening we'd all, patients and staff alike, sit around together and chat. Quoddy became a de facto therapy animal. She'd lie in the middle of the group, either with paws crossed and head up or doing her clever imitation of a dead dog. Sometimes, when we discussed difficult or painful things, one or another of the patients would get down on the floor with her and stroke her silky head while he talked. Most of the time we didn't talk about whatever substance addiction we were there to be treated for. Instead we talked about family, jobs, hobbies, and the like.

That was also very different from Bramley Heath. At Bramley Heath I felt like I was an addiction rather than a person. At Brattleboro I was a person first. The fact that I was blind was not important. The fact that I had been addicted to narcotics was not the most important part about who I was. We were all people first who had come to get help from the Retreat.

The patients were different too. I don't remember doing 12 step meetings at The Brattleboro Retreat although we must have had them. I contrasted the attitude of the other patients to the patients at Bramley Heath where I had treatment for my eating disorder. At the beginning of Overeaters Anonymous meetings each participant has to introduce herself by first name only and then say what she is addicted to. In one meeting at Bramley Heath I said my name and then said I had an eating disorder. One of the other patients had a ten minute argument with me declaring that by identifying myself as someone with an eating disorder rather than a food addict I was clearly in denial. There was none of that pettiness at Brattleboro.

They had originally determined that I would need to stay for a month. By the end of the second week they told me I could leave at the end of my third week. Jim drove to Vermont from Maine and stayed in a hotel the night before I was discharged. Hugging Janice, I thanked her for being my walking partner. I hugged and thanked Matthew as well. Hand in hand and with Quoddy at heel, Jim and I walked back to the truck and headed home.

45 | a little humility

ETURNING TO LIFE AFTER THE BRATTLEBORO RETREAT was similar to my return to life after Bramley Heath. After the treatment at Bramley Heath I returned home with wild enthusiasm. I was free from the tyranny of bulimia, something from which I thought I would never be free. My return from Brattleboro had an additional element. Both of them, bulimia and addiction to prescription narcotics, had brought me to the brink of the whirlpool. If they could do it so could something else, as yet unknown, in my future. That additional element was humility.

I resumed my job and home responsibilities without adding anything to the mix for several months. I was releived that everything seemed to be on an even keel as summer approached.

There are loads of fairs of all different sorts in Maine during the summer. The community radio station, WERU, had a fair each summer called the Full Circle Summer Fair. WERU stands for We Are You. It's a commercial free radio station started by Noel Paul Stookie and run by volunteers. The fair was a fund raiser for the radio station. It was populated by new age hippie types and the artsie fartsie crowd.

We entered a shed containing booths of all sorts. As we walked away from a booth at which Jim had purchased some earrings for me a woman approached us. "Hi," she began. "I'm with the Christian Science booth over there. I'd like to invite you to come over and chat with us."

Guessing where this was going I said, "Oh, that's okay, I don't think we're interested."

Undeterred the woman said, "But our church can help you get your sight back. Surely you'd like to hear about that?" Firmly, I said that I did not want to hear about that, picked up Quoddy's harness and commanded her forward.

Catching up with me Jim said, "Wow, I've never seen you be so firm with folks like that. Well done." We continued our ramblings around the fair grounds but I couldn't get the woman off of my mind.

Finally I said, "Can you show me back to that shed. I've had enough of these people and I want to talk to that lady again."

"Are you nuts? That's the easiest you've ever gotten away in one of those situations. Why do you want to go back?"

"Because I want to set the record straight. She may be only one person and it might not make all that much difference but this is something I want to do."

"Okay," Jim replied, "I'll get you in the right neighborhood but then you're on your own."

I stood facing the Christian Science booth and looked expectant by raising my eyebrows. Sure enough, here came Christian Science lady. "Hi, I see you're back," she began. "You must have decided that you want to hear more about getting your sight back."

"Well no, not exactly," I told her. "I'm just wondering why it is that so many Christians assume that everyone who's blind must want to be able to see."

"I just assumed . . . "

I let her get no further. "Let me give you a different perspective. Did you ever think that maybe God has plans for me, plans for something that I can do only if I'm blind? Maybe he's already used me for something like that and maybe it's something in my future. Niether you nor I know that but maybe it's true." I paused. She said nothing so I continued. "Look, I know the next thing you were going to say to me. You were going to tell me that if I prayed and had faith I'd get my vision back, weren't you?"

"Yes, that's one of the things I was going to tell you," she replied. What's wrong with that?"

"What's wrong with that is that someone's already tried that. It was in the early days of my blindness and it was terrible. Of course, of course I wanted to see again in those early days. So, I prayed. I tried to have faith. Nothing happened. It clearly had to be because I didn't have enough faith. All it accomplished was to make me feel like a failure."

Again, the woman was silent so I continued. "That's destructive enough in itself. All of that praying and not having enough faith prevented me from facing the reality of blindness and getting on with the emotional adjustment and the learning of skills necessary to live with blindness. But there's something even worse. By approaching a stranger, someone you don't know, someone about whose journey in life you haven't a clue and introducing this concept of wanting to have vision, you're potentially causing even greater damage."

"I'm not following you," said the woman.

"Okay, think about this. Here I am cruising through life and feeling perfectly comfortable about who I am. And you come along and tell me I must, absolutely must, want to see. You're asking me to deny myself. You're asking me to deny who I am and telling me to yearn to be someone I'm not. Does that make it clearer?"

"Oh, well, yes . . . I guess I see what you mean.

"Okay," I replied. "Maybe you'll think twice before you do such an irresponsible thing again." Picking up Quoddy's harness I said, "Quoddy, right," followed by, "Quoddy, forward." Wow, what a feeling of accomplishment. I had made all of my points clearly. I had made reasoned arguments and not gotten angry in the process. The only emotion I showed was in my last sentence to the woman. I had done it at last. I had put those feelings engendered so many years ago by the ladies in Birmingham to rest.

That was a particularly hot summer. It had been so hot at the Full Circle Fair that the soles of my sneakers actually began to separate from the uppers as we walked on the hot concrete. Our house wasn't air conditioned and we were usually fine with that. However, that summer tried our patience. "Let's get some kayaks," I suggested one hot afternoon. Quoddy had learned the trick of lying on the cool tiles when it was this hot but somehow that didn't appeal to us.

"What?" said Jim. "don't you want to get a tandem kayak instead of one for each of us?"

"No, I want my own kayak. That way I can paddle as far and as fast as I like, you know, the way I can skate when the lake's frozen. Besides that I want to be able to do some of the stuff I used to do when I was whitewater kayaking, stuff like bracing and turning and, I don't know, maybe even rolling." So, we set out for the Old Town factory store. An hour later we headed home with two kayaks, a ten-foot yellow one for me and an eleven-foot green one for Jim. We stopped only long enough to run in the house and get changed. Then we headed for the lake at the end of the road.

It was just as I had hoped it would be. I could paddle and paddle and when ready, I'd brace hard with one blade of my paddle or the other, pivot right around and race back in the other direction. We swam from the boats, splashed each other with the paddles and had a grand old time. Over the years our paddling adventures took us further afield. One trip on the ocean was so wild that we had to get spray skirts for our next ocean adventure. We took loads of trips to Moosehorn Stream about ten miles from our house.

The Moosehorn Stream trip involved paddling down the river to where another stream joined the one we were on. They converged and went down a waterfall about twenty yards farther along. The streams had a very slow current so when they joined we paddled upstream for a while finally ending up in Hot Hole Pond. The pond had no vehicular access so it was like our own private world.

There was always a beaver dam or two to be crossed and that was the first time I heard a beaver tail slap. It sounded as though someone did a cannonball into a swimming pool.

"Oh, wow," said Jim, at the beginning of one trip on the Moosehorn, "there's a bald eagle." The eagle kept flying down the stream ahead of us, moving from tree to tree. "Wow," said Jim again, "there are," he counted them, "five juvenile eagles in that tree ahead of us."

It was on the way back that I had my own close encounter with one of the eagles.

"Stop paddling," Jim whispered. "The female eagle is on a big rock in the middle of the stream. She's right in front of us. Let's see how close we can get ." We moved forward slowly and silently.

The eagle took flight.

I listened in wonder to her powerful wingbeats taking her, in slow stateliness, into the air.

46 | her name is beverly

THAT FALL I REJOINED THE ACADIA CHORAL SOCIETY and sang with them for the next eight years. What a joyful experience. Over the years we sang in English, Latin, French, German, and Russian. My favorite spring concert was when we performed Handel's Judas Maccabaeus. What a thrill to arrive at the last chorus with the hundred other performers, "Alleluia Amen," we all sang together. My favorite Christmas concert was the one in which we sang Christmas carols from Russia, carols from colonial times in the United States, and some modern carols from England.

I applied for and got a position as a computer access specialist. In those days, if you wanted to teach assistive technology, you were pretty much on your own when it came to learning the technology. I thrived with the challenge of my new job. I read all of the help and documentation I could get my hands on. Along with the new job came new territory. I covered the five northernmost counties in the state. I divided the time on the road between practicing music and learning everythingI could about assistive technology.

Quoddy was slowing down. For the first time I was facing retirement of a working dog after a full working career. I signed up for a mailing list for Seeing Eye graduates. I started asking other graduates who had retired dogs how they had known it was time. Over and over again they told me that I would know. How I would know remained a mystery.

In February Quoddy began limping. I had spoken with Dave, a friend who worked at the school, at a conference the previous November and he had urged me to submit my application for retraining. Although the limping episode lasted only a week or two and was resolved with medication I decided to go ahead with the application.

"Here's a letter from The Seeing Eye," said Jim as he entered the house with the mail. "It's in braille too. Want to read it yourself or want me to read it to you?"

"Oh, please, go ahead and read it to me."

"They're offering you a place in the November class," said Jim, when he came to the end of the letter. The next week I called the school and discussed the offered class. "She's working fine now. Can I postpone?"

It was no problem at all. They offered me a class the following February and, again, I postponed.

It was summer when I knew the time had come. Every summer we took The South Ridge Trail up Cadillac Mountain. It's seven miles round trip and quite rough in places. "Come on Quoddy dog," I said over and over again.

"Wow," said Jim. "You're really having to encourage her a lot. I don't think I've ever seen you do such cheerleading." It was true. We completed the hike but it was exhausting.

"I think it's time," I said to Jim when we settled at Geddie's for a post hike pizza and beer. "I'm going to go ahead with the class at the end of August." Jim placed his hand on mine as it lay on the table. We both reached under the table and fondled Quoddy's ears.

On a Friday afternoon in late August I took Quoddy's harness off for the last time. I watched with affection and appreciation as she helped herself to a drink and settled in her accustomed place in front of the glass door. Placing his arm around my shoulder Jim said, "She's a great dog." I hugged him back with tears in my eyes.

~~~

"Hi, I'm Dave Johnson. I'll be your instructor."

Taking the proffered elbow we headed down the hall together.

"Things have changed since you were last here," he said. "We've dropped the surname thing so you can call me Dave."

We arrived at the bottom of the stairs. As we ascended Dave said, "Your room is upstairs this time and you'll have the room to yourself.

We entered the room. As Dave oriented me he stopped at the desk. "I see you've brought a laptop. Here's your dedicated phone line for going online if you'd like to. Okay, Juno walk time," and he placed the harness handle in my hand.

I came away from the Juno walk with the impression that my next dog was going to have a stronger pull than Quoddy. That night we gathered in the common lounge to receive our new leashes and introduce ourselves. Across the room a woman said, "I'm Maggie Ostrowski from Pittsburgh." It was Maggie, Maggie from the Pennsylvania goalball team on which I had played during the tryouts for the Barcelona Paralympics.

When my turn came I introduced myself. Smiling broadly I said, "Hi, Maggie." Maggie and I were next door neighbors. When the new dorm had been built, for some reason, they had not used insulation in the walls. Every morning for the next three weeks I cringed as Beverly awakened at three or three-thirty each morning and shook vigorously. Bang, bang, bang went her tail on the wall between my room and Maggie's. Every morning for three weeks I apologized for Beverly's tail.

The first week of training was characterized by hard work and death. The hard work concerned controlling Beverly every time she heard Dave's voice or saw him. She was very devoted to Dave. She was also very strong and I had a time keeping her under control. This was going to be a difficult turnover, the phrase used to describe when a dog turns her attention and devotion from her trainer to her new handler.

Death came in a triad. On the first Sunday morning we awakened to the news that Princess Diana had died. Jim's Aunt Jenny died a few days later, and Mother Teresa died on Friday. We all gathered in the common lounge to watch Princess Diana's funeral. Several of us quietly sang along with parts of Verdi's *Requiem*.

"Hey, Dave," I began. "I know you don't usually allow visitors on the first weekend but my husband's aunt died in Wilkes-Barre, Pennsylvania, a few days ago. He's going to her funeral and, well, we were wondering. If he flies into Newark and rents a car, would it be okay for him to visit me this weekend?"

"Yeah, sure, no problem," said Dave. "When's he getting into town?"

"On Friday," I said. "So, it's okay for him to visit on Saturday?"

"Sure, but if he's going to be in town on Friday there's no reason why he can't come on out on Friday evening between dinner and evening park time."

It was the Friday afternoon before Jim's visit when it happened. I was trying to get Beverly to play with me just before afternoon park time. Suddenly her play changed. In an instant I knew I had her full attention. Snatching the kong out of my hand she began dashing all around the room. She dropped the kong and ran in laps around the room leaping on and off the bed, now making wookie noises. I laughed and laughed. She barreled into me covering my face with long swipes of her tongue. I sat on the floor and we wrestled in joyful abandon.

"Hey, Sue," called Dave as Beverly and I arrived, ten minutes late, at afternoon park time. "What held you up?"

"It's this crazy dog. She's been dashing all over my room making wookie noises and being a total goof."

"Ah," quipped Dave. "It's just the brain tumor, don't worry about it." His joking tone belied what we both knew. Beverly was becoming my dog.

I waited in the lobby for Jim to arrive. As the frontdoor opened I crossed the room. "Hi, sweetie," I said as Jim hugged me. "This is Beverly."

We sat in the winged armchairs in front of the fireplace for our visit. After a few minutes Jim said, "You're going to have your hands full with that there dog Miss Sue."

"what do you mean? I mean how can you tell?"

"She's never still. Her head's always in motion looking here, looking there. It's like she's a coiled spring just waiting to be released." He looked at Beverly for a few minutes. I waited. "And then there's her ears. They're way too big for her and they make her look really young and cute. And she's smiling. I swear it looks just like she's smiling."

During the last week of training Dave and his wife Lea took both of their classes into Manhatten together. On the subway platform that had tracks on either side of it we proofed our dogs at the edge of the platform. One by one each student approached the edge and commanded his or her dog forward. Dave and Lea watched closely. They waited to see each dog intelligently disobey the command to go forward. As I waited my turn trains pulled in and out of the station. As the first train pulled in with a roar I waited for Beverly to cringe. That's what Quoddy would have done. Beverly took absolutely no notice.

"Okay, Sue, your turn," called Dave. "Tell that mangy cur of yours to approach the edge here."

"Beverly, forward," I said. Beverly approached the edge

and stopped.

"Command her forward," said Dave.

"Beverly, forward," I said in a firm voice. Instead of obeying my command Beverly crossed in front of me and prevented me from moving forward.

"Nicely done," said Dave, at my elbow. We moved back from the edge. About that time two trains came roaring into the station from opposite directions. Apparently all of the dogs except Beverly had reacted. I heard Dave say to Lea, "Look at Beverly." Lea looked in my direction and laughed.

"What's so funny?" I asked.

Dave said, "It's just that all of the dogs are looking a little disconcerted right 'bout now. But your Beverly is just standing there smiling. That's one solid little dog you have there."

Jim left Quoddy at home when he came to pick me up at the airport. Immediately I noticed different reactions to Beverly than those to which I had become accustomed with Quoddy. Over and over again people told me how young she looked and how cute she was. When we got home I took Beverly's harness off and we brought out the other dogs, one at a time, to meet her. First came Quoddy. When Beverly tried to greet her she pinned her ears back and turned her head away. Little Iris, the dog that looked like a fox was next. She simply ignored Beverly. By then we had Silver Girl, a gorgeous white and silver Alaskan Malamute. Silver Girl showed signs of wanting to play. They all got along fine and Beverly settled into life with the pack.

A month after I brought her home Beverly and I traveled to an assistive technology conference in Minneapolis. At the end of the first day of presentations, lectures, and the insanity that is an exhibit hall at an international conference we both needed some fresh air and exercise. Stopping at the concierge desk I asked about places to walk.

After exiting the hotel I pulled on my gloves, picked up

the harness and said, "Beverly, left. Atta girl. Okay, hup up." And off we went into the cool November air. We were moving through an office park which seemed almost completely deserted. It was great. We walked block after block, crossing streets with no traffic and no problem. After half an hour I stopped. Kneeling on the sidewalk I took Beverly's face in my hands. "Guess what little dog. I'm lost. Come on, let's head back. I hope your memory is better than mine!"

Off we went, back in the other direction. After three or four blocks Beverly's pull in the harness became strong. I went with her. In no time flat she stopped dead. Reaching down I found her nose pointing right at the handle of the door into our hotel. Kneeling again, I looked into her eyes and said, "You're a good girl."

47 | the ice storm

THE WARNINGS FROM THE NATIONAL WEATHER SERVICE and Storm Center on the NBC affiliate in Bangor, WLBZ, started several days before the storm hit. By Tuesday we had plenty of water, candles, batteries, and firewood. My assistant, Les, and I agreed to call it quits in mid-afternoon on Tuesday. Les' car slid as he turned onto Hanson's Landing road. "You're sure you've got enough supplies?" he asked, as he steered into the spin and got the car under control.

"Yep, we'll be fine." By this time the agency had given me a car phone which lived in Les' car. I had already called Jim and knew that he was home. "But you be careful Les," Les lived in Old Town and he had quite a drive ahead of him. "Call me when you get home, okay?" Assuring me that he would do that he took his leave.

I slipped on the ice as I approached the door and prevented a fall by catching myself with Beverly's harness. "Jim?" I called as I entered the house.

"Hi, yep, I'm upstairs."

"It's already getting slick out there," I said. I nearly fell between the car and the house. How long have you been home?"

Coming out of the upstairs room which, by this time, we used as a computer and TV room, Jim put his hands on the balcony railing and looked down at me. "They're saying this could go on for, like, four or five days."

"Yeah, that's what we heard on the radio on the way home. I took off Beverly's harness and leash and hung them up next to the door. I hung my coat on the hat rack shaped like a moose and dropped my mittens on the cedar chest. "Should we do stuff like fill up the bathtub and some buckets with water for toilet flushing purposes?"

Coming downstairs Jim said, "I've already done that. We're sure to lose power so I've got the lanterns and candles out and ready. I filled up all the empty bottles I could find with water as well. That's about all we can do for now. Want to come upstairs and watch the coverage?"

I went upstairs and settled in the recliner while Jim sat at his table beside the TV. He multitasked, looking at weather related web sites, while I listened to Kevin Mannix on Storm Center.

After listening to the kind of damage to expect I said, "We're going to have to bring Silver Girl in. Otherwise she might get squished by a falling tree."

I hauled myself out of the chair and went to get Silver Girl from the pen behind the house. Silver Girl performed her usual routine. She barreled in the house, leaping right over Quoddy's back, dashed in the living room and began to roll and roll on the dark red carpet. Ruefully I thought of her white fur turning the carpet pink.

A few hours later the power came and went in several quick successions, then we had a brown out, a power surge, and finally the power went altogether. It happened so fast that neither of us could do anything until it was all over. "Damn," said Jim. "I swear sparks were flying out of that outlet by the couch."

"I wouldn't doubt it. What's that smell?" I crossed to the surge suppressor that the TV was plugged into. Kneeling down I smelled it. "Yuck," I said, "This surge suppressor is blown for sure." I went around the house and checked all of the surge suppressors. All of them had an acrid burned smell. "I just hope they did their job," I said as we settled down in front of the fire.

At around midnight the limbs started falling in the woods all around us. There was a predictable sequence of sounds. First there would be a loud cracking sound, then a hesitation, more loud cracking sounds and a booming crash as the limb or, in some cases, the entire tree hit the ground. It was like living in a war zone.

Then there was a louder crash than any that preceeded it. A limb from the tree just outside the dining room hit the roof and skylight with a horrendous crash. "Damn," said Jim, getting out of bed.

"What are you going to do?" I asked. "You're not going outside are you?"

Grabbing a flashlight Jim said, "I'm just going to try to see if I can tell what happened," and he went out into the open part of the house.

Following him I said, "What can you see? Is there any damage?" Jim was quiet for a few minutes while he shone the flashlight around the dining room. Crossing to the window he shone the light outside and saw the big tree limb.

"I see the limb. It's leaning up against the dining room window but I can't see any damage. I'm going to see what I can see outside."

"Be careful," I called as he went into the breezeway.

When he came back in he said, "Part of the limb fell between the house and the barn. It brought down the power line between them. That's all I can really tell for now. Come on, let's go back to bed. We can check it more fully in the morning."

Back in the bedroom we found Quoddy in a state. I sat

down on the floor with her and felt her quivering. She was scared to death. I didn't blame her. The falling trees and limbs were disconcerting for all of us but it seemed to effect her the most. "Do we have some batteries for that tape player in the kitchen," I asked Jim. Jim got the tape player and found that the batteries in it were dead. He replaced the batteries and I found some soothing music. I popped the tape in and to the strains of a classical adagio we finally all fell asleep.

We lived in the war zone for three days. By now we had built a barn which was connected to the house via a breezeway. We took much of the contents of the refrigerator and freezer and put them in the car which was parked in the barn. We filled the hydrator drawers of the refrigerator with the icey snow to keep what we had in the refrigerator cool. We kept warm with the wood stove. I cooked on the wood stove. We melted water in the pressure cooker on the wood stove. Gradually life returned to normal.

We had survived.

48 | when your heart breaks

THE NEXT YEAR JIM DECIDED to get a second master's degree from Western Michigan. This time it would be a degree in rehab teaching. He did the distance ed program so most of the academic work he did from home. We spent loads of time working on braille together. He made it through all of the academics and as the summer approached he prepared to go to Kalamazoo for six weeks. This was the last part of the program before he did his internship. During those six weeks he'd take classes in living skills, such as cooking and cleaning, and another class in assistive technology.

A couple of weeks before he left for Kalamazoo Jim had an overnight business trip. Trisha, my assistant, came to pick me up the next morning. I went out to her car with computer case in hand. Opening the back door I let Beverly jump in. As I leaned forward to place the computer case on the floor the car door swung shut. The corner of the door hit me just above my right eye. In the usual manner of facial cuts it bled copiously.

"I think I'd better go to the emergency room before we go to Bangor," I told Trisha. "Not sure, but I think I might need stitches." We turned right onto 1A and headed for Maine Coast Memorial Hospital. It had been years since I had been to the ER for anything. How different this experience was.

Trisha and I sat in the exam room cracking jokes and laughing at the absurdity of the perfect timing of the car door swinging shut just as I was bending forward.

"Well this is certainly a change from when we used to see you here for migraines," began the physicians assistant as she entered the exam room. "What's happened with those anyway? Do you still get them?"

"Yes," I replied. "But I take this relatively new medicine called Zomig. It works almost every time. And if it doesn't I just have to put on my big girl panties and deal with it until the pain eases on its own." She put two stitches in my eyebrow and we departed.

That evening when Jim got home he took one look at me and said, "What the heck happened? Are those stitches above your right eye?" After I explained Jim said, "I don't know Miss Sue, I leave home for one night and look what happens. And I'm supposed to leave for six weeks. What am I going to do with you?"

The day after Jim left for Kalamazoo I flew to Birmingham. My father had just been diagnosed with systemic lupus, a tricky diagnosis as there's no one test that can determine if someone has it. Over the past year he had battled with a host of problems including pneumonia, pleuracy, skin lesions, and flare ups of his arthritis.

"Hi Mama," I said when my mother met me at the airport. "How are you? How's Daddy?"

After collecting my suitcase we found the car in the parking deck and headed home. "Daddy's having problems with pleuracy right now," began Mama. "It's just been one thing after another but this pleurisy is really bothering him. Be sure to be careful when you hug him. He's got a lot of pain in his ribs right now." She paused and then said, "I'm so glad you're here honey."

I stayed with my parents for a week. It was tough seeing

how my father had declined. He was now using a walker all the time. They had installed a ramp so that he could get down the two steps into the den. Another small ramp allowed him to get over the threshold of the glass door onto the patio. The one thing I remember that convinced me of how much he had declined was when my friend, Addie, came for a visit. We were all sitting on the patio and Daddy was wearing his bath robe. When I told him that Addie was coming he just said, "Okay, it will be good to see her." Ordinarily he would never have visited with anyone who was not a member of the family dressed in his bath robe.

It was this image that I took back to Maine with me, the image of my father in his illness, my father in his old age.

Over the next year my father was in and out of the hospital with some regularity. In March my mother hired round the clock sitters to help her with Daddy's comfort and safety. On a Thursday in July I called to check on Daddy. No one answered the phone. I knew that someone should be there. Daddy certainly wasn't going anywhere and either my mother or whoever was sitting with him should have answered the phone. I was uneasy.

Jim and I both worked out of the Ellsworth Career Center and we both happened to be in the office that Thursday. "Jim," I called to him. "I've just called the house and nobody answers. That can't be right."

Coming out of his office Jim took a seat in my visitor's chair. "What do you want to do?" he asked.

"I don't know. Something's wrong, I just feel like something's wrong." I tried calling my brother, Jimmy, and got no answer. I tried my mother's cell phone and got no answer. "I'm calling the hospital," I said.

When the switchboard operator answered I identified myself and explained the problem. The operator asked for my phone number and said she'd see what she could find out.

"Okay," she began when she called me back. "Yes, your father is being seen in the emergency room right now. Your mother and brother are with him. Your brother said he'd leave the ER for a few minutes and give you a call. " I thanked her and hung up.

"Hey," said Jimmy when he called a few minutes later. "We're in the ER with Daddy. We're not sure what's wrong but he seems to be in a lot of pain and he's pretty agitated."

"What," I said, "Are they doing some tests or something?"

"Yes," he replied. "They're doing a bunch of blood tests but we won't have the results for a while. They've told us that they're going to keep Daddy in the ER until they get the results of the tests."

"Okay, give me a call as soon as you know anything." Jimmy agreed and we hung up.

The next time the phone rang it was early afternoon. "Hi honey," said my mother. "You need to come." That's all she said. I didn't have to ask why.

"Jim," I said when I hung up the phone. "I've got to go to Birmingham. Mama said to come. I think . . . " I let the words trail off. Jim hugged me and we headed for home.

I arrived in Birmingham by mid morning the next day, Friday. "I'm so glad you're here," said my mother as she hugged me.

We went straight to the hospital. "Hi Daddy," I said as I entered the room. I crossed to the bed, leaned down to kiss my father on the cheek and said, "I love you Daddy." Mama and I stayed with him for the rest of that day and came back on Saturday. Mama arranged for the sitters to be there round the clock, just as they had been when he was at home. She wanted to insure that Daddy had someone with him all the time to see to his comfort and to act as his advocate with the hospital staff.

Just before we headed for home on Saturday afternoon

Daddy became agitated and upset. I held his hand. He began to cry. My strong father, my good, gentle, kind father was crying. I learned, at that precise moment, what it feels like when your heart breaks. As I held his hand the tears slid silently down my own cheeks.

Mama went out to the nurse's station and asked that my father be given the medicine that had been prescribed for anxiety. We stayed with him until the medicine worked and he settled down. There were many times, during those last days, when my father seemed agitated. He never said he was in pain but would sometimes move about as though he were in pain. I came to believe that, when he did this, when he seemed as though he was struggling, what he was struggling with was giving up his life.

On Monday, when the doctor came in to see my father, he asked my mother, brother, and me to step out in the hallway.

"I believe I'm correct in assuming that Harrison wants to die at home?" There, it had been spoken aloud.

"Yes," said Jimmy and Mama at the same time.

"Okay then," said the doctor, "I'll arrange for you to meet with hospice this morning. You should be able to take him home this afternoon."

By Monday afternoon everything was arranged. My mother left the hospital first so that she would be at home to take delivery of the new hospital bed. Before she left she showed me how to get to the pharmacy. My job was to take any prescriptions the doctor wanted Daddy to have down to the pharmacy and get them filled.

The doctor said, "Here you go. These are prescriptions for the antianxiety medicine and some pain medicine." Thanking him, I took the prescriptions and headed for the pharmacy.

When I returned to my father's room the ambulance crew was transferring him to a gurney. "Come on," said Ethel, the sitter on duty. Ethel and I drove home together, following the ambulance.

Once Daddy was settled in their bedroom in the new hospital bed he announced, "I would like three saltine crackers with peanut butter on them." We all looked at Daddy in some surprise. He hadn't wanted to eat anything in the hospital despite our wheedling. Delighted that he was showing an interest in food, any food, my mother headed back down the hallway to get the snack.

At around midnight on Wednesday Daddy became the most agitated we had seen him. For the first time he complained of pain. Mama called the hospice nurse. She arrived an hour later with the liquid morphine. Speaking to my mother she said, "Here's a medicine dropper. Any time he seems agitated or in pain use it to drop the morphine in his mouth. Don't be stingy with it. What we want to do from now on is keep him calm and pain free."

When the nurse left Mama and I sat with Daddy until he went back to sleep. Mama handed the liquid morphine to Robin, the sitter who was on duty, and both of us went to bed. By now it was 2:00 on Thursday morning.

Shortly before 6:00 that morning, Robin came to get us. "He's going," she said. "He's very close now."

Then we sat, my mother holding Daddy's right hand and I holding his left. His breathing faltered, resumed, and then stopped. Still holding his hand I said, "I love you Daddy." Then I leaned forward and gently kissed his cheek for the last time.

QUERCUS ALBA

white oak

PART FOUR

RESOLVE

~~~~~

You gain strength, courage, and confidence

by every experience in which you really

stop to look fear in the face. You are able

to say to yourself, "I have lived through

this horror. I can take the next thing that

comes along." You must do the thing you

think you cannot do.

Eleanor Roosevelt

49 | home calls

THE SATURDAY AFTER WE RETURNED FROM ALABAMA and my father's funeral we did the South Ridge Trail up Cadillac Mountain. It was when we were on the open ledges just beyond one of the rock faces that I thought of it, that I thought of the hymn, "For All the Saints."

I began singing it in my head as we made our way across the granite ledge. I stopped dead. I sang the verse again in my head. Standing right there on that open granite ledge looking out across the Atlantic Ocean I sang it again as the tears flowed freely.

"And when the strife is fierce, the warfare long,

Steals on the ear, the distant triumph song.

And hearts are brave again, and arms are strong.

Noticing that I had stopped Jim turned around and came back to me. "What is it," he asked. "You're crying. What is it?"

"It's, well it's just this verse of "For All the Saints." I was singing it to myself and I got to this one verse and, well, I thought of Daddy."

Brushing a tear from my eye Jim said, "Tell me about it. Here', let's sit down for a minute. Tell me about the verse of that hymn."

Sitting down I tried to sing it, but there was no way, so I just said the words. "That's what it was like when Daddy died.

It was so hard to see him so debilitated. But when he died, well, I could think of his brave heart and strong arms again."

Jim let me cry myself out. Then, standing up, he offered me his hand. "Ready?"

"Yeah, thanks sweetie."

As we made our way down the mountain I thought about our lives in Maine. I , we both, loved it here. But the past year had been tough. I had flown to Alabama every month or six weeks to see Daddy and to help Mama with his care. Now Daddy was gone and Mama was alone. And that disturbed me.

Then there was the uneasiness about my job. My supervisor had expressed frustration with many decisions made at the agency for months. Now she simply seemed resigned and not very hopeful. There seemed every possibility that the computer access department might be on the way out. If one of us lost our job we'd be in a world of hurt.

We came to a rough part of the trail and I had to concentrate on where I was putting my feet. When it smoothed out a bit I turned back to my thoughts. We only had a couple of months, maybe three, until we'd be facing winter again. November, rain, drizzle, and fog, oh my. Who knew what kind of winter we'd have. *Would it be mild with heavy wet snow? Would we have weeks with the temps dropping to twenty-below-zero every night?*

I thought of the two years we had spent in Tennessee, where we could do stuff outdoors year round. Where we weren't at the mercy of the capricious snow. Where we didn't have to shovel snow, worry about getting our driveway plowed, or drive on dangerous roads to see our clients. Tennessee. Sewanee. Mama. Home.

My mother had been 'getting the house in dying order', as she called it for years. She had given away what she could and thrown away what she couldn't. That made the process of getting the house ready to sell much easier. Nonetheless, there was a lot to do. "Mama," I began, "Do you need help sorting through everything and packing and stuff?"

"You know," she replied, "I thought I would need your help but Jimmy and Margaret have been helping and your cousin, Margaret, came over from Atlanta last weekend. She's positively ruthless. Honestly, I'm afraid to stand still for too long for fear she's going to pack me in a box."

The house sold quickly and my mother found a brand new garden home in Cahaba Heights, on the other side of 280. She moved in early December and was settled in nicely as we prepared to come to Birmingham for Christmas. By now Quoddy was in her fifteenth year and had just been diagnosed with partial renal failure.

"Jim," I said, one day in early December. "I'm afraid to leave Quoddy in a kennel for ten days. Remember how she was when we got home after Daddy died? I don't think she ate very much while we were gone and she seemed so weak."

"I know," he replied. "I've been thinking about that too. I'm thinking it would be better to drive and take her with us rather than fly."

A week before Christmas we threw our luggage in the car and bundled all four dogs in after it. We dropped Silver Girl and Iris at the kennel and headed south on I95. Following the directions that Mama had given us we pulled in the driveway of her new house.

"Oh, I'm so glad to see you," she said, as she came out of the house to meet us. We all hugged and then she said, "Come on in. I can't wait to show you the house." She was almost childlike in her enthusiasm and eagerness that we approve of her new house.

Although Mama had described the house and how she had arranged the furniture I hadn't really been able to get a clear idea of it. "Wow," I said, "This is great." We had just finished the tour and were standing in her bedroom. "The bed is spectacular," I told her. It was the mahogany four-poster that my great-grandparents had brought to this country from England. It was the first time I had seen the fretwork around the top. The ceilings in our old house had been too low for the fretwork to be attached.

"I can't wait for you to see the bank outside of the breakfast room window," Mama said. "I've planted it with winter blooming flowers and herbs. It's been so much fun. I even transplanted all of those wildflowers you brought me from Sewanee. For now, let's have a cocktail and sit down for a little while before dinner."

As we prepared to head back to Maine ten days later, my mother said, "Now don't forget, I'm having cataract surgery in two weeks." I hugged her and assured her that I wouldn't forget.

The weather grew worse and worse the farther north we got. We completed the trip in almost blizzard conditions. "Whew," said Jim as he pulled the car to a stop in our driveway.

Two weeks later I called my mother when I figured she'd be home after her cataract surgery. "Hi, how was it?" I asked.

"Oh, honey, it was so easy. Clara drove me to the hospital and they took me right in. It was so quick and there was almost no pain. Clara and I are just sitting here on the patio having a glass of iced tea together." Hearing the winter birds in the background I could just picture the two of them. Continuing, she added, "You know, the plan was for Clara to spend the night with me tonight but I'm sending her home. I'll be fine on my own."

After we hung up I called Jim. "And then she said they were sitting on the patio drinking iced tea," I concluded. "Sheesh, it was like torture hearing the birds in the background and imagining being able to sit outside comfortably. Since we got home from our Christmas visit the weather had been atrocious. For the entire two weeks it had had sleeted or snowed and even rained a few times, after which it would freeze solid. It was getting very old. The cataract surgery was one elective procedure which my mother had postponed during Daddy's illness. The next one was a hip replacement. In April I went to Birmingham to help her following that surgery. While I basked in the sun on Mama's patio Jim was shoveling snow following a late snowstorm. He took a picture of the snow covering our driveway and emailed it to me. "Look at this, Mama," I said, turning my laptop towards her. "Can you believe we're having snow this late in the year?"

After I had been at Mama's for a week, I called Gina at the Southeastern Blind Rehab Center. "Oh, my gosh," she said, after I identified myself, "I can't believe you're calling me at this particular moment."

"Well," I quipped, "I know it's been a while, but what's special about this particular time?"

"You've been working as a computer access specialist, right?" When I replied in the affirmative, she continued, "Because we're going to be hiring a subject matter expert for our computer access training section. And," she paused, "we're about to advertise two O&M positions."

Seeing where this was going I said, "You're thinking that Jim and I might apply?"

"Yes," she said, "it would be perfect. Do you think you'd consider it?" That simple question was a turning point. I thought back over the last year of my father's life. I thought about all of the trips between Maine and Alabama. I thought of my mother, who would turn eighty next month, and who was just beginning to deal with some major health problems.

"Yes," I said slowly to Gina. "Yes, I think we might be interested."

On a chilly and rainy May Saturday Jim and I both applied for jobs with VA.

We moved to Alabama In September.

50 | you *are* going to change

WE LEFT MAINE ON A GLORIOUS SEPTEMBER DAY with low himidity, perfect temperature, and a brisk breeze blowing the clouds about. It got hotter and hotter the farther south we went. By the time we hit Tennessee the humidity turned the heat into a wall that we hit each time we exited the car or the hotel. At a convenience store in north Alabama I was told I couldn't bring my dog into the store. I mentally scratched my head and wondered if this move had been such a good idea after all.

My doubts were erased as soon as we pulled into my mother's driveway. "Oh, I'm so glad to see you," she called as we decanted ourselves from the car. Her delight was manifest. She hugged us both and all of us, three humans and two canines, entered the blessed cool of Mama's house.

"How was your trip?" Mama asked as she got lunch on the table.

Following one of my mother's traditional chicken salad and deviled egg lunches, I said, "Can we go look at the house?" Mama had helped us locate a house to rent just down the road from hers. We were anxious to see where we would be living.

After taking a tour of the house, Jim said, "This will be okay for now, but I think we're going to have to put some of our furniture in storage. It was really nice of him to build the fence for the dogs. And look, this door here in the kitchen must be the one he said we could put a doggie door in." We were worried about Silver Girl and the heat, wanting her to be able to let herself in and out as she pleased.

Over the next two days, we prepared for the arrival of the moving van. We got the doggie door installed. We washed all of the windows and made sure the house was nice and clean. The morning the moving van was due, my mother looked pointedly at my cutoff jeans and said, "Just look at yourself. You are going to put on something a bit nicer than those aren't you?"

I burst out laughing and said, "Oh, here we go again, our eternal battle over what I'm wearing!" In my youth this would have been a bone of contention. Now, I could joke about it. "Just for you dearie," I said, and I hugged her and changed into lightweight slacks, throwing the ratty cutoffs into the back of the car.

Jim was already at the house waiting for the movers. Mama and I ran up to Bed Bath and Beyond at The Summit to grab something or other that she seemed to think was essential. Then we went to the rented house, arriving just ahead of the movers. I got Beverly off of the back seat and reached for my cut offs, meaning to get my keys out of the pocket. The only problem was that the shorts weren't there. I racked my brain. I knew I had put them on the back seat. Then it came to me. "Mama," I said, "I think Beverly pulled my shorts out of the car up at The Summit, you know, when I got her out of the car? My keys were in the pocket." Mama came and looked in the back seat but the shorts were gone.

"Okay, honey," she said. "I'll just run back up to The Summit and see if I see them. You stay here and help with the placement of the furniture and such."

Mama was gone for almost an hour but returned, triumphantly, with the shorts and the keys. I asked what had taken so long. "Well, when I got there I found the shorts immediately. The problem was that someone had parked their car right on top of them. I asked the security guard to help me but he said he couldn't do anything, that I'd just have to wait for the owner of the car to return and move it. So, there I was, a little old gray haired lady looking wistfully down at your ratty old shorts, waiting until I could retrieve them for you." We all burst out laughing.

"Oh, Mama," I said, "I'm so sorry. Thanks for getting them back."

"I can see that my life will never be boring again," she replied laughing ruefully."

Taking stock of the situation, Mama said, "Sue, can you bring out one of those kitchen chairs for me to sit in? I'm not as spry as I once was you know. This unpacking is going to take a while and I'll need to sit down." I ran in the house and brought out one of the kitchen chairs. "Okay, honey, put it right over here. I'll tell the movers which door to bring things in and you and Jim can direct them once they get things in the house." And my mother sat regally in the chair like a queen directing her subjects.

When we had gotten everything we planned to put in the house off of the truck Jim said, "I'll take them over to the storage unit, okay? You and your mother can stay here and start getting things organized," and he left.

"Okay, honey," said my mother, "Where do you want to start?"

Standing in the middle of the living room I scratched my head and tried to think. "My plants," I said, "I want to make sure my plants all made it okay." By now we had moved so many times that we had it down to a science. My hanging plants were in wardrobe boxes with other plants held steady in boxes of their own by life preservers, old quilts, towels, and bubble wrap. The boxes were clearly labeled and all of the plant boxes were still outside.

"How about this," said Mama, "I've been out there in the heat for about as long as I can take it. While you do the plants I'll get started in the kitchen."

I dug my Swiss Army knife out of my purse and headed outside. All of the plants had made it just fine. I positioned the aloe and jades on the front porch and, retrieving a stool from the house, hung the streptocarpus, Swedish ivy, and Bolivian Jew from hooks under the eaves.

"How's it going?" I asked when I entered the kitchen. "Want help or should I go work on the bedroom and bathroom?"

"Tell me where you want these things I've unpacked and put on the kitchen table. It's the food processor, the coffee maker, these blue and white canisters."

"I trust you," I replied. "Put them wherever you think they should go. It'll be fun to see if we agree." Laughing, I made sure that Silver Girl and Beverly, who were in the pen, had plenty of water and made my way around the boxes, down the hall and into the bedroom.

"Sue," called Jim as he came back in the house. "Where are you Miss Sue?

"Back here," I yelled from the bedroom. Jim made his way back and asked what I wanted him to do.

"Mama's unpacking in the kitchen and I've unpacked some of these boxes. Maybe, first, if you don't mind breaking down the empty boxes and putting them somewhere out of the way, well, that would be great. Then maybe you can start on the smaller bedroom across the hall. Most of the boxes in that room look like your clothes and stuff. There's a closet in there and your two wardrobe boxes should be in there as well."

The rest of the afternoon passed agreeably enough. Each of us worked on our own tasks, calling out to each other whenever we had a question. We finally called a halt at around six o'clock. "Mama," I said, coming into the dining room where she was unpacking crystal and china and placing it in the oak corner cabinet, "is it okay if we spend tonight back at your house? I never did get the bed made and there's no way I'm cooking anything tonight."

"Of course, honey," she replied. She seemed quite delighted by the prospect. We ended up spending the next two nights at Mama's before things were orderly enough to move into the rented house. Once we got moved in we took our time. We had a full two weeks before we had to start our new jobs. My best friend from childhood, Addie, came over one afternoon and helped me get the room we were using as an office squared away.

"How did you learn how to do all of this computer stuff," she asked, as I emerged from under the desk where I had been connecting cables to the back of Jim's computer.

"I don't know," I answered distractedly, trying to remember which box had Jim's scanner in it. "I mean, well, this is what I've been doing for the past six years. Setting up computer systems and teaching people to use them." Then we sat down in the middle of the floor and just talked.

"You know," began Addie, "When you were first blind, you know, before you learned how to do all the stuff you do now, well, you know, at first I thought everything was going to be different for you. But now it's just like blindness doesn't matter. You're still the same old Sue." She laughed self-consciously.

"You know, I said, "That's music to my ears. It's taken a while to get here but honestly, I really am the same old Wig, as Jane would say."

Addie hesitated. Then she said, "Do you remember what we used to do sometimes at your house when we were children? You know, we'd close all the doors in the hall at your house and turn off the lights. It was completely dark. And then we'd try to play with each other, you know, like playing tag or just wrestling in the dark?" Who knew? Who knew that, well, it was sort of like, I don't know, a foreshadowing or something."

I laughed. "And remember when one of us, I don't even know who it was now, I think it was me, I banged my head on your knee or something and bled all over the pale green carpet." Then I stopped. "It's so hard to believe it's not there anymore.

"I know," said Addie. "None of us could believe it when they tore down your house." We were quiet for a few minutes, sitting there with our shared memories.

51 | where it all began

TWENTY YEARS AFTER WORKING THERE AS A VOLUNTEER I entered the Southeastern Blind Rehab Center as a member of the staff. George, the chief of service, was my direct supervisor so I headed to his office that first morning. After about half an hour I realized that this job was going to be whatever I made it. It appeared that I had complete freedom to structure my activities however I liked within certain boundaries. "Come on," he said, "Let me Show you your office."

We took the stairs to the sixth floor and George showed me into a small interior office smack dab in the middle of the manual skills department. "There's a lot of equipment in here for you to sort through," George began. "We weren't sure what to do with it so we left it for you to deal with."

Just then one of the pieces of power equipment in the wood shop across the hall started up. "Good thing my office has a door," I said.

Laughing, George closed the door. "Your NT computer is here on the desk. Over here," he walked to the back of the office, "Are several other computers and various components." Making my way to the back of the office I found a high work bench with a clutter of equipment, piled higgledy-piggledy on the work surface and on the floor below the bench. "There's no rush of course," George continued, "You can do whatever you see fit with this stuff."

When George left I sat down in front of my computer. I pulled out the index card on which Gina had brailled my ID and temporary password and logged on. I spent most of the rest of the day getting familiar with the programs on my computer. Coming up for air I pressed a couple of keys and the computer spoke the time. Wow, the workday was almost over. Leaning back in my chair I sat quietly for a few minutes. That's the position in which Jim found me fifteen minutes later.

"Ready to go Home?" he began. "What are you doing?"

Turning to him I said, "What do you mean, what am I doing?"

"Well you're just sitting there like a lump on a log. What are you thinking about?"

"Oh," I said, pulling myself together. "I was just thinking how nice it is to be alone on the job, you know, with no driver or assistant. It's great."

Jim said, "Well you look like you're in a trance. Come on, let's go home."

George assigned one of the O&M instructors to help me get oriented to the layout of the hospital. Aside from that, and an orientation to each of the training sections of the blind center, I was free to do whatever I wanted to do whenever I wanted to do it. I sorted through the stuff at the back of my office and threw most of it away. Realizing that I needed to become an expert in the function of both the screen reader and screen magnifier issued to the veterans I started at the beginning and worked my way right through the training and manuals for both products. That's how I got started six years ago when I got my first assistive technology job in Maine but I hadn't had, or taken the time, to do it as new versions of the software were released. What a lot I had been missing. I had completely missed several new features in JAWS. I spent extra time with Zoomtext, working out how I was going to teach a program I could barely see.

Someone knocked on my door and Beverly barked. Shushing her I opened the door. "Hi," said the man. "I'm John, I've got your printer and scanner."

I had put in a request to the IT department for the equipment. "Wow, that was quick," I said. "I only requested it this morning. As John came in my office Beverly barked at him again. "Phooey on that," I said, grabbing Beverly by the scruff of her neck and giving her a little shake. She subsided with a grumble. We both laughed.

"What's her name?" asked John.

"Beverly, and she's my mouthy little bitch. Here, give her a treat and see if that'll shut her up."

I handed John a few tiny milk bones and he knelt on the floor and gave them to her one by one.

"She's really pretty," began John. Then he sat down in my other chair and told me about his dogs. "They're all Chihuahuas and, you know, show ring quality. But that doesn't really matter, we just love them all." He continued and I sat back and listened.

After a while John said "I was wondering, can you show me how you use the computer?"

"Sure," I replied. I opened Outlook and showed him how I handled email. I went on the Internet and showed him how easy it was to navigate a well-structured web page and how poorly coded pages gave me trouble. He listened and watched, apparently enthralled.

Finally he said, "Well I guess I'd better get this equipment set up for you." I helped him unpack the printer and scanner and decided where I wanted them on the desk. "Scooch over," he said, "I'll install the drivers before we plug them in." I was perfectly capable of installing drivers but I moved over and let him do it.

"Okay, I think that's got it," said John. "You know, it was kind of cool to see how you use that screen reader. If you need anything else here's my direct extension."

I wrote it down and he left.

After those first two weeks I got out of my office. I began observing the CATS instructors as they taught. Keenly aware of being the new kid on the block I simply listened at first. Eventually, at the end of the class and once the veteran had departed, I began to ask questions and make suggestions.

"You did a really good job teaching Mr. Jones to spell check. Let me try something." I moved to the keyboard and performed a spell check in a slightly different way. "I don't know," I concluded, "It might be a little easier. What do you think?"

One thing was becoming clear to me. Being a CATS instructor at a VA blind center is hard work. There were seven classes a day. If an instructor had a full schedule there was little time left over for anything except teaching and documentation in the Computerized Patient Record System, CPRS. If something went wrong with the computer it might take an entire class to figure out the problem and fix it.

I called a meeting of the staff. "I've been watching you folks dashing hither and yon, you know, setting up equipment, trouble shooting problems, and teaching every single class period. I was wondering if I could make things easier on you." I looked around but nobody said anything. "Here's what I was thinking. What if I set up the computer systems for each new guy just before they come in. That way you'd have a little more time to review the patient chart in CPRS or the referral information from the VIST coordinator. Then I was thinking that I'd set up one Zoomtext and one JAWS computer in that office at the end of the hall. If you've got some problem with the veteran's own computer you can take him in that room and use one of those computers while I fix whatever's wrong with his machine. What do you think?"

After some discussion we agreed to give it a try.

When an instructor had a problem he turned the problem over to me. When a veteran had already gone home with his equipment and had a problem he called me. I became an expert at teasing out the details of the problem so that it could be solved. I became the one who seemed always to be dashing about, fixing a recalcitrant printer on the fifth floor, running up the stairs to see what was wrong with a JAWS installation on the sixth floor, dashing back to my office just in time for a conference call. I loved it. I thrilled to the challenge and I thrived.

52 | girls' night out

JIM AND I SPENT EVERY WEEKEND THAT AUTUMN looking for a house to buy. We finally found it just south of Springville. The house was in the middle of thirteen wooded acres and it was the last house on a dead end road. The entire property was steeply sloped with the house about halfway up the hill. "Good thing this place isn't in Maine," commented Jim as we rounded the hairpin bend in the steep driveway." We had lived in Maine for so long that it was instinct to consider what a driveway would be like when the snow flew. "I mean, if this place was in Maine I think you'd just be stuck until the spring thaw."

We had just closed on the house and wanted to walk around inside while it was still empty. We had decided where most of the furniture should go but were still in a quandary about which room to make our computer room. We entered the house through the back door into a sun room. The sun room was divided from the kitchen by a breakfast bar but the two rooms were essentially one big open area. I had decided to put our whicker furniture in the sun room. Noticing that Jim wasn't following me to the upstairs bedroom where we had discussed setting up our computers I asked, "What are you thinking about?"

"Well, I was thinking, let's use the sun room as our

computer room."

I gazed at him in amazement. "You're a genius, an absolute genius. Of course that's where we should put the computers. It's so obvious. Can't believe I didn't think of it."

After touring the house we went out on the front porch. "Wow, listen to the stream," I began. "I don't remember hearing it when we've been here before. I love it."

Yeah, it must be seasonal. It'll probably flow in the winter mostly but, yeah, what a great sound."

When we moved we changed a lot more than our address. Springville is about thirty miles northeast of Birmingham. It's very hilly, very rural, and exactly what we like. Our tour of duty ended at four o'clock, so, if we left right after work, we could avoid rush hour. Having lived in rural areas most of our lives we had developed a real aversion to being stuck in slow moving traffic. We found amenities closer to home such as grocery stores, building supply places, and a great nursery so we pretty much just headed out of town as soon as the work day was over.

Until we moved I had been going to my mother's hair dresser whose shop was in the same little community where my mother's house and our rented house were located. We had lived in Springville for two months when I realized I needed a haircut.

"Mama," I began, when she answered the phone. "I need to get my hair cut. The problem is that, if Jim brings me down there and waits for me, it'll put us on the road at around five o'clock, right smack in the middle of rush hour. I was wondering, if I could get Carolyn's last appointment of the day, if maybe I could just spend the night at your house?"

"Sure, honey," my mother replied, with enthusiasm. "Carolyn's late afternoon is on Thursday. Want to do it this week?"

"Sure, that would be great. I'll give her a call and see if

we can line it up."

"No need," Mama said. "I'm seeing her this morning. I'll get it all set up for you." Mama called me back that afternoon and said it was all set. "Her latest appointment is for four o'clock. Can you leave work at three-thirty? I'll pick you up then if that's okay."

"Oh, that feels so much better," I said as mama and I left Carolyn's shop.

"Yes, she did a really good job," replied Mama. She added, "Look, Miss Myra's is in this same little complex, just around the corner. How about some barbecue for dinner?"

We entered Miss Myra's restaurant and found Myra herself behind the counter. "Well hi Sue," she said.

Myra worked as a volunteer at the blind center and I recognized her voice at once. "Myra," I began, "this is my mother, Frances Wiygul."

Mama and Myra both laughed. Then Myra said, "Well now I know the connection. Frances, you and your family have been coming here for years of course, but I didn't know the connection with Sue." After visiting for a few minutes Myra fixed two plates for us and we headed home.

Entering the house from the garage Mama said, "I'll put the barbecue aside for now. Let's get something to drink and sit out on the patio."

"Great idea," and we settled in wrought iron chairs on Mama's patio. "You know, the birds you have here are the birds I remember from when I was growing up. But we have some different birds at home. We don't hear robins or red winged blackbirds. But we do hear brown cowbirds and my favorite, the wood thrush, and I don't remember ever hearing them around here before.

"Yes," Mama said, "That's true. It's just the difference between an urban or suburban area like this and a rural area like where you live."

We sat listening to the birds for a while, and then Mama said, "Do you remember that time we took Tony the pony to Mississippi?"

I laughed and replied, "Like it was yesterday. Remember how I used to climb up in the pecan tree before we went over there?"

Laughing in her turn, Mama said, "Do I remember that? Of course I do. You used to call it your thinking tree didn't you?

"I did," I said. "And it was so much fun having Tony on the farm. Remember Daddy kept getting after me for chasing the cows? I was pretending to be a cowboy and that's what cowboys do, right?"

We were silent with our own thoughts for a few minutes. Then I said, "Tell me again why you and Daddy decided to keep the farm as a working farm after Granny and Grandaddy Jim died? I mean it was so cool being able to go over there and have free run of the entire four hundred acres. And learning to fish and knowing where our food came from, it was just wonderful. But why did you decide to do that?"

"Well," Mama began. "When Daddy and I were first married, the first time we went to the farm to visit Granny and Grandaddy Jim, well, your grandfather presented me with a bushel of turnip greens. All he said was that I should wash them well before I cooked them. So, your city mouse mother brought them home and put them in the washing machine with some Tide."

"You what?" I gasped, trying to control my laughter.

"It's true, and we decided that having the opportunity for you children to go to the farm, to learn about things like where your bacon, butter, and turnip greens came from, well, we wanted to give you that gift. Oh, not to mention, I never wanted you to try to wash the turnip greens in the washing machine."

After I finished laughing, I said something to my mother I had never said before. "Thank you. Thank you and Daddy for giving us that wonderful gift."

"Oh, those were halcyon days, weren't they?" said Mama. Then she added, "Come on, let's have some barbecue."

53 | a new passion

"HEY GINA," I SAID WHEN SHE ANSWERED THE PHONE. "Did you get this memo from the hospital director?" "Yeah, why?" Gina replied.

"Well I can't read it," I said. "I open it and JAWS says 'empty document'. What's that all about?" We had been speaking on the phone but, at that point, Gina hung up and came around the corner to my office.

"It's a definite problem," she said, sitting down in the chair on the other side of my desk. "These memos and directives; they have to be signed by whoever is issuing them. Apparently they create these things in Word, print them out and sign them, and then scan them into an image in a PDF document. It's so that people can see the signature."

"Get out of here. Are you serious? That's ridiculous. They take a perfectly accessible Word document and turn it into an image just so people can see the signature? You know, when I came to work for the Federal Government I thought my dealings with inaccessible technology were over. I thought 508 meant that everything would be accessible. How can they get away with this stuff?"

"Mostly I think people just don't know about 508," Gina replied.

Shaking my head I said, "How can they not know about

it? It's the law."

"Okay," Gina soothed, "Just as an example, look at the signature block on that message. Who sent it out?"

I closed the useless PDF and scrolled to the bottom of the message to which it had been attached. "Alice somebody, I don't know if I can pronounce her last name, JAWS certainly can't."

"And what's Alice's title?" Gina continued.

"Administrative assistant to the Hospital Director," I answered.

"Over there on the ninth floor," Gina began, "they probably have a dozen admin assistants, I don't really know. But with that many people working on the executive staff, well, that's a lot of people who have to be educated. And then there's the matter of turnover. Even if you went over there and taught each one of them how to produce an accessible PDF or taught them to always include the Word source document from which the PDF got created, before you know it somebody gets promoted or moves or retires or something. That's why all of us who have tried to take up this battle have pretty much given in. We don't have the authority to . . . "

I held up my hand for permission to interrupt and Gina stopped. "But Section 508 is the law," I said. "How can they get away with ignoring it?"

"Like I was saying, we don't have the authority to tell them they have to produce stuff in a way that's accessible. Really, we've all tried and we've all pretty much given up the fight."

I hesitated for a minute and then said, "Okay, if I take up the fight?"

"Of course you can. I can see that you're passionate about this. Go ahead, but be prepared for disappointment."

I quipped, "Okey-doke. Now, where's my sword?" Laughing, Gina left my office.

I was vague about the details of Section 508 so I decided to look it up. I opened my browser to a search engine and entered the terms I thought might get me what I wanted. The first hit was a Department of Justice site so I activated the link. In short order I found what I was looking for.

"Section 508 of the Rehab Act requires that Federal agencies' electronic and information technology is accessible to people with disabilities, including employees and members of the public."

That was pretty straightforward and perfectly clear.

Switching back to the email I checked Alice's extension and placed the call. "Hi Alice," I began, "I'm Sue Martin and I work at the blind center here. I've just received your email and I can't read the attachment. I'm blind and use a screen reader to access my computer"

"Oh, wait a minute," Alice interrupted me. "I forgot about the problem with scanned PDFs. Hang on, I'll resend it and include the original Word document this time. Will that work?"

"Well yes," I replied. "That would be great." I was surprised. It had been so easy to get what I needed.

Two weeks later Alice sent out another inaccessible memorandum. I didn't bother to call her, just replied to the email asking for the accessible alternative. I was beginning to understand why Gina and everyone else had given up. It was certainly an uphill battle. As time passed I found myself walking the tightrope between the idealism of all IT being accessible and reality. There were plenty of times when I just had to lay down my accessible IT sword and do my job.

I didn't have any authority to insist that employees make their IT accessible but I could advocate. I could also figure out ways around inaccessible IT. The company that made JAWS also had a program called OpenBook, an optical character recognition program. Using OpenBook I could convert scanned images of print to actual text. . If my efforts to get accessible alternatives failed I'd convert things to text with OpenBook and share with other employees at the blind center.

The next hurdle I ran into was mandatory training. All employees were required to complete forty hours of training per year and the training was completely inaccessible. "Hey Lynn," I said to my colleague, "Why has no one complained about this training?"

"Oh, we've complained," she said, "but it hasn't done any good."

"So, you've had to have somebody sighted sit beside you to complete this training all along? That's unbelievable."

"Yeah, we know it's unbelieveable; but all of our complaining hasn't done any good, so we've pretty much given up."

Back in my office, I picked up the phone and called the head of Employee Education at the medical center. "Hi , Susan," I began, "This is Sue Martin from the blind center. I'm wondering if you could help me find out who develops this Synquest training. It's not accessible and it really needs to be addressed." Susan said that she thought the company in Nashville that created the training had been taking a lot of heat recently due to the problems with accessibility. The only phone number Susan had for the company was the main switchboard number so she gave it to me and we hung up.

I sighed. Main switchboard numbers were bad news. I picked up the phone and dialed. On my first try I got transferred six times. I finally hung up after being on hold for a solid five minutes. How could I approach this differently?Instead of explaining ad infinitum to someone who didn't have a clue what I was talking about I decided to try working my way up the food chain. This time I got lucky. I spoke with a manager in the software development department.

"Are you a Section 508 coordinator," he asked.

Not sure what a Section 508 coordinator was I replied, "No, I'm just an employee at the Department of Veterans Affairs who wants to take her mandatory training independently."

"Well we think we have a fix for the problem," he replied. I waited. "Yes," he replied confidently, "I think we're almost there." I waited some more. Finally he said, "Look, if you use one of those programs that," he paused and finally said, "Sightless people use, give me your phone number or your email address and we'll get in touch with you when we've got this figured out."

Disliking euphemisms for blindness I replied, "Yes, okay, I am blind and here's my phone number and email address." I recited the information and he assured me he'd get in touch with me within a week. "Wait, wait a minute," I said. There was no way I was letting this guy hang up without learning how to contact him directly. He gave me his contact information and we hung up.

Two weeks later I called him back. They weren't ready. Two weeks later they still weren't ready. It ended up being two months before they had a solution. Finally, Synquest was accessible. I made the changes on all of the computers of assistive technology users in the blind center. A colleague told someone at the Augusta blind center about it and I helped the AT users there get squared away. I was on a roll. Word spread.

As Jim and I walked to the parking deck that afternoon I said, "You know what? I love teaching and trouble shooting and doing tech support and stuff but I'm really getting into this accessibility business. You know, making sure that email attachments are readable and stuff like that. Then, this afternoon, I worked with the Synquest folks and actually got Synquest to work with JAWS."

"I know," he replied.

I was surprised. "How'd you know?"

"I stuck my head in your door just to say hello. You were

so absorbed in whatever you were doing that you didn't even notice." "Jim laughed and took my right hand. I dropped Beverly's harness and we walked, hand in hand, to the parking deck.

54 | her name is kismet

EVERLY WAS REALLY SLOWING DOWN. I was surprised because she was only eight years old. By the end of the summer I knew it would be the last summer I could work her. In autumn I applied to train with a new dog. I made it clear that I felt Beverly could work through the winter and spring so I wasn't expecting to hear from The Seeing Eye any time soon.

"Sue Martin," I said, as I answered the phone.

""Hi Sue, it's Pete at The Seeing Eye. Look, I know you said that Beverly would be able to work until next summer but I want to let you know that we have two shepherds going into the March class. We think one of these dogs would be a good match for you."

Hesitating, I said, "Wow, thanks Pete. I, well I guess I'll see you in March then."

"There's no pressure you understand," said Pete. "We just want to offer you a spot in the March class if you'd like to take it."

In truth I was a little shocked. I had never been invited to attend a specific class in which the school had a specific dog in mind for me. Yes, I'll come into class in March, and thanks Pete, thanks so much."

On March 7th Ralph handed me her leash and said, "Her

name is Kismet." I was sitting cross legged on the floor of the main lounge. Kismet took one look at me and turned back to Ralph, jumping up as though she was saying, "No way, you're my person. I'm sticking with you buddy." Kneeling up on my knees I wrapped my arms around the squirming little dog and brought her down to sit on my lap. She paused for a moment and then raised her head and licked my chin. Ralph told me later that it was at that moment that he knew the match was going to work.

Kismet combined the great qualities of both of my other shepherds. She was keenly focused when she worked and she worked with panache. She was also very affectionate and playful. Quite simply, she was a joy, in and out of the harness.

That August there was a conference in Kansas City to introduce assistive technology users in Blind Rehab Service to the new accessibility built into the Computerized Patient Record System, CPRS, and the new Blind Rehab data base. Both of these programs, in particular the data base, could have been poster children for accessible software design. Accessibility was considered early and often during the development process.

When I answered the phone in late July the caller said, "Hi Sue, this is Ellen Crowe. Todd, in Augusta, suggested that I call you. We need a driver for the presentations next month and Todd said you'd be a good person to ask."

I hesitated. Knowing that she wasn't talking about driving a vehicle I was confused. "What's a driver?" I asked.

"During the presentations one person reads from the script while another person carries out the steps on the computer. The presentations will be in a lab setting with each person in the audience having their own computer to use while you demonstrate the steps on a computer hooked up to a projector. Think you can do that?"

"Sure, yes, I'll be glad to be a driver."

"Okay, fabulous," replied Ellen. "I'm sending you the script now. See you next month."

My co-worker, Mark, and I were on the same flight to Kansas City. The first flight was late getting into Atlanta, and we only had fifteen minutes to make our connection. After we landed the flight attendant approached and told us to wait until all of the other passengers had deplaned, and then they would assist us in getting to our next gate. "No way," I told her. "We've only got fifteen minutes. There's no way we'll make our next flight if we wait until everyone else has deplaned."

"Don't worry," she said, "It's airline policy that you have to wait. "We'll be sure you make your next flight."

I knew there was no such policy but I decided to take the path of least resistance. I didn't argue with her. Turning to Mark I said, "As soon as they turn off the seatbelt sign we're gonna make a break for it, okay?" As we moved into the aisle I told the folks in front of us that we had a very tight connection and asked if they minded if we went ahead of them. We worked our way forward and were almost the first to deplane.

"Wait a minute," said the flight attendant.

I whispered to Mark, "Hang on."

Turning to the flight attendant I simply said, "Goodbye," and we took off.

At the end of the jetway an airline representative asked if we needed any help. "Yes," I said, "where's gate b23?"

"Take a right when you get to the concourse and it's the last gate on the right, at the end of the concourse."

We were off. Mark and I slalomed through the airport, found the correct gate on the second try and made the flight.

The next day the conference began. I didn't have to drive the computer until the last day and found myself in the audience with several familiar friends. Vicke and Kathy, the two with whom I had played in my first ever goalball tournament were in the row behind me. Rita was on the other side of the room and I was sitting next to Ellen Crowe.

"Hey," she began, "Thanks for agreeing to drive on Thursday."

"Thanks for asking me," I replied. "Should be fun." Over the next two days we worked hard and really did have fun. I drove during the presentations on Thursday and it went very well. I returned from the conference with even more passion for accessibility.

"Hi sweetie," I said to Jim when he met me at the airport.

"Gosh," he replied, "You look like you've just come back from a vacation instead of a workshop."

"It was fabulous," I told him. "I really had fun."

"Fun?" Jim quipped. Don't know about you Miss Sue. You're the only person in captivity who goes to a workshop and has fun."

About a year later Ellen contacted me again. "There have been some huge changes in CPRS," she began. "We're working with the developers in Salt Lake to come up with a Delphi accessibility framework. It's a huge undertaking. I was just wondering if you'd be interested in working on the project?"

"Well sure," I said. "I'll have to clear it with George of course but it sounds great.

When I had George's blessing I called Ellen back. "Let's do it," I said.

"okay, cool," she said. "The first thing we're going to do is bring a few JAWS users to Salt Lake and work with the development team to identify as many problems with CPRS as we can. Then we'll have monthly conference calls to test the fixes as they make them. You did such a good job as a driver at the conference in Kansas City that I was wondering if you'd drive for those conference calls?"

The trip to Salt Lake City was just as challenging and just as much fun as the Kansas City trip. We worked hard but had fun with the work.

The following summer Ellen invited me to work with her on a project in the DC area. It was on that trip, when we were in the bar, that we started talking about people that we both knew. There were a lot of them.

"Do you know Maggie Ostrowski?" I asked.

"Oh, yes," I know Maggie," Ellen said. "Like Maggie, I'm originally from Pennsylvania. In fact, Maggie and I played together during the tryouts for the Barcelona Paralympic goalball team."

I gasped. In my mind I went back to the Paralympic trials.

"But," I hesitated, "That was the team . . . Oh, my God, you must have gotten married. Are you, I mean, were you Ellen McMahon?"

"One and the same," she said. Then she got it too.

"You played on that same team. You're that Sue Martin," she said, emphasizing the word, 'that'.

~~~

When I got home from that trip I started thinking about my career. I had been teaching for over twenty years. Becoming the subject matter expert for the computer training program had been a big change in itself, but I was beginning to think it was time for an even bigger change. I started keeping an eye on the USA Jobs web site. Two months later, there it was. A Section 508 job in the Veterans Health Administration.

"I'm going to apply for this job," I said to Jim.

"Really?" he replied. "Are you sure? Are you sure you want to leave rehab?"

"Yes, I'm sure. I still love this job and maybe that's the best time and the best way to leave a job. You know, leave when you still like it and you're doing a good job at it. All I can do is apply and see what happens. It's all good because if I

312 | PART FOUR: RESOLVE

don't get it I've still got this job and that'll be okay too."

In October I left the field of blind rehab to become a Section 508 analyst.

The best part of the deal was that my boss became Ellen Crowe.

55 | the 508 dream team

E LLEN FILLED THREE POSITIONS and we all joined the Veterans Health Administration Section 508 office at the same time. The very first week we all traveled to Salt Lake City. The trip had been planned for months and it was coincidence that it happened just as we became a team. We were coming together for our first objective: to test the bug fixes the developers had made in CPRS.

We settled in. We began working as a team. Each person brought strengths and skills, and we all learned from each other. There were times when I thought I must be crazy, changing careers in my fifties. I felt challenged beyond, well, beyond anything I can ever remember. We worked hard though, all of us did.

At the end of the week we all went our separate ways, Ellen to Chicago, Mary Lou to Syracuse, Mia to Seattle, and I to Birmingham. Since we also had a dispersed contractual staff—mostly located in the DC area—we had to set up a regular schedule of conference calls. The topics of these calls ranged from project tracking to one that we called "the water cooler call" . . . to share ideas and just to catch up. In addition to these regular contacts there were others, some planned and others ad hoc, and most of these were with the development teams we worked with. Often, at the end of the day, I felt like I needed to have the telephone surgically removed from my ear. But these early days were enormously challenging for me and, well, big fun.

In late March Ellen called me.

"Hey woman," she said, "we've got the coolest opportunity coming up. There's a conference in May called GIE Tech. Stands for something like Government Information Executives or something like that. It's a conference for CIO's across the Federal Government, and we've got a chance to have a booth in the exhibit hall."

"Wow," I said. "That does sound good. "What do you want to do in the booth?"

"Well, I was thinking of demonstrating J-Say," she said. "When you did that J-Say demo at Tech Talk last September, before you joined the team, well, you had about 350 developers and project managers spellbound for an entire hour. Honestly, they were on the edge of their seats. I just think this is a super opportunity to get some way cool AT in front of CIO's in the Federal Government."

"Okay, sounds like a plan."

"There's just one thing," she added. "I can't expect you to demo for three straight days without a break. So, I was thinking, do you think you can get ML up to speed with J-Say by then?"

"Well, sure, no problem, but she'll have to get her hands on the software first."

Ellen laughed, "To tell you the truth I've already bought it for her. Hang on, I talked to her earlier, let me conference her in."

When Mary Lou, or "ML," as we called her, came on the line I said, "It'll be no problem to get you up to speed and it's kind of fun."

"You know," said ML, "This is such a good opportunity for me. Remember last year when my husband hurt his hand?

Remember helping me get the software ordered for him? He can use it fairly well but he's not the geeky type. If I get really good with it I can help him with his installation so everybody wins."

"Yep, sounds like a good plan all round. I'll call Ed Rosenthal at NGT when we hang up and see if he can expedite getting the software to you."

I had learned to use J-Say when I worked at the blind center. There were plenty of veterans with visual impairments who could not use a keyboard due to injury or a variety of diseases. J-Say allows someone who can neither see the screen nor use a keyboard to effectively use a computer. A year earlier I had been invited to become a beta tester for the software and by now I knew it inside and out.

Once ML received her software we got to work and were ready by the time the conference rolled around. I was thankful that ML and I could switch off at the GIE Tech conference. Word spread about the cool software over at the 508 booth and we stayed busy the entire time, often demonstrating non-stop for hours while Ellen answered questions and chatted with folks.

A year later our office was given authority for e-learning content within the VA learning management system. Veterans Affairs is composed of three administrations, Veterans Health, Veterans Benefits, and Cemeteries and Monuments. Since we were within the Veterans Health Administration, VHA, our authority was for e-learning content that was clinical in nature or for which the VHA was the business owner. VHA is huge and there's a lot of e-learning content out there.

On our next team call we discussed the new project. Ellen began, "This is a big project. It's going to take a lot of work to test this volume of material. First thing we need to do is decide which one of us is going to manage this thing."

Thinking back to my work at the medical center with the

Synquest e-learning application and my passion for teaching I said, "I'd like to take this on. I'll need help but I'd like to take this on as my primary project." The rest of the team agreed

I had never done anything of this magnitude and it was our contractual partner, Fred, to whom I turned. Fred had been the 508 coordinator for the US Patents and Trademarks Office until his retirement. He worked part-time on our project and his experience and guidance was most welcomed.

"Okay, Sue," he began, "the first thing you need to do is set up your procedures. As manager of this thing, you need to learn how to delegate. You need to figure out how the testing will be done, who's going to do what, and then you need to write it all down."

With Fred's guidance, I came up with a draft for the procedures of testing the e-learning materials. I would be the overall manager and the primary contact for the developers and project managers who submitted courses for review. Our contractual partners at the SSB BART Group would do the actual testing and deliver the results.

"Hey, Cammie," I began, "I've got a rough draft of procedures for this process. Can you take a look and see if it all makes sense? Here, I'm sending it to you now. You'll see that I've designated you and Mike as the technical leads."

Cammie and I worked on the document together, and she helped me iron out the wrinkles.

So, we began. At first the courses were terrible. No one had ever held the developer's feet to the fire in terms of accessibility and, over the first year or so, not one course passed 508 testing on the first go. It became clear that remediation was going to be a big part of this project. Mike and Cammie began asking me to make technical decisions that were beyond me.

"Mia," I began when she answered the phone, "You're far and away the best technical person on our team. We need someone with more technical skill than I to make decisions and provide guidance in the remediation phase of this project. Can you take on the role of remediation coordinator?"

"Yeah, sure," she replied.

"Okay, great. I'll make the changes to our process document and send it to you for your approval."

~~~

"I want to produce an e-learning course on producing accessible e-learning."

It was our regularly-scheduled program planning call, and it was Ellen who threw out the ultimatum. Ellen seldom made ultimatums but she was firm on this.

"We've got to teach developers to fish if they're ever going to understand how to create accessible content. I want to start with a course on HTML and then do one on Software and operating systems."

My current project demanded most of my time, and I wasn't sure how much I'd be able to contribute to this initiative, but early in the planning we decided we needed to have some videos of AT in action.

"I'll do that part," I said.

"That would be great," Ellen replied.

The production of the actual training courses became ML's baby and Mia was involved in just about everything. Whenever any of us had a technical question we couldn't answer we went to Mia. Ellen rode herd on the lot of us, encouraging, correcting, and allowing us to develop professionally in our own areas of strength.

56 | mama's decline

IN JULY, IN THE MIDDLE OF THE NIGHT, MAMA FELL in the bathroom and hit her head on the floor. She began having periods of confusion during which she'd take her medications incorrectly or forget to turn off the stove. Jimmy and I took her to see her primary care physician, Dr. Houston. He ordered head and neck films. "I want you and Sue to come to see me by yourselves," he told Jimmy a few days later.

When we were seated in Dr. Houston's office he began. "Your mother's situation is very grave. She has arthritic nodes that are pressing on her brain stem. Eventually the pressure will kill her. You have two choices. You can get her on hospice and keep her as comfortable as possible until she dies or she can have brain surgery."

We were stunned. Jimmy and I looked at each other in silence. Eventually I said, "Dr. Houston, Mama is 87 years old. I, I just can't see her having brain surgery at her age."

Then Jimmy spoke. "What are the chances of success if she has the surgery?"

"I honestly don't know," said Dr. Houston. "I want your mother to see a neurologist. He's a brain surgeon here at the medical center."

I'll never forget Mama's appointment with the neurologist. It was the last time she dressed with the same care she had her whole life. She donned a linen suit and had a silk scarf at her throat. During the appointment she handled herself with grace. It was her one last time for being the gracious confident woman who had raised us and made a home for us. When the neurologist came to the end of his explanation about the benefits and risks of the surgery, Mama, her voice strong and confident, said, "Thank you so much for your time and your clear explanations. I elect not to have the surgery."

I was so proud of her. I had tried hard not to influence her decision. I, personally, thought the surgery would be a mistake but I tried to let her come to her own decision. There we were. The road to the end of my mother's life lay before us.

Through Dr. Houston we met Cassandra who organized round the clock sitters. Hospice delivered a hospital bed and established a schedule for a nurse to come twice a week and for home health aides to come to bathe Mama. The sitters were phenomenal. They cooked and kept the kitchen tidy. Jackie stayed with Mama each weekday and we hired her sister, Joyce, to come once a week and do the housecleaning.

With the logistics in place Jimmy and I returned to Dr. Houston's office. "Can you tell us what to expect?" I asked.

"I know you want to know what's to come, Dr. Houston said. Here's how I see things. Unfortunately the pressure of the nodes in your mother's neck are causing angulation of her spine. Those same nodes are gradually increasing the pressure on her brain stem. The brain stem is responsible for autonomic nervous system function. You know, things like breathing, heartbeat, digestion, all of those things our body does without us having to think about them. When the pressure reaches a certain point those functions are going to begin shutting down. In the meantime the angulation of her spine is going to cause gradual paralysis. Those are the two things you're dealing with and there's no way to know how far the paralysis will go before the pressure on her brain stem kills her. Does that all make sense?"

"Yes, I understand it perfectly well," I replied. "It's just so, bleak, I guess is the word I'm looking for."

Jimmy asked about pain. "There's definitely going to be some pain," Dr. Houston said. "I'll prescribe something in the valium class of medications to help your mother with the inevitable anxiety that comes at the end of life. I'll also prescribe narcotics, one oral narcotic but, most importantly, liquid morphine."

Thinking back to Daddy's death I said, "Hospice prescribed liquid morphine at the end of Daddy's life too. He never even said he was in pain but they brought it to us the last night of his life and told us not to be stingy with it. I had the feeling that they gave it to us, as much to help him stay calm, as to help with pain. Do I have that right?"

"Yes, you've got that right. Between the valium and the liquid morphine you should be able to keep your mother as calm as possible and help her to the place where she can let go of her life."

Then Jimmy and I sat down together. "Look," he began, "There's a lot that you can't do, like taking care of Mama's mail and bills. I'll be happy to take that on. I think we should both have access to Mama's bank accounts. You can do that online banking, right?"

Relieved I said, "I'm so glad you'll take over those responsibilities. And yes, the online banking site is well done, I'll have no trouble with that."

Continuing Jimmy said "Since we live so close I'll stop by every day and check on how things are going. I can write the checks for the sitters each day and pick up the mail."

Jimmy and I discussed my role in Mama's care. What could I do?

"Ellen," I began, "My mother is dying. I don't know what to expect really but she is dying."

"Oh, Sue," and for once Ellen dropped all of the professionalism from her voice. With compassion she said, "I'm so sorry, Sue. What can I do to help you?"

"Well, you know how Mama and I were having our girl's night out from time to time?" By now I was working from home two days a week and it was clear that I could do my job anywhere. "Instead of girl's nights out I want to start spending the night at Mama's, I don't know, maybe three or four times a month. I was thinking that Jim could drop me off on his way to work in the morning and I could stay the night and the next day. That way I can be with her when she's awake and alert but I can work when she's asleep or when we have a call scheduled. We have round the clock sitters but this is the only way I can be there enough to really know what's happening. I can help direct her care."

"Sure thing," said Ellen instantly. "Tel you what, depending on whether it's a time card week just work as much as you can and then figure out how much leave to enter afterwards. If it's a time card week and you end up having to take time Thursday afternoon or Friday unexpectedly we'll just work with the time keepers and do a corrected timecard as we need. That work?"

"Oh, Ellen, thank you so much. This is going to be difficult and there's no way to know how it will all play out. Without going into the medical details I can tell you that this isn't going to be pretty.

"I know," Ellen replied. "Look Miss Suzy Cue, we've all got your back. We'll make this work for you, okay?" With relief I hung up the phone. I was so far beyond grateful to Ellen that I might as well have been in another country.

Jim drew the car into Mama's driveway and leaned over to kiss me. "See you tomorrow afternoon. Take good care. Call me and let me know how things are going, okay?" I kissed him, grabbed my backpack and computer case and let Kismet out of the car. Shouldering my backpack I passed through the open door of the garage, slipped past Mama's car and entered the kitchen through the laundry room.

"Jackie?" I called, finding the kitchen empty.

"We're in here," called Jackie, "In your mother's bedroom." Dropping my backpack and computer case by the blue chair I entered Mama's bedroom.

Mama was in bed and Jackie was tucking in her blanket. I leaned over and kissed Mama's cheek. "What kind of night did you have?" I asked her. Mama wasn't lucid so Jackie answered.

"She had a fairly anxious night. That's why she seems so groggy right now. She had two of those episodes where she seems to think she's going on a trip. You know how she gets, she keeps talking about her suitcase, asking if it's packed, that kind of thing."

"Hmm," I said, "I'm going to open the draperies, okay?" We had taken great pains, the sitters and I, to keep Mama's home like a home. The only thing that spoke of her illness in her bedroom was the hospital bed itself. Otherwise, all of her mahogany furniture was still there and it glowed in the early morning light. With the draperies opened I called Kismet and let her jump her front paws up on the railing of Mama's bed. Mama loved Kismet and sometimes seeing her or patting her seemed to give her great satisfaction. She reached up weakly and rubbed her hand over Kismet's head. The paralysis had taken almost all of her dexterity away but patting Kismet was something that she could do just fine. She murmured and then lay back in the bed.

Turning to Jackie, I said, "When was her last dose of Ativan?" Jackie went in the kitchen to check the log.

Coming back in the bedroom she said, "At five this morning."

"With or without morphine?" I asked.

"With," replied Jackie, looking at the log. "With her

normal dosage."

"Okay, thanks, Jackie," I said. "She'll probably be fairly groggy for a while. She must have been pretty agitated earlier." I went back in the kitchen to fill Kismet's water bowl and then took my computer case into Mama's bedroom. I settled in the winged armchair in the corner and started my work day.

I worked steadily for two hours and then Mama said, quite lucidly, "Well hi there honey, I'm so glad you're here."

I put my computer down on the floor and crossed to the bed. "Hi sleepyhead, glad you decided to join the land of the living." Hearing our voices Kismet came in the bedroom and jumped her front feet up on the rail.

Mama spoke to her and then said, "Come see your old grandmother," and Kismet jumped neatly over the railing and settled beside Mama's legs at the foot of the bed. The first time this happened it was quite by accident and apparently entirely Kismet's idea. By now it was a well established routine. Kismet settled at the foot of the bed beside Mama's legs. She stretched out her paws and laid her chin on them so that Mama could reach her head easily when she wanted to pat her. I stood beside the bed, placing one hand on the rail. Mama placed the hand that wasn't patting Kismet on my hand. I placed my other hand on top of hers. She took her other hand off of Kismet's head and put it on top of the stack. I pulled out my bottom hand and put it on top of hers. Mama laughed. She laughed with such gayetty and abandon that, for a moment, she sounded like her old self. Laughing together, with me standing beside her hospital bed, we played a game of "Stack the hands'. As our laughter died Mama patted my hand and lay back. Biting my lip I turned and went into the living room.

"What was that all about?" said Jackie. She was seated in one of the yellow silk chairs just outside the bedroom.

"We were just playing a game together. At the end of it she patted my hand. It was like, well, like she was comforting me or something." Look, I've got a conference call in half an hour. I'm going to just take a quick walk and I'll be back in time for the call." Harnessing Kismet I left through the front door.

As Christmas approached I decided to plant the large planter on the patio with fresh winter blooming flowers. Wanting Mama to have something pretty outside of each window I also purchased several hanging pots and poles to hang them on. Two bags of soil completed the order and Little Hardware delivered the lot a week before Christmas. I took Christmas Eve off and got to work. Thinking of my mother and of how she always had flowers blooming in the yard, no matter the time of year, I lovingly planted flowers in the planter and each of the hanging pots. By early afternoon I was done. I drove two of the poles into the soft earth outside Mama's bedroom and two into the bed of Hosta outside her sunroom. Then I hung the pots of flowers up.

By now my hands were freezing. I came back in the house and ran warm water over them until they thawed. Mama loved the flowers. She laughed in delight when Jackie rolled her into the sunroom in her wheelchair and she caught sight of the hanging pots. Then I started cooking. I planned to cook the turkey and make the sweet potato casserole that day and then cook the rest Christmas morning. When everything was in the oven I sat down at the table with Mama.

"Let's have a drink," she said. So, we did.

By the time Mama finished her drink the turkey was done. She had a slice and went right to bed.

When Jackie came back from helping Mama into bed I said, "You've sat with people who were dying before. How do you do it?"

"Oh, Sue," said Jackie, "It's completely different when the person is not a member of the family. I know this is hard for you, but you're doing really well, you really are." I sighed and puffed out my cheeks.

"I'm going to go read for a while. Let me know if you need anything."

I had fallen asleep before Jackie left and awakened when I heard raised voices. I went into Mama's bedroom to find Ranadia trying to calm Mama down.

"She keeps talking about your father and your grandmother," said Ranadia. "She seems sure that they're in the next room. Nothing we did eased her agitation."

"When was her last dose of Ativan," I asked.

"It was just two hours ago," Ranadia replied. "She's not due for another dose for two more hours."

"Give it to her now," I said. "Give it to her now, along with half her usual dose of morphine."

"But," began Ranadia, "but it's too soon."

"I don't care. Do it on my authority. I'll take the heat if anybody questions it." Ranadia dissolved the Ativan in the liquid morphine and gave the medicine to my mother.

I stood beside the bed until she calmed down and drifted off to sleep again.

57 | mama passes

IN EARLY JANUARY MARY LOU SENT ME AN EMAIL and said she wanted to chat. She said that something was bothering her and she wanted to clear the air. I was clueless. The next morning, when she called, I was truly shocked. "Right before the Christmas break," began ML, "I wished you a merry Christmas, and you sort of blew me off."

I hesitated. I racked my brain, but honestly had no memory of the blow-off. "I . . . I'm so sorry, ML. I just don't remember that. I must have done it though, and I'm really sorry."

"Let's talk about the elephant in the room," said ML. I waited. "You've got a really tough situation with your mother. I know you're trying your best to compartmentalize things and you're doing a good job given the circumstances. But, in truth, you've got a bad situation that's only going to get better when something else bad happens, when your mother dies."

As the tears came to my eyes I said, "Oh, ML, you're right." In silence, I pondered what she had said. It was true. The terrible uncertainty of how much worse my mother's situation would get would end in one, and only one, way, with her death. I thought of everything I was juggling, work, Mama's care, everything in my personal life. No wonder I hadn't realized that I had blown ML off right before Christmas. It was too much, too much to keep track of. "ML," I finally said, "you've just dragged the truth out of the darkness. I've just got to slow down. I've just got to slow down and realize that I'm not super woman. I can't do it all and I can't do it perfectly. Thank you, thanks for what you said, for what you've just helped me realize."

"Okay, Sue," she said. "Just hang in there, okay?"

I sat with my elbows on the desk gazing out the window. I thought about everything that was going on. Pulling myself together I got up and opened my office door. Instead of turning right back to the computer and attacking whatever I had been working on when ML called I thought carefully about how I was working. Not the work I was doing but how I was doing it. Until half an hour ago I thought I was doing just fine. Thinking back, I recalled several mistakes I had made recently, none of them huge but mistakes all the same. These, combined with the fact that I had been rude to a valued friend and colleague, added up to a professional who was distracted and not at the top of her game. Maybe it wasn't necessary or even possible to always play at the top of my game.

All those months ago, when I first told Ellen about my mother's situation, hadn't she told me that the team had my back? There it was. I was part of a team. I wasn't out there all by my lonesome. The least I could do was slow down and not make mistakes. *So what if I didn't respond to that email thirty seconds after it arrived?* Surely it would be better if that PDF got finished tomorrow morning, free of errors, instead of this afternoon, with errors in its structure?

"Come on little dog," I said and Kismet got up, stretched, shook, and ambled over. "Let's go for a walk," I said. After I snapped on her leash and buckled her harness she shook one more time and we set out. As I walked I thought about the balancing act in which I was engaged. Was I pushing myself too hard? My mother was without a doubt, the most important ball I had in the air. Although her situation sometimes took me way out of my comfort zone I was satisfied that I was doing what I could do for her. What could I do differently in my job? Well, that was simple really, ask for help. I could ask for help and take my time with things.

Kismet suddenly came to a halt. Jerking out of my reverie I realized I had come to the end of the sidewalk. Kismet was waiting for me to tell her what to do next. "Kismet, right," I said and we continued. I turned my thoughts to my personal life. *Yeah, right, what personal life?* I said to myself. Jim was being enormously supportive. It felt like all I was doing in the relationship was taking. I didn't have a solution for that. I'd just have to try to remember to thank him more often.

The most difficult task with my mother was fast becoming keeping her calm. She often wanted to go somewhere. Where this place might be was a mystery but she felt, quite strongly, that she wanted to go there. Sometimes just going to a different room was enough. Usually Jackie and I could transfer Mama from the bed to her wheelchair but more and more frequently we had to use a hydraulic lift. One of us would wheel her from room to room in the house. In the room she called her 'Hidey hole', she would sometimes ask to be taken up to the wall covered with framed photographs of the family. Everything was there, Mama and Daddy's wedding, pictures of Jimmy and me as children, everything from me on Tony the pony and Jimmy holding a football to pictures of me at my debutante ball. I'd go over to the wall and place my hand on one of the pictures and ask her which one it was. Mama would tell me what was in the picture and we'd remember together.

"That's the one of you wearing that hat with the feather in it. You're holding that broom handle that you used to pretend was a sword."

Laughing, I said, "I remember that. That was when I used to pretend to be d'Artagnan with the Three Muscateers. And which one is this?"

"Hmm," she said, "I'm not . . . oh, that one is of Granny and Grandaddy Jim."

"Is it the one of them on the front porch of the house in Mississippi? I asked.

"Yes," she replied. "Oh, those were halcyon days."

If the weather permitted, we'd take Mama outside in her wheelchair. I'd walk around her small back yard, touching the various plants and we'd talk about them. "This is the "Leather leaf viburnum. Snapping off a leaf I took it to her saying, "Name really fits doesn't it?" She laughed, fingering the thick leaf.

"Oh, look," she said, with more animation than I had seen for weeks, "there's the first daffodil."

"Really?" I was surprised. Then I realized I shouldn't have been surprised at all. It was late February—of course there would be daffodils. *How had I lost touch with the natural world I loved?* Pushing that thought aside I said, "I want to bring it to you. Where is it?" There then ensued one of those hilarious ballets in which a sighted person, not used to directing a blind person to as small a target as a single flower, gives directions. "A little to the left, no not that far, okay now forward, forward, wait, too far, back up a little, right there." We got there in the end and I triumphantly presented the flower to my mother.

"Oh, thank you, honey," she said as I held out the flower. By now I knew enough not to let go of it completely. Mama had so little dexterity left that there was a good chance she'd drop it.

I heard her inhale the flower's fragrance and then I said, "Let's take it in the house and put it in a bud vase." I placed the bud vase, with its single daffodil, on the table in the sunroom. There it sat for several days, symbolizing the cycle of death and rebirth of the natural world.

Mama's periods of agitation gradually took on a diffeerent quality. There was less coherence and more desperation. By now Dr. Houston had prescribed a different medication for anxiety. It didn't seem to be working. I read everything I could find about the medication and had an idea. "Dr. Houston," I began, "I've been reading about this medicine for anxiety. You know it's not really doing the trick. I have some ideas but I'm no doctor."

"Shoot," said Dr. Houston. We discussed several alternatives and when he came to a conclusion he said, "I'll get Sheri to call it in to Rich's and they can deliver it this afternoon." It worked. Mama was calmer. Whenever she got agitated though, the agitation gradually became focused on one thing, on going somewhere.

I hit the internet again, this time looking for anything about the process of letting go of life. Then I found it. The book was entitled *Final Gifts: Understanding The Special Awareness, Needs, and Communications of the Dying.* It was all there, the focus on 'going somewhere,' the desire to 'have the suitcase packed,' the conviction that people she loved, people who were already dead were in the next room, the restlessness, it was all there in the book.

Then I got to the part about what a dying person needs. Sometimes a person who is near the end of life needs assurance, assurance that it's all right for them to die, assurance that the people they leave behind will be okay.

Once again, I was in the chair in the corner of her bedroom working away. She made that sound that I had learned, over the long months, meant she wanted me to be near her. I put the computer on the floor and went to her bedside. We simply held hands. I waited for her to say something. She simply held my hand, with the diminished dexterity she had, she simply held on.

Finally, I said, "Mama, you can go now. It's all right for you to go. You can go and be with Daddy again. He's waiting for you, you know. I'll miss you when you're gone, but, I promise, it's okay for you to go."

On May 5th Mama was, at last, able to let go of her life.

58 | whatever it takes

JIMMY SAT DOWN, HOLDING A PIECE OF PAPER. We were going through Mama's papers in her hidey hole. "Look at this . . . This document is about your birth mother. Did you know anything about this?"

"No, not a thing." I replied. "Why don't you read it to me?"

When he finished reading the one-page document, Jimmy said, "I didn't know that Mama and Daddy had any information at all about either of our birth parents."

"Yeah, neither did I."

Jimmy and I had always known that we had been adopted as infants, but that topic fell into the category of "No talk" subjects.'

"You know," I began, "I wrote to the Cradle Society back when we lived in Maine to try to get health information about my birth parents. You know, because working in a quasi-health care field, I've learned so much about inherited diseases and stuff."

"Wow," Jimmy replied, "you really did that? How'd you know what to do? I mean, how'd you know that you could even do that?"

"A lady that I worked with in Camden had been a volunteer there and she told me what to do. It's easy, all I had to do was send a letter to the agency giving them my date of birth and Mama's maiden name."

"And what did you find out?"

"Not much. They just said that both of my birth parents had had all the usual childhood diseases and recovered fully, that was about it."

"Did they say anything else; you know, anything about who they were?"

"No, and I didn't bother with the mutual consent form either."

"What's that?" Jimmy asked.

"It's a form that you can sign if you want to get in touch with your birth parents. If they sign the same form, then they give you each other's contact information." I paused, thinking back, and then I continued. "I've never had the least curiosity about my birth parents, you know, except that health stuff. Mama and Daddy were always my parents, they always will be."

At that moment Margaret stuck her head in the door, "Hey Sue," she began, "Can you come take a look in your mother's closet. There might be some things you want to keep."

"Sure thing, be right there." Turning back to Jimmy, I said, "You can just throw that document away. I don't need it." Then I left Mama's hidey hole.

Before joining Margaret in the walk-in closet, I checked on Jim. He was in the bathroom sorting through the contents of drawers and cabinets. "Having fun yet?" I asked him.

"Oh, barrel of laughs," he replied. "I'm throwing most of this stuff away, okay?"

"Yeah sure, feel free to be ruthless."

"Whutcha got?" I asked Margaret, as I walked into Mama's closet. The four of us worked on into the evening.

Later, in the car on the way home, I placed my hand on Jim's as it rested on the gear shift. I felt Daddy's jade ring and smiled. "I love it that you wanted Daddy's ring," I said.

"I know, I'm surprised that Jimmy didn't want it.

We drove on in silence. Eventually I said, "It was so hard seeing Mama struggle like that. I sure as hell don't want to go through anything like that when my time to die comes along." We drove the rest of the way in silence. Looking out at the darkness I pondered. If I knew I was going to die what unfinished business did I have? What thoughts kept me awake at night?

Once we were settled in bed that night I lay with my hands folded behind my head. It was clear to me that my mother was unsettled at the end of her life. Thinking back to my father's death I suddenly remembered that he, too, seemed to have some internal anguish. He too seemed to be struggling to let go of life. His struggle wasn't as long or as intense as my mother's had been but it was still there.

I stopped dead in my mental tracks. Thinking back to when I thought I was about to end my own life. Yes, of course it had been a struggle. And maybe that's just the point. It's risky, this death thing.

Turning to Jim I whispered, "Awake?"

Hmm," he muttered. "Sorta."

"I'm determined not to approach the end of my life with unfinished business."

"Good . . . " he murmured.

SALIX BABYLONICA (SUB LUNA)

weeping willow

PART FIVE

RECONCILIATION

~~~~~

Do not stop thinking of life as an
adventure. You have no security
unless you can live bravely, excitingly,
imaginatively; unless you can choose a
challenge instead of competence.

Eleanor Roosevelt

59 | the company of friends

WANT YOUR SHEPHERD FIX?" It was August, and Mary Lou and I were at Caesar's Palace to exhibit at a Veterans Affairs conference. ML's current dog, Charlie, was a nine year old Lab, who was close to retirement. Her previous dog had been a shepherd, and she enjoyed getting her shepherd fix when we traveled together. She gave me her room number, only three doors down, and I knocked on the door. "Hi," I said when she opened her door. We gave each other a quick hug then I took off Kismet's harness.

Sitting down in the chair in front of the desk ML said, "Come here little Kizzy. Come over here and say hello."

Trotting across the room Kismet went to ML.

"Oh, hello, you," said ML. "Just look at those shepherd ears. You're such a cutey, Miss Kizzy."

Kismet looked around and pounced. She snatched Charlie's toy and took it to Mary Lou.

"Oh," said ML, "are we going to play fetch?"

They did; ML threw the toy over and over for Kismet to fetch. After a while Kismet lay down on the floor and chewed on the toy.

"So, how are you doing?" ML asked.

"You know, ML, I'm getting there. Those last months with Mama really were tough. Looking back on it, though, I honestly don't think I would have done anything different."

"I know it was tough," said ML, "but that's really good. If you can look back over a difficult time in your life with no regrets, well, that's a good thing.

"Yeah, and the other thing is, you know, watching Mama go through such a struggle, well, it made me want, no, need, to get my own house in order. It's amazing the stuff I'm discovering. Secrets I didn't even know I was keeping. Anger that I thought I had put to rest a long time ago, stuff like that. Emotional housecleaning I guess you'd call it."

"You know, Sue, that's such a good thing to come out of all of this. It really is. To see something so positive come out of such a difficult time. It's just great."

We sat in silence for a long time.

As I was sitting there, I realized it was really more than emotional housecleaning I had been doing. In those early months of my blindness my self-concept had been that of a damaged version of my sighted self. When that didn't fit anymore—when blindness became just a part of who I was, but not the most important part—that self-concept faded away. The fact I had attempted to kill myself took a lot longer to fade. For years, that persisted, always an important part of my self-concept. Back in Michigan, after I had apparently dazzled Jim by so handily identifying that black cherry during our tree identification expedition, I had told him about having attempted to kill myself. When he had simply said, "Oh, okay," I had been startled. Clearly, the fact that I had attempted suicide wasn't the most important part of who I was to Jim.

Now another self-concept was shifting. When asked to describe what suicidal depression felt like I had always described it as a whirlpool, as being sucked down into a whirlpool. I had thought of other major challenges I had faced in the same manner, my eating disorder, my troubles with prescription narcotics, even the death of each of my parents in turn. But a whirlpool has an out-of-control feeling. Being sucked into a whirlpool implies helplessness. I was far from helpless. Instead of being buffeted about by the currents of life, I had held on to life. I had done more than merely hang on, I had sailed out, out onto a calm sea.

At last, I was well—*truly* out of the whirlpool.

ML broke the trance. "Wanna talk about what we're doing tomorrow?"

"Sure thing," I said. "What'd you have in mind?"

"Well," she began, "We've demoed JAWS and Dragon running together so much that people are beginning to think we can't use a keyboard."

Nodding in agreement I said, "I know. Impressive as it is to use a computer without looking at it or touching it maybe it's time we just demo the screen reader and use the keyboard. You know, the way we use it every day. One thing I could do is toggle between my normal speech rate and one that mere mortals can understand."

"Great idea," she said. "I'm thinking we should maybe just demo in Word and Outlook. The last time I demoed web browsing it kind of fell flat."

"Really," I replied. "How come?"

"I think it's because there's nothing to look at. Even when I tell people to listen to the speech they never quite get the hang of it. Oh, I mean it's okay when I scoop up the links and put them in a list or something. That's something they can see. But hitting a single keystroke to jump to the first heading on the page goes right over their heads."

Sitting up I said, "I know, I'll run MAGic at 1X. That way the focus rectangle and spotlight will give them something to goggle at."

At that moment Charlie pounced. He snatched the toy from Kismet and took it to Mary Lou. Kismet just lay there, apparently bemused.

Leaning down ML tugged the toy out of Charlie's mouth and threw it across the room. Charlie and Kismet both went for it but Charlie got there first. He leaped right over Kismet's back, grabbed the toy and presented it to ML.

"Goodness me, old man," she said, caressing Charlie's head, "Didn't know you had it in you."

Looking at ML, I smiled. Kismet came over to me to get her own ears scratched. "They never cease to amaze us do they?"

Charlie stood patiently, getting his ears scratched while Kismet tried to climb in my lap.

60 | ecce quam bonum

I ADJUST THE STRAP OF MY HIKING STICK, making sure it sits snugly around my wrist. Turning to Jim I say, "Ready?"

We set out together. We're on the Rock Harbor trail, walking three abreast with Lake Superior rolling onto the rocky shore to our left. I take deep lung fulls of the cool air tinged with the scent of balsam fir. Our boots crunch on the trail as we stride out. Kismet's harness jingles as she trots along.

We stop dead.

"A loon," Jim whispers.

"Two of them," I whisper back. We listen until the pair is silent.

"Cool," and we continue.

The gravel thins and, soon, instead of crunching on gravel our footsteps thud solidly on rock. The titanium tips of our hiking sticks begin to ting as we plant them on the rocky trail. What started as a casual stroll turns into a hike. My muscles stretch and flex as I begin to reach for footholds. "It's starting to get narrow," says Jim. "Want to lead?"

"Sure," I reply." I click my tongue, encouraging Kismet. "Come on little dog, hup up."

I take the lead. The trail rises. Kismet slows as she shows me the rough spots along the way. When she stops completely

I probe the trail with my hiking stick to discover what lies ahead. There's a huge boulder ahead and slightly to the right but to the left it seems clear. "Left?" I tell Kismet with a question in my voice. Yes, it's clear to the left and we continue.

At one spot I simply can't figure out the best way to proceed. I stop.

"Down to the left," Jim says. "Then up. A big up."

Experience tells me that 'a big up' probably means that I'll need to let Kismet go.

"Hup," I say. She scrambles up the rock face. As soon as I feel the leash begin to tighten I let it go so that I don't impede her progress. "Good girl, now wait for me." Letting my hiking stick dangle from my wrist I scramble up after my dog. She whines softly until I join her. As I stand she moves smartly behind me finishing at my left side. My hand drops right onto the harness handle and I take it up once again. With things back in their proper places I say, "Okay, hup up."

We continue, our breathing becoming slightly labored. We use our special shorthand.

"Don't fall to your left," says Jim.

"She correct?" I ask.

"A big down," he says.

"Got it," I murmur as I feel the trail level out beneath my feet.

Then the trail rises. We stop at a wide open place high above the water. The wind blows, the waves crash.

"I see a pair of loons out there," Jim says, "Well, there was a pair, one of them just dove under." I smile. "Want me to lead now?" Jim asks.

Nodding in agreement I say, "Yep, your turn. Go ahead."

With Jim in the lead we continue.

"Another big down," says Jim. "Hmm, how are we going to do this one?" After a couple of minutes he says, "I'll go first. Might want to let her go."

I unsnap Kismets leash and drape it over my shoulder so it won't get in the way. "Okay, Kiz, hup." She bounds down the rocks, landing with a humph at the bottom.

"Humph," says Jim, laughing.

"Which way?" I ask.

"Straight," he says.

"Here?" I ask.

"Yep, then right."

"Okay . . . ."

"Got it," and Kismet leaps up to greet me as though we've been separated for days. "Okay, settle down you." And we continue.

We're moving more quickly now, the trail has smoothed out for a bit.

"Yikes!" A very pissed off red squirrel has just made his displeasure at our presence known. "Be still my heart," I add, hand over heart, pretending to faint.

Looking back, Jim says, "I know, it's like they plan it. They're quiet for just long enough that you forget they're there. Then they scare the bejesus out of you."

Two hours and a little over three miles later we reach the turn to the Mount Franklin trail. "Let's rest," says Jim. Sitting down gratefully I unzip the backpack and extract a water bottle and Kismet's bowl. After she's had a drink Kismet dashes off to investigate something or other.

"Kismet!" I call. "Come back here."

Nothing.

"Kismet, phooey on that, come!"

She dashes back, bounces off of my chest and runs away again. When I get her back this time I tell her to lie down. She does, embellishing the act with a dramatic groan.

"Sheesh," I say, "Where's she getting this energy?"

"Dunno," Jim replies. "But she better hang on to it, she's gonna need it for this next part."

After we're rested Jim, who has been carrying the backpack until now hands it over, saying, "Want to lead?"

"Yep, Kismet, hup up," and we begin the two mile ascent to Mount Franklin.

"Doesn't seem too bad," I say.

"Not yet, looks kinda gradual for a while," Jim says.

"Okay, Good girl Kizzy, steady, atta girl."

I had been walking, harness in hand, with a dog guiding me for over twenty-five years. All those years ago, when my first orientation and mobility instructor back in Birmingham, Oscar Thompson, taught me to use a cane and carry myself with grace, that had been the beginning. How could I have known that those lessons would lead to the graceful unconscious ballet that I was doing right now, right here with my beloved dog.

"Watch it on your left," says Jim.

"Got it," I say.

And the man who walks beside me. When he pulled down that branch of black cherry for me to identify in the Michigan forest, who knew that that act was the beginning of a quarter century of joy, love, trials, resolve, reconciliation.

Where had the courage, the determination come from when I could only see the road through a glass darkly. Wherever it had come from, come it had. My mother told me that she had dared to believe I would be okay. On that day long ago in that hospital room she dared to believe. She didn't know, how could she, that I would once again climb mountains.

Pulling me back into the present Jim says, "We've got another one of those bridges." We had encountered them before, two wide planks of wood, side by side, across wet lands. We continue.

After a while Jim stops. "This is going to be interesting," he begins. "It narrows to one plank as far as I can see. How do you want to do this?"

"I step forward and investigate with my hiking stick.

"Oh, joy," I mutter. I hesitate but not for long. Standing still has never gotten me anywhere. "Guess I'll just drop the harness, put her on long leash, and try to stay right behind her. I can trail the right side of the bridge with my hiking stick and just take it slow."

It works for a while. Then, for no apparent reason Kismet falls off the left side of the bridge. "Whoa!" I cry. Jim pivots, just in time to see her fall into the marsh. Thankfully she scrambles back onto the bridge by herself because with our precarious footing we can't offer her much help.

"Sheesh Little dog," I say "You're the one with the functional eyeballs. What are you doing falling off?"

Looking at Jim I say, "I don't even want to know how muddy she is."

Laughing we continue. Then my right foot misses the plank, and I, in my turn, fall into the marsh. I feel my left foot sink into the mud. I scramble back onto the bridge as quickly as I can but not before the mud closes over the top of my boot.

"Oh, good grief," I mutter in disgust.

Looking us over, Jim says, "Now you're a matched set."

Glaring at him I say, "Watch it or I'll boot your butt off this here bridge."

Finally arriving at the end of the marshy part, I heave a sigh of relief at having both feet, albeit one covered in mud, back on terra firma. We continue.

Noticing a change in the aromas from Balsam Fir and heath, the trail rising more steeply now, I say, "What's changed? What kind of trees are we in now?"

Pausing, Jim looks around and says, "Yeah, we're in a stand of Quaking Aspen with some White Birch thrown in for good measure. How'd you know?"

"For one thing, the smell changed. It puts me in mind of fall in a deciduous forest. The sound did too. Listen."

We listen together. Kismet whines. She pulls gently on

her leash.

"See what you mean," Jim replies. "Sounds almost like rain."

We listen to the wind in the trees, the sound of a stream trickling over rocks, a raven overhead.

"Ready?" And we continue.

"Going up," Jim intones in the manner of elevator operators of yore.

"Whoa," I say, as my foot slips off a rock and I catch myself with my hiking stick. The wind picks up. I stop for a minute, letting it cool my sweaty face. I continue, now breathing hard. Following Kismet as she turns to the right I step up onto a rock with my left foot. Kismet pokes her head under my leg and looks back at Jim. I burst out laughing.

"What?" questions Jim.

"Think she wants to wait for you," I reply. After I catch my breath we continue.

Mud splattered, sweaty, and winded I stride out onto the Greenstone Ridge.

Then the magic happens.

My spirit soars out, out into the vastness that lies before me. The three of us stand together, the dog who has guided me to this place and the man who has made the journey with me. We stand together beneath the blue vault of the sky, above the blue water of the lake, the only sound, that of the wind. I couldn't have done it alone. And how much richer to have done it together, together with the dog and the man who stand beside me.

I don't know what lies ahead.

Ecce Quam Bonum.

I believe it will be good, whatever it is.

acknowledgments

First, I wish to thank Dr. Paul Ponchillia, professor emeritus at Western Michigan University. Paul believed in this book before I believed in it myself, yet I owe Paul thanks for so much more than could be contained in this book. Thanks for bringing me into the world of adaptive sports. Thanks for helping me keep an open mind about the profession of blind rehab. Due to your patience and understanding I learned that I am a true teacher and enjoyed over twenty years in the field.

Another person who believed in this book came along much later—my thanks to Trisha Terwilliger. Your belief in my story and your belief in my skill as a writer fueled my enthusiasm to keep me writing this book to its conclusion.

I wrote the story of my own rehab process several years ago. I did nothing with it however, as I instinctively knew that I couldn't tell my story until I could be honest about the cause of my blindness. That moment came a year and a half ago when I learned of the death by suicide of someone I didn't know; but, I did know many of her friends, and it was their feelings of bewilderment and sadness that impelled me to write the rest of the story.

I owe a huge debt of gratitude to Patty Newbold who helped me realize that I had to tell the story of my suicide attempt with stark honesty. I had to reveal the feelings of isolation and alienation that accompanied that act of desperation. I hope that my honesty will let others who may feel that life is not worth living know that they are not alone. There is always hope. As long as there is life there is hope. Patty also helped me draw out and capture all of those emotions and struggles with my new blindness. My first draft made it sound like adjusting to blindness was a walk in the park, which it most definitely is not. Patty helped me with much more than just the beginning of the book and I grew, as a person, through all of her assistance and input.

This book began its life as a blog. I had no idea that I was eventually going to write a book. It was because of my blog that I met Michelle Laramie. Michelle read every word of this book and gave me invaluable guidance, suggestions, and, yes, criticism. Thanks, Michelle, for the thousands of words that have passed between us. Thanks for the music. You've made my world a richer place.

April Martin, no relation, but possibly the closest to a sister I'll ever have, listened to every one of the early recordings of this book. Thanks, April; thanks for ensuring that all of my expletives got deleted along with the many, many times I got tongue-tied.

And, then, there's my way cool boss, Ellen Crowe. Apart from hiring me for a job that has been hugely challenging and rewarding, Ellen had my back during a very difficult time in my life. I'll be forever grateful. Two others who work with me at Veterans Affairs deserve special mention, Alan Greilsamer and Lara Dolin. Lara and Alan became my biggest cheerleaders.

My thanks to Daphne Wood and Norm Fine, both Masters of the Foxhounds. It's been over thirty years since I have been fox hunting and I had forgotten some of the terminology. Norm very patiently helped out a total stranger when I found him through his web site, www.FoxHuntingLife.com. Joanne Boyd wondered why there was nothing else in the book, after the first chapter, about horseback riding. I took up almost all of my outdoor adventures again after becoming blind and even added to the list. And I did, of course, get back in the saddle. Thanks, Joanne, Chapter 31s for you.

And then there's Addie McGriff Walters, my best friend, beginning at the age of three or so. A long time ago I wrote three stories about the farm in Mississippi where my father grew up. Addie and I spent a lot of our childhood on that farm, playing, learning to fish, chasing the cows. When I posted those three stories to my web site I dedicated them to Addie. Then she started reading the blog posts. She said, "You just have to publish these in a book." By then I was thinking along the same lines but I told Addie I had no idea how to go about doing that. "No problem," she said. And then she introduced me to my editor. Thanks for your belief in me Addie.

There's no doubt that this book is tighter and more coherent than it ever would have been without the help of professionals and friends. I have learned invaluable lessons about the world of publishing and the craft of writing. I have so much more confidence in my abilities as a writer because of the time and effort that so many have put into bringing this book to reality.

Finally, I want to thank my husband, Jim Martin. Jim had encouraged me to write this book long before anyone else. He, more than anyone, fully understands my look of intense concentration as I would pound away on the keyboard. He never minded my interruptions of whatever he was doing when I went to him to get the facts about some scene or other. He fully understood my need for getting the facts as true as I could. He graciously took himself back into those experiences we had shared and talked about his feelings at the time. These discussions brought a new level of intimacy into our relationship.

Jim even put up with my state of "Missing in action" during the hours and hours I spent in our media room recording the book. Whenever I'd come out he'd crow, "Aha! It's a Sue-sighting." Thanks sweetie. It's been a wonderful twenty-eight years. Let's get out there and have some more adventures! There are new mountains to climb.

CPSIA information can be obtained at www.ICGtesting.com
Printed in the USA
LVOW13s0115301113

363195LV00002B/5/P